AF344423

Charles Spurgeon, 1854

the LOST SERMONS *of*
C. H. SPURGEON

the LOST SERMONS *of*

C. H. SPURGEON

His Earliest Outlines and Sermons Between 1851 and 1854

Vol. 4

Edited with Introduction and Notes by JASON G. DUESING

B&H
ACADEMIC
NASHVILLE, TENNESSEE

The Lost Sermons of C. H. Spurgeon, Volume 4
Copyright © 2020 by Spurgeon's College
Published by B&H Academic
Nashville, Tennessee

All rights reserved.

Standard Edition ISBN: 978-1-4627-5934-7
Collector's Edition ISBN: 978-1-4627-5936-1

Dewey Decimal Classification: 252
Subject Heading: SPURGEON, CHARLES H. \ SERMONS \ CHRISTIAN LIFE–SERMONS

Special thanks to Spurgeon's College, spurgeons.ac.uk

Scripture quotations are taken from the King James Version.

The web addresses referenced in this book were live and correct at the time of the book's publication but may be subject to change.

The marbled paper for the cover of the collector's edition was created by Lesley Patterson-Marx, lesleypattersonmarx.com

Printed in China
1 2 3 4 5 6 7 8 9 10 RRD 25 24 23 22 21 20

To

Jim Baird and Chris Thompson,
for their steadfast commitment
to this project
and
to all who have contributed to it.

CONTENTS

CONTENTS

CONTENTS

FOREWORD

The genius of Charles Spurgeon endures. But why?

Definitely a man of his time, singularly constituted for fruitful gospel ministry in the Victorian era, Spurgeon nevertheless seemed built for all times. He endures because while cultural and sociopolitical seasons change, his message did not. Today's preachers could learn a lot more than they might think from this prince.

A little over ten years ago, my family made the difficult decision to leave a church in which we'd invested a decade. This was largely precipitated by a noticeable decline in biblical teaching. I feared I was wrong, but the downward slope proved too slippery: today that church has fully embraced a New Age brand of "evolutionary Christianity" tuned to the ephemeral whims of vague spirituality. When I first discovered that their theological deconstruction had run its course, I thought of Spurgeon navigating resolutely through the choppy waters of Downgrade Controversy, holding firm to biblical truth amid the modernistic and humanistic challenges to the Christian tradition. The gospel may have become "out of season," but Spurgeon refused to disobey the evergreen commandment to "preach the word" (2 Tim 4:2). Thus, his genius endures when the new ideas of the culturally captive church do not.

Spurgeon was ridiculed by critics in the press. His "old-fashioned" brand of Christianity was marked out of step with progress. They lampooned him in magazines, caricatured him in newspapers, skewered him in academic lectures. They called him backwards, superstitious, uncouth. Still he preached on. I think of him nearly every time the latest mouthpiece from the cultural elite shrilly announces that evangelicals are "on the wrong side of history." The fact that Charles Spurgeon's name is remembered while his critics' names seldom are tells me otherwise. His genius transcends the latest version of progress.

Even when his own theological countrymen wavered in loving application of gospel truth, Spurgeon did not neglect to see his deeds match his creed. While many sought to justify the unjust treatment of the poor and the oppressed, sometimes even twisting Scripture to do so, Spurgeon championed the cause of the orphan and the slave.

Some Christians in the United States burned his books and threatened his life over his position on slavery in particular. But he never wavered in his campaign against social ills of all kinds. His orphanage, in fact, is still in operation. And his brave and principled position in the midst of the slavery issue is still instructive for our ethnically divisive times as well. His genius endures in part because the problem he identified at the heart of it all—sin—still endures in every culture today.

But there is more. We may see much to adapt for our day in how Spurgeon applied the unchanging gospel to his own era, but the biggest reason his genius endures is that the biggest theme of his ministry endures. Like Paul the apostle before him, Spurgeon had resolved to know nothing "save Jesus Christ, and him crucified" (1 Cor 2:2). We remember this preacher—we revere this preacher—because his commitment to the centrality of the Savior Jesus is undeniable and uncanny. The cross illuminates the abundance of Spurgeon's sermons and other writings, and we have still not outrun their shadow 200 years later. His way of "finding the road" from every text to the great metropolis of Christ informs every one of us committed to Christ-centered exposition today. While you may not preach with Spurgeon's style, wit, or rhetorical acumen, you'd best preach with Spurgeon's Christ! His genius endures because Christ endures.

Even Spurgeon's simplicity and pithiness serve this greatest of ends, of making Jesus look glorious. This is why he endures, and this is why he is a deceptively and staggeringly complex figure himself. Through his travails and suffering, despite his depression and disease, in the face of ridiculous criticism and malicious attacks, in the midst of a progressive culture and in the context of a spectacularly growing congregation, Charles Spurgeon's ministry continued to bear fruit, to multiply, to take dominion for Christ's cause all around the world.

Because of all this and more, I am in awe of Spurgeon's genius. Echoing Barth's classic appraisal of Calvin, I am compelled to say of Spurgeon that he is an overflowed dam, an oasis, something directly down from Mount Moriah, a heavenly agent in the Col 1:6 sense, a power unleashed in the world, bearing fruit and growing, some alien force that is wonderfully cheering. I am lacking completely the vocabulary, even the heart, to merely absorb the gigantic phenomenon that is Charles Spurgeon—let alone to present it correctly.

Because Christ is all to Spurgeon, Spurgeon is all things to all people. Because the gospel is Spurgeon's unwavering center, his particular genius endures along with it. This is why recovering the sermons you hold was an especially precious undertaking.

As those in The Spurgeon Library at Midwestern Seminary are fond of saying, we do not look finally *to* Spurgeon, but *through* Spurgeon to Christ. You hold in your hands a new window on our Lord Jesus. Friends, let's keep on marveling.

JARED C. WILSON
Assistant Professor of Pastoral Ministry and Author in Residence
Spurgeon College and Midwestern Baptist Theological Seminary
Kansas City, Missouri

EDITOR'S PREFACE

Lector, si monumentum requiris, circumspice

— *Epitaph of Christopher Wren, 1723, St. Paul's Cathedral*

Twelve years after the completion of the beautiful and historic St. Paul's Cathedral in London, its architect, Christopher Wren, died. Following the destruction caused by the Great Fire of London in 1666, Wren had played a vital role in designing many of the rebuilt buildings. Much of London today is shaped by his vision, and this is seen most prominently in St. Paul's.

When Wren died, in fact, he was entombed in the bottom of St. Paul's; his resting place was marked with a modest plaque. His son, desiring to pay tribute to the lasting mark his father left on the city through his buildings, inscribed on the plaque the words "*Lector, si monumentum requiris, circumspice,*" which translates to: "Reader, if you seek a monument, look around." The idea, clearly, is that Christopher Wren's lasting legacy is in the iconic and culture-transforming structures that serve as the backbone of London architecture.

Within these pages reside some of Charles Haddon Spurgeon's earliest transforming structures of his own design. They are not physical buildings; rather, they are the recorded words and notes of a young preacher during his first pastorate in Waterbeach. Spurgeon preached these sermons during the autumn and winter of 1852–1853 when he was eighteen years old, having served just one year at the Baptist church. When Spurgeon first arrived at Waterbeach in 1851, he wondered:

Would God save any souls through me? They called me a ragged-headed boy, and I think I was just that; I know I wore a jacket. After I had preached for some time, I thought, 'This gospel has saved me, but then somebody else preached it; will it save anybody else now that I preach it?' Some Sundays went over, and I used to say to the deacons, 'Have you heard of anybody finding the Lord under my ministry? Do you know of anyone brought to Christ through my preaching?"[1]

Waterbeach was a rural community that Spurgeon described as "a village notorious for its drunkenness and profanity."[2] Yet, eventually Spurgeon would learn of those converted, and—in his words—his "heart leaped for joy when I heard tidings of my first convert!"[3]

As Spurgeon continued to preach his sermons and record them in his Notebooks, he discerned a significant spiritual roadblock within the congregation: antinomianism. He relates, "In my first pastorate, I had often to battle with Antinomians—that is, people who held that, because they believed themselves to be elect, they might live as they liked. I hope that heresy has to a great extent died out, but it was sadly prevalent in my early ministerial days."[4] As a result, many of the sermons in this volume address topics related to the gospel of Jesus Christ and sanctification, perseverance, holiness, and hypocrisy. During his years at Waterbeach, the Baptist church grew; many from the town came to hear Spurgeon and were converted. As Spurgeon's *Autobiography* relates, "[I]t pleased God to turn the whole place upside down. In a short time, the little thatched chapel was crammed, the biggest vagabonds of the village were weeping floods of tears, and those who had been the curse of the parish became its blessing."[5]

Whether in Waterbeach or London, Spurgeon did not leave behind a city of beautiful buildings like Christopher Wren; nevertheless, his legacy is, in fact, greater. For Spurgeon dedicated his life to the building of the household of God, built on "the foundation of the apostles and prophets," with Christ Jesus "himself being the chief corner stone" (Eph 2:20).

So, reader, if you seek a monument for Spurgeon, take up and read these sermons, look around, and from there see the gospel of Jesus Christ that changed lives then and changes lives now.

JASON G. DUESING
General Editor
Ascension Day 2019

---

1   *Autobiography* 1:232.
2   *Autobiography* 1:227–28.
3   *Autobiography* 1:232.
4   *Autobiography* 1:232.
5   *Autobiography* 1:228.

PROJECT RESEARCH TEAM

General Editor

Jason G. Duesing

Volume Editor

Jason G. Duesing

Project Coordinator

Phillip Ort

Spurgeon Library
Research Assistants

Timothy Gatewood
Ronni Kurtz
Drake Osborn
Ed Romine
Adam Sanders
Devin Schlote
Garrett Skrbina
Tyler Sykora

Spurgeon Library
Student Scholars

Austin Burgard
Jordan Wade

With Special Thanks To

Jason K. Allen, President, Midwestern Baptist Theological Seminary
The Spurgeon Library

Midwestern Baptist Theological Seminary
Kansas City, Missouri

Spurgeon's College
London, England

ABBREVIATIONS

ARM	*An All-Round Ministry, Addresses to Ministers and Students.* London: Passmore & Alabaster, 1900. Reprint: Pasadena, TX: Pilgrim Publications, 1983.
Autobiography	*C. H. Spurgeon's Autobiography. Compiled from His Diary, Letters, and Records, by His Wife, and His Private Secretary.* 4 vols. London: Passmore & Alabaster, 1899–1900. The Spurgeon Library.
Lectures	*Lectures to My Students: A Selection from Addresses Delivered to the Students of the Pastors' College, Metropolitan Tabernacle.* London: Passmore & Alabaster, 1893. The Spurgeon Library.
MTP	*The Metropolitan Tabernacle Pulpit: Sermons Preached and Revised by C. H. Spurgeon.* Vols. 7–63. London: Passmore & Alabaster, 1861–1917. Reprint: Pasadena, TX: Pilgrim Publications, 1970–2006.
Notebook	*Spurgeon Sermon Outline Notebooks.* 11 vols. Heritage Room, Spurgeon's College, London. K1/5, U1.02.
NPSP	*The New Park Street Pulpit: Containing Sermons Preached and Revised by the Rev. C. H. Spurgeon, Minister of the Chapel.* 6 vols. London: Passmore & Alabaster, 1855–1860. Reprint: Pasadena, TX: Pilgrim Publications, 1970–2006.
ST	*The Sword and the Trowel: A Record of Combat with Sin and Labour for the Lord.* 37 vols. London: Passmore & Alabaster, 1865–1902. The Spurgeon Library.
TD	*The Treasury of David: Containing an Original Exposition of the Book of Psalms; A Collection of Illustrative Extracts from the Whole Range of Literature; A Series of Homiletical Hints Upon Almost Every Verse; And Lists of Writers Upon Each Psalm.* 7 vols. London: Passmore & Alabaster, 1869–1885. The Spurgeon Library.
LS	*The Lost Sermons of C. H. Spurgeon.* 9 vols. Nashville, TN: B&H Academic, 2016–.

INTRODUCTION

WHO IS
CHARLES SPURGEON?[1]

---

1   This section was originally written by Phillip Ort for The Spurgeon Library as "Who Is Charles Haddon Spurgeon?"; available from https://www.spurgeon.org/.

Known as the "Prince of Preachers," this Victorian, Calvinistic, Baptist minister testified as a powerful gospel witness in his time, but his influence endures today. So much so that Carl F. H. Henry, the dean of twentieth-century evangelical theologians, once called Spurgeon "one of evangelical Christianity's immortals."[2]

But what makes Charles Haddon Spurgeon immortal? Born on June 19, 1834 in Kelvedon, Essex, to John and Eliza Spurgeon, he was the firstborn of seventeen children—although unfortunately only eight survived adolescence.[3] A boy who loved books, he quickly became fascinated with John Bunyan's *Pilgrim's Progress*. However, Spurgeon did not lose his own burden at the foot of the cross until January 6, 1850. Soon thereafter he moved to Cambridge, joined St. Andrews Street Baptist Church, and began his ministry as an itinerant preacher. In October 1851 Spurgeon was called to preach at his first church, Waterbeach Chapel, and soon thereafter accepted the pastorate of New Park Street Chapel in Southwark, London, in April of 1854. In 1861 the Metropolitan Tabernacle opened, and his ministry expanded, resulting in

2   Carl F. H. Henry, quoted in Lewis Drummond, *Spurgeon: Prince of Preachers* (3rd ed.; Grand Rapids, MI: Kregel, 1992), 11.

3   Photograph of genealogical record, "Pedigree of the Spurgeon (Spurgen, Spurgin, Spirgon, Spirjon, Etc.) Family of Halstead, Co., Essex, cited with permission by David Spurgeon in Christian T. George, *The Man and His Times: Charles H. Spurgeon in Context* (a timeline graphic displayed at The Spurgeon Library at Midwestern Baptist Theological Seminary, Kansas City, MO). Elsewhere, C. H. Spurgeon recorded the names of the eight surviving children: Charles Haddon, Eliza, James Archer, Emily, Louisa, Charlotte, Eva, and Flora (*Autobiography* 1:10).

the founding of sixty-six parachurch ministries.[4] His remarkable ministry in London would last thirty-eight years before his death on January 31, 1892, in Menton, France.

Spurgeon lived during the Victorian age where "progress" was the prized virtue of the day. Though born in the country, the nineteen-year-old moved to London in 1854; he was entering the largest and most powerful city in the world. However, in London he found himself on the *south side* of the river, in Southwark borough. According to Helen Douglas-Irvine's work, *History of London*, Southwark enjoyed "the infamous distinction of a pre-eminently evil reputation"[5] and a "meanness which proceeds from extreme poverty and decay."[6] To complicate matters, Spurgeon arrived at New Park Street Chapel only to find that the dwindling congregation could not pay him a regular salary; rather, he was paid by the fluctuating and meagre seat rent.[7] When the congregation—and the giving!—revived after three months of his ministry, he declared, "I will pay for the cleaning and lighting myself."[8] Indeed, from that day forth, he covered all the incidental expenses of New Park Street Chapel and the Metropolitan Tabernacle until his death.[9] But Spurgeon did more than cover the "incidentals." By

4   See the following list of the sixty-six ministries reproduced from *ST* July 1884:373 on the occasion of Spurgeon's Jubilee, celebrated on June 18, 1884 (see also, Marianne Farningham, *Spurgeon: The People's Preacher* [London: Walter Scott, n.d.], 251–52): The Almshouses; the Pastors' College; the Pastors' College Society of Evangelists; the Stockwell Orphanage; the Colportage Association; Mrs. Spurgeon's Book Fund, and Pastors' Aid Fund; the Pastors' College Evening Classes; the Evangelists' Association; the Country Mission; the Ladies' Benevolent Society; the Ladies' Maternal Society; the Poor Ministers' Clothing Society; the Loan Tract Society; Spurgeon's Sermons Tract Society; the Evangelists' Training Class; the Orphanage Working Meeting; the Colportage Working Meeting; the Flower Mission; the Gospel Temperance Society; the Band of Hope; the United Christian Brothers' Benefit Society; the Christian Sisters' Benefit Society; the Young Christians' Association; the Mission to Foreign Seamen; the Mission to Policemen; the Coffee-House Mission; the Metropolitan Tabernacle Sunday School; Mr. Wigney's Bible Class; Mr. Hoyland's Bible Class; Miss Swain's Bible Class; Miss Hobbs's Bible Class; Miss Hooper's Bible Class; Mr. Bowker's Bible Class for Adults of Both Sexes; Mr. Dunn's Bible Class for Men; Mrs. Allison's Bible Class for Young Women; Golden Lane and Hoxton Mission (Mr. Orsman's); Edbury Mission and Schools, Pimlico; Green Walk Mission and Schools, Haddon Hall; Richmond Street Mission and Schools; Flint Street Mission and Schools; North Street, Kennington, Mission and Schools; Little George Street Mission, Bermondsey; Snow's Fields Mission, Bermondsey; the Almshouses Missions; the Almshouses Sunday Schools; the Almshouses Day Schools; the Townsend Street Mission; the Townley Street Mission; the Deacon Street Mission; the Blenheim Grove Mission, Peckham; the Surrey Gardens Mission; the Vinegar Yard Mission, Old Street; the Horse Shoe Wharf Mission and Schools; the Upper Ground Street Mission; the Thomas Street Mission, Horsleydown; The Boundary Row Sunday School, Camberwell; the Great Hunter Street Sunday School, Dover Road; the Carter Street Sunday School, Walworth; the Pleasant Row Sunday Schools, Kennington; the Westmoreland Road Sunday Schools, Walworth; the Lansdowne Place Sunday School; Miss Emery's Banner Class, Brandon Street; Miss Miller's Mothers' Meeting; Miss Ivimey's Mothers' Meeting; Francie's Mothers' Meeting.

5   Helen Douglas-Irvine, *History of London* (New York: James Pott & Company, 1912), 364.

6   Douglas-Irvine, 364.

7   *Autobiography* 2:123.

8   *Autobiography* 2:123.

9   *Autobiography* 2:123–24.

the age of twenty-seven, the young pastor had donated approximately $1,325,378 of the required $3,690,913 toward the construction of the Metropolitan Tabernacle.[10] He earned this money from speaking fees and from the sale of his wildly popular sermons and books. He didn't even take a salary from his new megachurch.

Charles Spurgeon was a truly unique instrument of the Lord Jesus Christ. One of the most remarkable aspects of his life and legacy is that he holistically exemplified Christian virtue in his ministry. With respect to evangelistic zeal, Spurgeon's passion for evangelism is seen in every Christ-centered facet of his life, ministry, and sermons. During his lifetime, he preached the gospel to more than a million people and personally baptized 15,000 new believers converted under his ministry. Furthermore, his sermons were translated into nearly *forty* languages, including Arabic, Armenian, Bengali, Bulgarian, Castilian, Chinese, Congolese, Czech, Dutch, Estonian, French, Gaelic, German, Hindi, Russian, Serbian, Syriac, Tamil, Telugu, Urdu, and Welsh.[11]

Called a "nine-days wonder"[12] by the *Sheffield and Rotherham Independent*, this "boy preacher of the fens" took the world by storm when he arrived in London in 1854. The young speaker was a force to be reckoned with and provoked polarized reactions. *The Ipswich Express* said his sermons were "redolent of bad taste" and "vulgar and theatrical."[13] On the other hand, Elymas L. Magoon—his first biographer—said that when Spurgeon arrived in London, "A burning and shining light [had] suddenly burst upon the moral

---

10 *Autobiography* 3:12 records that on January 22, 1862, the Building Committee of the Metropolitan Tabernacle Church finished their audit and presented the final expense report to the church with a total cost of £31,332 4s. 10d. ($3,630,913.30). Among the list of receipts, the following entries are made: "collectors' accounts, £7,258 5s. 2d. [$841,117.82]; donations and subscriptions, £9,034 19s. 2d. [$1,047,009.38]; per Pastor C. H. Spurgeon £11,253 15s. 6d. [$1,304,135.34]" (*Autobiography* 3:13). However, this number must be considered alongside the testimony of deacon William Olney, who testified on the twenty-fifth anniversary of Spurgeon's ministry that "During those three years [of construction] Mr. Spurgeon paid over to the treasury of the church, for the building of this Tabernacle, just upon £5,000 [$579,424.28], all of which belonged to himself" (*Autobiography* 2:124). However, this too must be weighed carefully, as Olney's remarks refer to the seat rent collected during the building/fund-raising years of the Metropolitan Tabernacle. Thus, it is possible that the difference of £6,253 15s. 6d. [$724,714.06] was contributed by Charles from the sale of his sermons and books. With this in mind, the emphasis on "per Pastor C. H. Spurgeon" implies Spurgeon donated the entire £11,253 15s. 6d. [$1,304,135.34]. Even if the difference of £6,253 15s. 6d. [$724,714.06] was funded through gifts, these gifts would have been understood as having to pass through the pastor's hands personally. Additionally, the numbers above have been calculated using the following equation: (GBP(RPI-1984)/(RPI-Year)) x (GBP-USD-1984(RPI-2016)). January 1, 1984, has been chosen here as the control date for conversion from GBP to USD with the original GBP adjusted for inflation and the subsequent USD adjusted for inflation as of September 2016, when the equation was formulated. The following online sources were used for the calculation: www.parliament.uk/briefing-papers/RP99-20.pdf (accessed 5/31/2019); http://www.tradingeconomics.com/united-kingdom/currency (accessed 5/31/2019); http://www.usinflationcalculator.com/inflation/consumer-price-index-and-annual-percent-changes-from-1913-to-2008/ (accessed May 31, 2019).

11 *Autobiography* 4:291.

12 *Autobiography* 2:55.

13 *Autobiography* 2:44.

world."[14] His voice was "full, sweet, and musical,"[15] and the massive crowds he drew by open-air preaching led Magoon to title his biography of Spurgeon, *The Modern Whitfield* [*sic*].[16]

But how was Spurgeon viewed by the people, by the "least of these" to whom he ministered in his blighted community? In 1855 one anonymous writer, *Vox Populi*, the "voice of the people," wrote, "Mr. Spurgeon institutes a new era, or more correctly revives the good old style of Bunyan, Wesley, and Whitefield, – men whose burning eloquence carried conviction to the hearts of their hearers, – men who cared naught for the applause of their fellow-mortals, but did all for God's glory."[17] Indeed, Spurgeon gave fresh voice to the stream of rich theology that flowed through Calvin, Owen, Bunyan, Edwards, Wesley, and Whitefield. He knew that Christ had not commanded him to "feed [his] giraffes," but rather to "feed [his] sheep."[18] Thus, in preaching he insisted that, "We must not put the fodder on a high rack by our fine language, but use great plainness of speech."[19] And Spurgeon did speak plainly and often about his favorite theme, "Jesus Christ and him crucified." Indeed, it is for his richly theological, exceptionally vivid, and dogmatically Christocentric preaching that Charles Spurgeon is known.

But Spurgeon was not just a preacher: he was also a college president. In 1856, he founded the Pastors' College, a free seminary designed to help "rough and ready" ministers sharpen their skills for the ministry. Within the first twenty years of operation, his students planted fifty-three new Baptist churches in London—not counting the missions planted around the world or across England.[20] Nevertheless, Spurgeon serves as an example of theological integrity. Near the end of his life, in 1887, the Downgrade Controversy erupted as the theological decay of Britain was exposed. At that time, many had abandoned the authority, inspiration, and inerrancy of the Scripture; furthermore, others began to reject the bodily resurrection of Jesus Christ.[21] He saw this decay in the Baptist Union and called for a direct response—the drafting of an

---

14   E. L. Magoon, *Sermons of the Rev. C. H. Spurgeon, of London; With Additional Discourses, and an Introduction and Biographical Sketch. First Series–Twentieth Edition* (New York: Sheldon & Company, n.d.), v.

15   Magoon, x.

16   E. L. Magoon, *"The Modern Whitefield." Sermons of the Rev. C. H. Spurgeon, of London; With an Introduction and Sketch of His Life* (New York: Sheldon, Blakeman, and Company, 1857).

17   *Autobiography* 2:50-51.

18   C. H. Spurgeon, *The Salt-Cellars: Being a Collection of Proverbs, Together with Homely Notes Thereon. A. – L.* (New York: A. C. Armstrong and Son, 1889), 56.

19   Spurgeon, 56.

20   *ST* Annual Report of the Pastors' College 1877–8, 1878:240–63.

21   "A new religion has been initiated, which is no more Christianity than chalk is cheese. . . . The Atonement is scouted, the inspiration of Scripture is derided, the Holy Spirit is degraded into an influence, the punishment of sin is turned into a fiction, and the resurrection into a myth" (*ST* August 1887:397).

evangelical statement of faith.[22] However, his call was not heeded, nor was a statement drafted. In the end Spurgeon submitted his letter of resignation to the Baptist Union on October 28, 1887,[23] only to find himself censured by the same body a few months later.[24] Prophetically, he said, "I am quite willing to be eaten of dogs for the next 50 years; but the more distant future shall vindicate me."[25] Today his prophecy rings true.

Finally, Charles Spurgeon exemplified the Christian virtue that David Bebbington has termed "activism," the passionate belief that the gospel must be expressed in action.[26] In addition to the Pastors' College, he also founded a ministry to prostitutes, a ministry to policemen, two orphanages, and seventeen almshouses for widows. Research conducted at The Spurgeon Library has shown that a *conservative* estimate of his net worth ran about $50 million, yet only about $250,000 was left in his bank account when he died. What does one do with $49,750,000? For Charles Spurgeon, the answer was simple: invest it in God's kingdom. Orphans had to be fed, the houses of widows subsidized, and the Home Rescue Society for women suffering from domestic abuse had to be funded somehow.

Any one of these qualities—evangelistic zeal, theological integrity, or evangelical activism would have been sufficient to earn Spurgeon recognition as an exemplary Christian man. Yet, God was pleased to work all these things through his chronically depressed, arthritic, and gout-smitten servant, Charles Haddon Spurgeon. It was not Spurgeon who made Spurgeon great; it was God who made Spurgeon great: God magnified his own greatness through Spurgeon's weakness. In Spurgeon's words, it was "all of grace." Faithfulness to the Lord Jesus Christ above all other things was the chief goal.

Spurgeon's Sincere and Pure Devotion to Christ[27]

When thinking how best to assess and categorize the life of Charles Haddon Spurgeon, a phrase used by the apostle Paul in 2 Cor 11:3 may come to mind. For the totality of

---

22 *Autobiography* 4:263.

23 G. Holden Pike, *The Life and Work of Charles Haddon Spurgeon* (London: Cassell and Company Lim., n.d.) 6:287.

24 Spurgeon's censorship occurred in two stages, first privately among the council of the Baptist Union (*ST* February 1888:81) and second by the Union as a whole (*Autobiography* 4:254).

25 *ST* August 1889:420.

26 See Phillip Ort, Timothy Gatewood, and Ed Romine, "Charles Spurgeon: The Quintessential Evangelical," in *Midwestern Journal of Theology* 18:1 (Spring 2019), 104–25.

27 Portions of this section were originally published by Jason G. Duesing, "The Conversion of C. H. Spurgeon: A Lecture," in *Midwestern Journal of Theology* 17, no. 2 (Fall 2018): 77–84.

his life as a Christian, Spurgeon had "a sincere and pure devotion to Christ." His sight was set on Jesus Christ from the moment he looked to him in his conversion.

As a young boy, Spurgeon remained close to his grandparents. His grandfather, an Independent minister, had a study in his home that was filled with books. Thus, reading filled much of Spurgeon's young life. When others were outside, Spurgeon was always with books. This relationship with written words found further reinforcement at home. Spurgeon's mother regularly gathered the children on Sunday evenings to explain Scripture, read aloud books, and pray. In his *Autobiography*, Spurgeon recounts,

> I cannot tell how much I owe to the solemn words of my good mother. It was the custom, on Sunday evenings, while we were yet little children, for her to stay at home with us, and then we sat round the table, and read verse by verse, and she explained the Scripture to us. After that was done, then came the time of pleading; there was a little piece of Alleine's *Alarm*, or of Baxter's *Call to the Unconverted*, and this was read with pointed observations made to each of us as we sat round the table; and the question was asked, how long it would be before we would think about our state, how long before we would seek the Lord.[28]

Often Spurgeon's mother would pray this way: "Now, Lord, if my children go on in their sins, it will not be from ignorance that they perish, and my soul must bear a swift witness against them at the day of judgment if they lay not hold of Christ."[29] This thought of his mother standing against him was unbearable and prompted Charles to seek the Lord early. Spurgeon would later say,

> Fathers and mothers are the most natural agents for God to use in the salvation of their children. I am sure that, in my early youth, no teaching ever made such an impression upon my mind as the instruction of my mother; neither can I conceive that, to any child, there can be one who will have such influence over the young heart as the mother who has so tenderly cared for her offspring. A man with a soul so dead as not to be moved by the sacred name of 'mother' is creation's blot. Never could it be possible for any man to estimate what he owes to a godly mother.[30]

---

28   *Autobiography* 1:68.
29   *Autobiography* 1:68.
30   *Autobiography* 1:69.

His mother's prayers were answered when Spurgeon was fifteen. At this time Spurgeon was experiencing deep conviction of sin, saying, "I do speak of myself with many deep regrets of heart. I hid as it were my face from Him, and I let the years run round."[31] As the Holy Spirit pressed conviction for sin upon Spurgeon's soul, he realized his "heart was fallow, and covered with weeds; but, on a certain day, the great Husbandman came, and began to plough [his] soul. Ten black horses were His team, and it was a sharp ploughshare that he used, and the ploughshare made deep furrows."[32] (The team of "ten black horses" equaled one horse for each Commandment under which Spurgeon stood condemned.)

In this state, Spurgeon sunk lower and saw himself to be nothing but "rottenness, a dunghill of corruption."[33] While he would later acknowledge that "A spiritual experience which is thoroughly flavoured with a deep and bitter sense of sin is of great value to him that hath had it," it was overwhelming for young Spurgeon.[34] In late 1849, Spurgeon visited different churches in and around Colchester, but without much relief or encouragement. He explains: "From chapel to chapel I went to hear the Word preached, but never a gospel sentence did I hear; but this one text preserved me from what I believe I should have been driven to,—the commission of suicide through grief and sorrow. It was this sweet word, 'Whosoever shall call upon the name of the Lord shall be saved.'"[35]

When Spurgeon was in the "hand of the Holy Spirit" and experiencing a "clear and sharp sense of the justice of God," he could not believe in *substitution*: the "sum and substance of the gospel."[36] For Spurgeon, the central question was, "Who would or could have thought of the just Ruler dying for the unjust rebel?"[37] Yet, while Spurgeon then did not believe that "it was possible that [his] sins could be forgiven," soon the "Great Change" would take place.[38]

During this period, Spurgeon was employed as an usher for a private school in Newmarket. As an usher Spurgeon was both student and tutor for this school, paying

31 *Autobiography* 1:67-68.
32 *Autobiography* 1:75.
33 *Autobiography* 1:93.
34 *Autobiography* 1:76.
35 *Autobiography* 1:95.
36 *Autobiography* 1:98, 113.
37 *Autobiography* 1:98.
38 *Autobiography* 1:97, 103.

for his tuition by his work. When the school closed temporarily in December due to an outbreak of fever, Spurgeon returned home to Colchester.

One Sunday morning Colchester was hit with a substantial snowstorm. Spurgeon, while en route, stumbled into a private Methodist church hidden in a back alley.[39] The regular minister was unavailable that morning, and an unidentified lay preacher took the pulpit. By Spurgeon's account, this person spoke ineloquently for about ten minutes on the passage, "Look unto me, and be ye saved, all the ends of the earth" (Isa 45:22).[40]

Thanks to the providence of a snowstorm, Spurgeon found himself subject to the so-called preaching of a man whom he claims was "really stupid" and "did not even pronounce the words rightly."[41] Nevertheless, the message from this crude preacher effectually struck a chord in Spurgeon's anguished soul. At the end of the service, the preacher looked squarely at Spurgeon and said, "Young man, you look very miserable." Spurgeon recounted his thoughts:

> Well, I did but I had not been accustomed to have remarks made from the pulpit about my personal appearance before. However, it was a good blow, struck right home.
>
> He continued, "and you will always be miserable—miserable in life and miserable in death—if you don't obey my text; but if you obey now, this moment, you will be saved." Then lifting his hands, he shouted, as only a Primitive Methodist could do, "Young man, look to Jesus Christ. Look! Look! Look! You have nothing to do but look and live."
>
> I had been waiting to do fifty things, but when I heard that word, "Look!" what a charming word it seemed to me! Oh! I looked until I could almost have looked my eyes away. There and then the cloud was gone, the darkness had rolled away, and that moment I saw the sun; and I could have risen that

---

39 In recent years, three pews from this Primitive Methodist Chapel on Artillery Street, Colchester, where Charles Spurgeon was converted, were kindly donated by the current congregation of Artillery Street Evangelical Church to The Spurgeon Library at Midwestern Seminary. Library visitors can see an artist's depiction of the scene described here as well as see the actual pews on which many people of this era sat to hear preaching like Spurgeon heard on that day.

40 *Autobiography* 1:105.

41 *Autobiography* 1:105–6.

instant, and sung with the most enthusiastic of them, of the precious blood of Christ, and the simple faith which looks alone to Him.[42]

And at that moment, Spurgeon saw clearly the way of salvation. He *looked* to Jesus Christ and *lived*. Henceforth Spurgeon knew he was no longer under the "frown of God," but could say, "My Father smiles." The joy of that day was "utterly indescribable" as the teenage Spurgeon rejoiced, "I am forgiven, I am forgiven, I am forgiven!"[43] He later would say,

> When I first received everlasting life I had no idea what a treasure had come to me. I knew that I had obtained something very extraordinary, but of its superlative value I was not aware. I did but look to Christ in the little chapel, and I received eternal life. I looked to Jesus, and He looked on me, and we were one forever. That moment my joy surpassed all bounds, just as my sorrow had before driven me to an extreme of grief. I was perfectly at rest in Christ, satisfied with Him, and my heart was glad, but I did not know that this grace was everlasting life till I began to read in the Scriptures, and to know more fully the value of the jewel which God had given me.[44]

What Spurgeon discovered on January 6, 1850, was the "sum and substance of the gospel . . . *Substitution*." On this subject, he would later comment:

> If I understand the gospel, it is this: I deserve to be lost forever; the only reason why I should not be damned is, that Christ was punished in my stead, and there is no need to execute a sentence twice for sin. On the other hand, I know I cannot enter Heaven unless I have a perfect righteousness; I am absolutely certain I shall never have one of my own, for I find I sin everyday; but then Christ had a perfect righteousness, and He said, 'There, poor sinner, take My garment, and put it on; you shall stand before God as if you were Christ, and I will stand before God as if I had been the sinner; I will suffer in the sinner's stead, and you shall be rewarded for works which you did not do, but which I did for you.'

---

42   *Autobiography* 1:106.
43   *Autobiography* 1:108–10.
44   *MTP* 31:395.

I find it very convenient everyday to come to Christ as a sinner, as I came at the first. 'You are no saint,' says the devil. Well, if I am not, I am a sinner, and Jesus Christ came into the world to save sinners. Sink or swim, I go to Him; other hope I have none. By looking to Him, I received all the faith which inspired me with confidence in His grace; and the word that first drew my soul—'Look unto Me,' — still rings its clarion note in my ears. There I once found conversion, and there I shall ever find refreshing and renewal.[45]

That morning, Charles Haddon Spurgeon looked to Jesus Christ and was saved. He found the joy of Christ, and as he put it, "I could have danced."

Interestingly, Spurgeon returned to that same chapel the next week and took issue with the pastor's preaching on Romans 7.

The next Sunday I went to the same chapel, as it was very natural that I should. But I never went afterwards, for this reason, that during my first week the new life that was in me had been compelled to fight for its existence, and a conflict with the old nature had been vigorously carried on. This I knew to be a special token of the indwelling of grace in my soul, but in that same chapel I heard a sermon upon "O wretched man that I am! Who shall deliver me from the body of this death?" And the preacher declared that Paul was not a Christian when he had that experience. Babe as I was, I knew better than to believe so absurd a statement.

What but divine grace could produce such a sighing and crying after deliverance from indwelling sin? I felt that a person who could talk such nonsense knew little of the life of a true believer. I said to myself, "What! Am I not alive because I feel a conflict within me? I never felt this fight when I was an unbeliever. When I was not a Christian I never groaned to be set free from sin. This conflict is one of the surest evidences of my new birth, and yet this man cannot see it, he may be a good exhorter to sinners, but he cannot feed believers." I resolved to go into that pasture no more, for I could not feed therein. I find that the struggle becomes more and more intense, each victory over sin reveals another army of evil tendencies, and I am never able to sheathe my sword, nor cease from prayer and watchfulness.[46]

45   *Autobiography* 1:113.
46   *MTP* 31:395–96.

On May 3, 1850, Spurgeon received baptism in the River Larke. As his family were Congregationalists, his mother was saddened to learn her son would pursue believer's baptism. She said to him that while she prayed for his conversion, she did not pray he would become a Baptist. Spurgeon responded, "Ah, mother! the Lord has answered your prayer with His usual bounty, and given you exceeding abundantly above what you asked or thought."[47]

By August of 1850, Spurgeon preached his first sermon and then was called, in 1851, as pastor in Waterbeach, a village near Cambridge. For the next three years, he would hone his craft and record his sermons in nine notebooks. These were lost to publishing history, until now, with the publication of these volumes as *The Lost Sermons of C. H. Spurgeon*.

While lecturing on Spurgeon, Andrew Atherstone, of Wycliffe Hall, Oxford, made a very helpful observation about that sermon Spurgeon heard in Colchester and how God used it in his conversion. He recounts that there are three key elements of Spurgeon's conversion. First, God's sovereignty over the circumstances of it. Second, God's powerful Word that convicted him. Third, God's use of Christ-centered preaching.[48] Atherstone observes that all of these would remain the key components of Spurgeon's ministry throughout his life—God's sovereignty, God's Word, and Christ-centered preaching.

From his conversion in the chapel on Artillery Street, Spurgeon kept his gaze set on his devotion to Christ. As such, much like that preacher, Spurgeon pointed many others to "look" as well. It is our hope that *The Lost Sermons of C. H. Spurgeon* will further Spurgeon's pointing and direct the gaze of all readers to Jesus Christ.

Sources and Method of *The Lost Sermons*

The publication of Volume 4 of *The Lost Sermons of C. H. Spurgeon* marks a change in the general editor of this series as well as a refocusing of the editorial task and method for the remaining volumes. The Introduction to Volume 1 of the *Lost Sermons* projected the series to run to twelve total volumes.[49] However, as that was a reflection of a large endeavor just embarking, the work and reception of the first three volumes has allowed the project's

---

47 *Autobiography* 1:69.
48 Andrew Atherstone, "Andrew Atherstone on C H Spurgeon," at the 2018 Evangelical Ministry Conference. Available from http://acl.asn.au/andrew-atherstone-on-c-h-spurgeon/.
49 *LS* 1:22.

research team to refine the total scope to a new total of nine volumes. Within that space the entirety of Spurgeon's earliest unpublished sermons, totaling 400, will still appear.[50]

To that end, the remaining volumes of *The Lost Sermons of C. H. Spurgeon* are still committed to finishing what Spurgeon left unfinished. As his wife, Susannah, shared in the *Autobiography*, "Mr. Spurgeon had himself intended, long ago, to publish a selection from [his first outlines]; in the Preface to *The New Park Street Pulpit* for 1857, he announced that he hoped shortly to issue a volume of his earliest Sermons, while Pastor at Waterbeach, but this was prevented by the pressure of his rapidly-increasing work."[51]

To the end of continuing what Spurgeon started, Volumes 4–9 follow the same research method and consultation of sources as Volumes 1–3, with only a few adaptations.[52] The overall aim is still to offer the reader "a critical work that can be accessed by academics and laity alike."[53] In sum, the remaining volumes will:

- continue to consult primary and secondary sources in addition to the Notebooks themselves. These include, in part, the books Spurgeon owned that now make up the collection of The Spurgeon Library at Midwestern Baptist Theological Seminary in Kansas City, Missouri.[54]
- continue to minimize any technical adjustments to preserve Spurgeon's original voice. However, simple typographical errors or misspellings are corrected to aid in reading and comprehension. Moreover, whereas every ink smear or page discoloration was noted in Volumes 1–3, the editorial work of the remaining volumes has refrained from highlighting such minutiae unless it bears a significant contribution to the content.
- continue to provide definitions of words likely unfamiliar to a modern audience, using Spurgeon's personal copy of Samuel Johnson's dictionary.
- continue to provide explanation for cultural references, using contemporary secondary literature.
- continue to mark any connection between Spurgeon's earliest sermons and those preached later and recorded in *The New Park Street Pulpit* and *The Metropolitan Tabernacle Pulpit* series.

---

50   What remains for a future project is the analysis and presentation of Notebooks 10 through 12, which contain non-sermonic material.

51   *Autobiography* 1:213.

52   See "Sources and Method," in *LS* 1:29–33.

53   *LS* 1:31.

54   See https://www.spurgeon.org/.

- Continue to cite Scripture references from Spurgeon's personal copy of the King James Bible.[55]
- Continue to provide references to Scripture when the editor concludes that Spurgeon was directly or indirectly citing specific passages or related doctrines from the Bible.

Finally, here is a representation of the contents of the sermon Notebooks housed in the Heritage Room Archives at Spurgeon's College in London that form the substance of the *Lost Sermons of C. H. Spurgeon* project:

Notebook 1: 90 total pages
(81 pages of sermon text, 4 blank pages, and 5 miscellaneous pages)

Notebook 2: 140 total pages
(135 pages of sermon text, 2 blank pages, and 3 miscellaneous pages)

Notebook 3: 140 total pages
(135 pages of sermon text, 2 blank pages, and 3 miscellaneous pages)

Notebook 4: 123 total pages
(114 pages of sermon text, 7 blank pages, and 2 miscellaneous pages)

Notebook 5: 123 total pages
(115 pages of sermon text, 5 blank pages, and 3 miscellaneous pages)

Notebook 6: 128 total pages
(120 pages of sermon text, 6 blank pages, and 2 miscellaneous pages)

Notebook 7: 125 total pages
(113 pages of sermon text, 11 blank pages, and 1 miscellaneous page)

Notebook 8: 178 total pages
(167 pages of sermon text, 11 blank pages, and 0 miscellaneous pages)

---

55   See *The Illustrated Family Bible* (London: Fisher, Son, and Co., n.d., The Spurgeon Library).

Notebook 9: 164 total pages
(147 pages of sermon text, 17 blank pages, and 0 miscellaneous pages)

As *The Lost Sermons of C. H. Spurgeon* finally reach publication, we join Susannah Spurgeon in her assessment that these earliest sermons "are valuable, not only because of their intrinsic merits, but also as the first products of the mind and heart which afterwards yielded so many discourses to the Church and the world, for the glory of God and the good of men."[56]

JASON G. DUESING
General Editor

PHILLIP ORT
Project Coordinator

56   *Autobiography* 1:213.

THE SERMONS

NOTEBOOK 4 (SERMONS 188–232)

1. The Roman numeral IV indicates that this is the fourth Notebook in the series. For an account of similar inscriptions in each Notebook, see *LS* 1:51; 3:28. The majority of the front flap of this Notebook has been removed.

[blank]

bol IV.
I hope to die skipping.
Skeletons. 188 to.
In this volume may   the pen of a ready writer
I have

Vol IV.

I hope to die singing.[1]

SKELETONS 188 *to* [232][2]

In this volume, may I have the pen of a ready writer.[3]

1. In "The Beloved of the Lord in Safety" (Notebook 2, Sermon 100), Charles reflects on the sweetness of Moses's sermon in Deuteronomy 33 as a farewell song sung before his death. See also "Oh that Men Would Praise the Lord" (Notebook 2, Sermon 105).

2. This volume concludes with Sermon 232.

3. With this statement, Charles is referring to Ps 45:1: "My heart is inditing a good matter: I speak of the things which I have made touching the king: my tongue is the pen of a ready writer."

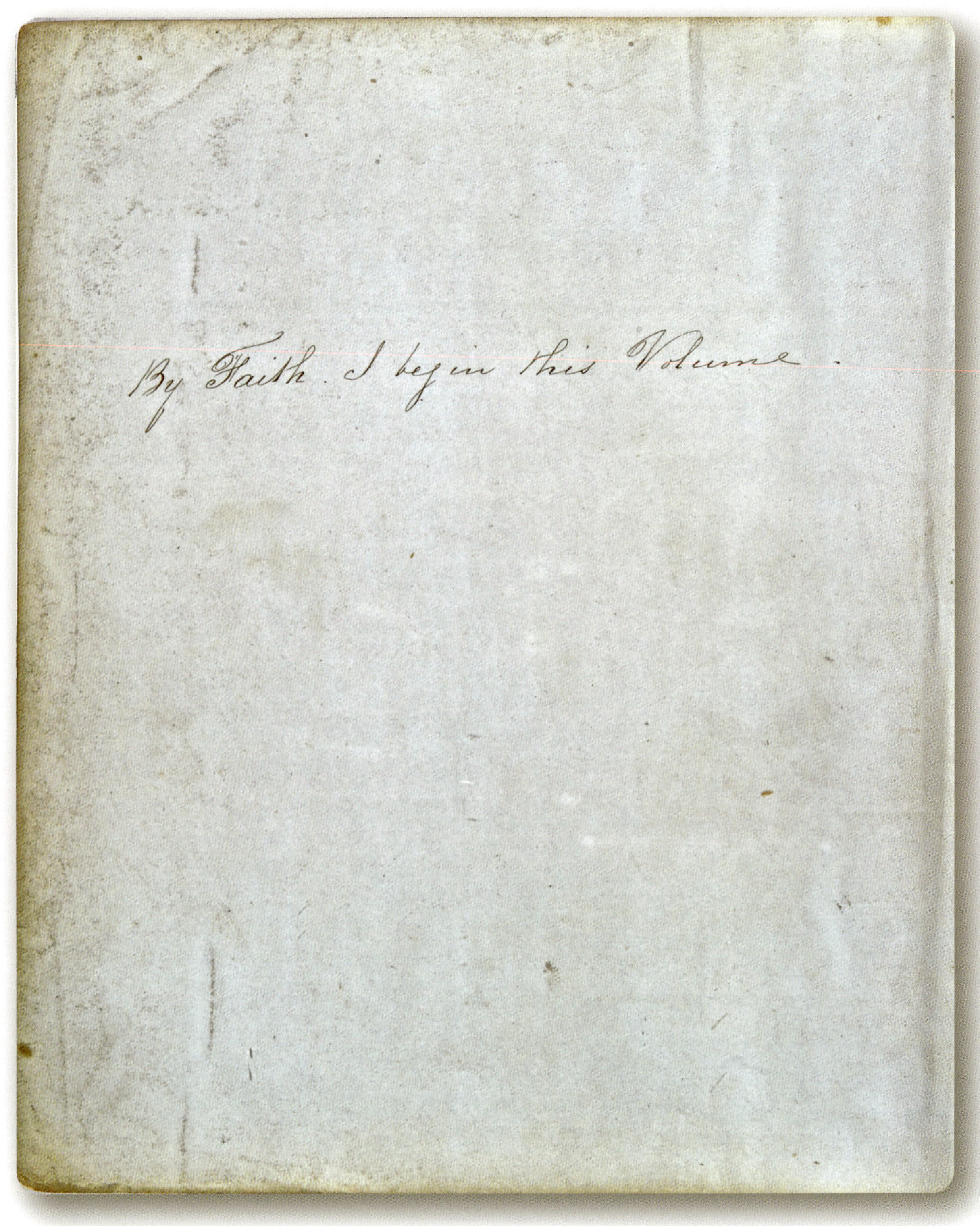
By Faith. I begin this Volume.

By Faith, I begin this Volume.[1]

1. Reminiscent of the commendation of the ancients listed in Hebrews 11, Spurgeon is setting forth "by faith."

Prov. II. 4. 5.   The spiritual miner.   188

Diligence in order to the attainment of true religion
& happiness is often commended & commanded in the
Sacred Scriptures.   "to labour", "to strive", "to run",
"to search diligently",   "Go to the ant." —— "make calling &c sure"
We who preach grace much are accused of being
cool in our exhortations & not pressing on men
the necessity of immediate duty.   Some of us
may deserve it, but it is not the effect of our creed
but of our hearts coldness .... We love however
to see all exhortations to duty cleared of any
of the dust of legality & man's merit & we wish
ever to make prominent the fact, that is
of grace, through faith, not of ourselves but
the gift of God.   May the good Spirit help me.

I. Let us Examine the treasure spoken of.
We would not dig for a thing that may be work-
-less.   Well Solomon was a good jeweller & we
will stand or fall by his opinion, what says he?
Better than silver, gold, rubies, or all desirable things.
What is it? What is the name of it?

1. **Wisdom.**   Well a good education is something but
after all not so wonderful a jewel.   College learning
say you, is something, but a man may be bad or
poor & yet have learning, we want something
that will abide & be more precious than that.
     Right friend — but this is another kind of wisdom
to all these. It will help you to understand

THE SPIRITUAL MINER
Proverbs 2:4–5

"If thou seekest her as silver, and searchest for her as for hid treasures; then shalt thou understand the fear of the LORD, and find the knowledge of God."

Diligence in order to the attainment of true religion[1] and happiness is often commended and commanded in the Sacred Scriptures. "To labour,"[2] "to strive,"[3] "to run,"[4] "to search diligently,"[5] "Go to the ant."[6] "Make calling etc. sure."[7]

We who preach grace much are accused of being cool in our exhortations and not pressing on men the necessity of immediate duty.[8] Some of us may deserve it,[9] but it is not the effect of our creed but of our heart's coldness[10] . . . We love however to see all exhortations to duty cleared of any of the dust of legality and man's merit[11] and we wish ever to make prominent the fact that [it] is of grace, through faith, not of ourselves but the gift of God.[12] May the good Spirit help me.[13]

I   LET US EXAMINE THE TREASURE SPOKEN OF.

We would not dig for a thing that may be worthless. Well Solomon was a good jeweller [*sic*][14] and we will stand or fall by his opinion, what says he?

Better than silver, gold, rubies, or all desirable things. What is it? What is the name of it?

1. **Wisdom**. Well a good education is something but after all not so wonderful a jewel. College learning, say you, is something, but a man may be bad or poor and yet have learning.[15] We want something that will abide and be more precious than that.

    Right friend—but this is another kind of wisdom to all these. It will help you to understand

the heights & depths of the love of Christ, & the science
of salvation. — it will get you a degree in heaven
By it a crown of glory may be won, & a throne
may be your resting place. Heavenly wisdom.

2, **Fear of the Lord.** This is another name for
the treasure to be sought. It is to be carefully distinguished
from another article in the market called Slavish fear.
fear of man, fear of hell, fear of disgrace; Those other
things are mere gilt, Birmingham trinkets, done up
with exquisite art, scarcely to be detected, but
really not worth the carriage. Do you dig for the
true gem, the true pearl. mind **of the Lord**

3. **Knowledge of God.** The third name, this implies
not alone the knowledge derived from nature &
going into the intellect, but heart-knowledge
Knowledge of God as a lawgiver, just & true.
As an offended judge — yet as a tender Benefactor
As the giver of his son Jesus. & thro' him as our
Friend, Father, Blessed Lord.

This is the true treasure since we can carry
it with us, it will be current in heaven, it is
eternal, gives present peace & future glory.

II The way of obtaining the treasure,
"seeking as for silver" "searching as for hid treasure"
But let us be careful.

1. To seek in the right place, sink not a shaft
where there is no treasure, as some have done.

the heights and depths of the love of Christ, and the science of salvation[16]—
it will get you a degree in heaven. By it a crown of glory may be won, and a
throne may be your resting place. Heavenly wisdom.

2. **Fear of the Lord**. This is another name for the treasure to be sought. It is to
   be carefully distinguished from another article in the market called slavish
   fear, fear of man, fear of hell, fear of disgrace.[17] Those other things are
   mere gilt, Birmingham trinkets,[18] done up with exquisite art, scarcely to be
   detected, but really not worth the[19] carriage. Do you dig for the true gem, the
   true pearl,[20] [the] mind **of the Lord**[?]

3. **Knowledge of God**. The third name, this implies not alone the knowledge
   derived from nature and going into the intellect, but heart-knowledge.[21]
   Knowledge of God as a lawgiver, just and true. As an offended judge—yet
   as a tender Benefactor. As the giver of his son Jesus, and thro' him as our
   Friend, Father, Blessed Lord.

   This is the true treasure since we can carry it with us, it will be current[22] in
   heaven, it is eternal, gives present peace and future glory.

II. THE WAY OF OBTAINING THE TREASURE, *"seeking as for silver" "searching as for hid treasures"*

But let us be careful.

1. To seek in the right place, sink not a shaft where there is no treasure, as some
   have done.

If in yourself, or your works your pit be dug, you will find, just nothing at all. Find a fit spot —
As we can learn from miners let us do so.
2. They find not ~~gold~~ coal, iron or metals on the surface, they dig deep, through rocks & find down below. So must we wait for salvation, striving & not staying till we find it — Using labour & perseverance.
3. They do not find it all pleasure — they are in peril of their lives, they sit in a constrained position, descend the dark shaft, & sweat much in toil. but they look at the pay. So expect to be ill-treated, to encounter trouble, hardship & loss. *To be on your knees.* Look to labour at all times.
4. They go up & down by a strong chain. Christ is our shaft & faith the chain. Trust no tow rope of thy own invention & spinning
5. They traverse untrodden paths & cut every inch of their way by incessant labour, so too we are led in paths we have not seen & none but we know of & we have to fight, toil & labour for every inch of our way — Many rocks to blast. & bad earth to turn out.
6. They have double labour of getting the treasure & pumping out the water & removing the earth So we also, ever find there is the water to be got out & our filth to be purged away.
7. They carry a stout hammer & pick-axe so must we use the Bible or no treasure will ever be gained, Creeds of man are wooden mallets the Bible is the rock-breaking hammer,

If in yourself or your works your pit be dug, you will find, just nothing at all. Find a fit spot—as we can learn from miners let us do so.[23]

2. They find not ~~gold~~[24] coal, iron or metals on the surface[. T]hey dig deep through rocks and find down below. So must we wait for salvation, striving and not staying[25] till we find it—using labour and perseverance.

3. They do not find it all pleasure—they are in peril of their lives,[26] they sit in a constrained position, descend the dark shaft, and sweat much in toil. [B]ut they look at the pay. So expect to be ill-treated, to encounter trouble, hardship and loss. To be on your knees. Look to labour at all times.

4. They go up and down by a strong chain. Christ is our shaft and faith the chain. Trust no tow rope of thy own invention and spinning.[27]

5. They traverse untrodden paths and cut every inch of their way by incessant labour. So too we are led in paths we have not seen and none but we know of[,] and we have to fight, toil and labour for every inch of our way. Many rocks to blast and bad earth to turn out.

6. They have double labour of getting the treasur[e] and pumping out the water and removing the earth. So we[,] also, ever find there is the water to be got out and our filth to be purged away.

7. They carry a stout hammer and pick-axe.[28] So must we use the Bible or no treasure will ever be gained. Creeds of man are wooden mallets, the Bible is the rock-breaking hammer.

8. The miners want a light, candles would set the foul air on fire & ruin them, so they have a safety lamp. So carnal-reason will but ruin, only the Spirit guides us securely. —

III. The assurance of success.

In earthly mines there is some uncertainty but here none at all. He who seeks shall find.

Some have found, who are of the same flesh & blood as you. They used these tools. went to work thus & have succeeded, so shall you 'f you do likewise. None ever failed.

Men work hard for uncertainties then why despise a certain treasure. Mark it will not pass in the ale-house, card-table, bowling yard, brothel, theatre, or race ground: But it will in heaven, in eternity. 'Tis of grace however

1. Believer thou hast found, seek more, go on — make not a sufficiency alone but a fortune. Be grateful that thou hast found the treasure.
2. Sinner, I use allegory to draw thee 'f thou wilt come, I lose no stone unturned. I love thee more, than thou dost thyself.
Seek & find. God help thee
amen.

299.

8. The miners want a light, candles would set the foul air on fire and ruin them,[29] so they have a safety lamp.[30] So carnal-reason will but ruin[. O]nly the Spirit guides us securely.

III. THE ASSURANCE OF SUCCESS.

In earthly mines there is some uncertainty, but here none at all. He who seeks shall find.[31]

Some have found, who are of the same flesh and blood as you. They used these tools, went to work thus and have succeeded. So shall you if you do likewise.[32] None ever failed.

Men work hard for uncertainties[. T]hen why despise a certain treasure[?] Mark[33] it will not pass in the ale-house, card-table, bowling yard, brothel, theatre, or race ground. But it will in heaven, in eternity. <u>Tis of grace however.</u>

1. Believer[,] thou hast found, seek more, go on—make not a sufficiency alone, but a fortune.[34] Be grateful that thou hast found the treasure.[35]

2. Sinner, I use allegory to draw thee if thou wilt come.[36] I lose no stone unturned.[37] I love thee more, than thou dost thyself.

Seek and find. God help thee[.]

Amen.

299.[38]

1. Cf. Jas 1:27.   2. Cf. Heb 4:11.

3. Cf. Luke 13:24.   4. Cf. 1 Cor 9:24.

5. Cf. Heb 11:6.   6. Cf. Prov 6:6.

7. Cf. 2 Pet 1:10.

8. A recurring issue Charles addresses in Notebook 4 is antinomianism, both in terms of those who accuse him of adherence to that system and to those who hold to and practice it, whether with intention or by default. In his *Autobiography* Charles notes, "In my first pastorate, I had often to battle with Antinomians,–that is, people who held that, because they believed themselves to be elect, they might live as they liked. I hope that heresy has to a great extent died out, but it was sadly prevalent in my early ministerial days. . . . From my very soul, I detest everything that in the least savours of the Antinomianism which leads people to prate about being secure in Christ while they are living in sin. We cannot be saved *by* or *for* our good works, neither can we be saved *without* good works. Christ never will save any of His people *in* their sins; He saves His people *from* their sins" (*Autobiography* 1:258, italics in the original). "I am rather fond of being called an Antinomian, for this reason, that the term is generally applied to those who hold truth very firmly and will not let it go. But I should not be fond of being an Antinomian. We are not against the law of God. We believe it is no longer binding on us as the covenant of salvation; but we have nothing to say against the law of God. 'The law is holy; we are carnal, sold under sin.' None shall charge us truthfully with being Antinomians. We do quarrel with Antinomians; but as for some poor souls, who are so inconsistent as to say the law is not binding, and yet try to keep it with all their might, we do not quarrel with them! They will never do much mischief; but we think they might learn to distinguish between the law as a covenant of life and a direction after we have obtained life" (*NPSP* 2:132).

9. "I have sometimes been greatly obliged to a wicked world for what it has done to inconsistent professors of religion. . . . In those early days, I had sometimes to contend with the Antinominian [*sic*] preachers as well as with their people. I once found myself in the midst of a company of ministers and friends, who were disputing whether it was a sin in men that they did not believe the gospel.

Whilst they were discussing, I said, 'Gentlement [*sic*], am I in the presence of Christians? Are you believers in the Bible or are you not?' They said, 'We are Christians, of course.' 'Then,' said I, 'does not the Scripture say, "of sin, because they believe not on Me'"? And is it not the damning sin of men, that they do not believe on Christ?' I should not have imagined, if I had not myself heard them, that any persons would be so wicked as to venture to assert that 'it is no sin for a sinner not to believe on Christ'" (*Autobiography* 1:260).

10. Later in his ministry, Charles often contended with the accusation that his doctrinal views would beget antinomianism. Rather, for Charles, the fullness of God's grace in pardoning sin caused the opposite reaction, creating an aversion to sin. In his sermon "None But Jesus–Second Part" Charles expressed this sentiment by asking, "My Lord, have I sinned against thee so many times, and yet hast thou freely forgiven me all? What stronger motive could I have for keeping me from sinning again?" (*MTP* 7:119). Charles believed that faith in Christ and his completed work produced this gratitude, saying, "And so faith, leading us by the way of gratitude up to the standpoint of love begets in us a desire to please him, and also a desire to imitate him; for love, somehow, always grows like its object. You cannot love a thing without becoming something like it, in proportion to the force of love; and just in proportion as you love Jesus you must get like him" (*MTP* 22:117–18). Thus, any coolness in evangelistic zeal, for Charles, is an issue of the heart, not of doctrinal commitment.

11. The idea of man's merit being salvific was abhorrent to Charles. Throughout his ministry he rejoiced in that "the law's demands were met and fulfilled for believers by Christ," but warned his listeners that "God cannot accept anything but a perfect obedience; and if you are hoping to be saved by your own sincere endeavours to do your best, your hopes are rotten things, delusions, falsehoods, and you will perish wrapped up in the shrouds of your pride" (*MTP* 8:28).

12. Cf. Eph 2:8.

13. Charles utilizes invocations like this one throughout his sermon writing. It is not known whether this would have been spoken in the delivery of the sermon.

14. Cf. 2 Chr 9:13–29.

15. In February of 1852, just months after Charles had started at Waterbeach and was preaching the sermons from Notebook 2, he wrestled with whether to leave the church to pursue college training. Joseph Angus, the tutor of Regent's Park College, asked to meet with him, and while Spurgeon sought to accept his invitation, Providence intervened, and Spurgeon remained at Waterbeach. "Soon after I had begun to preach the Word in the village of Waterbeach, I was strongly advised to enter Stepney, now Regent's Park, College, to prepare more fully for the ministry. Knowing that solid learning is never an encumbrance, and is often a great means of usefulness, I felt inclined to avail myself of the opportunity of attaining it: although I hoped that I might be useful without a College training, I consented to the opinion of friends that I should be more useful with it. Dr. Angus, the tutor of the College, visited Cambridge, and it was arranged that we should meet at the house of Mr. Macmillan, the publisher. Thinking and praying over the matter, I entered the house exactly at the time appointed, and was shown into a room where I waited patiently a couple of hours, feeling too much impressed with my own insignificance, and the greatness of the tutor from London, to venture to ring the bell, and make enquiries as to the unreasonably long delay. At last, patience having had her perfect work, and my school-engagements requiring me to attend to my duties as an usher, the bell was set in motion, and on the arrival of the servant, the waiting young man was informed that the Doctor had tarried in another room until he could stay no longer, and had gone off to London by train. The stupid girl had given no information to the family that anyone had called, and had been shown in the drawing-room; and consequently, the meeting never came about, although designed by both parties. I was not a little disappointed at the moment, but have a thousand times since thanked the Lord very heartily for the strange Providence which forced my steps into another path" (*Autobiography* 1:241–45). Charles would have preached this sermon after he had decided not to go to college.

16. Charles used this phrase one other time in his preaching: "[Jesus] came to teach us the science of life, and in him was life; he experienced life in all its phases, and was tempted in all points like as we are, though without sin. The highest were not above him, the lowest he did not regard as beneath him, but he condescended to their infirmities and sorrows. There are no dreary glens of melancholy which his feet have not trodden, nor lofty peaks of joy which he has not scaled; wondrous was the joy as well as the sorrow of our Lord Jesus Christ.

He leads his people through the wilderness, and, like Hobab of old, he knows where they should encamp in the wilderness, and understands all the way which they must traverse to reach the promised land. He was made 'perfect through suffering.' He teaches us no truth as mere theory, but as matter of actual experiment on his own person. The remedy he gives to us he has tested. If there be bitterness for us, he has quaffed full bowls of it, and if there be sweetness in his cup he gives us of his joy; all things that have to do with this life and godliness, the whole science of salvation from the gates of hell up to the throne of God, he understands right well, by personal acquaintance therewith. There is not a single chapter of the book of revelation which he does not comprehend, nor a solitary page of the book of experience which he does not understand; and therefore he is fit to teach, having both a master mind and a master knowledge of that which he comes to inculcate" (*MTP* 20:579).

17. Charles preached against these types of fear often: "The fear which is to be avoided is *slavish fear;* the fear which perfect love casts out, as Sarah cast out the bondwoman and her son. That trembling which keeps us at a distance from God, which makes us think of him as a Spirit with whom we can have no communion; as a being who has no care for us except to punish us, and for whom consequently we have no care except to escape if possible from his terrible presence. This fear sometimes arises in men's hearts from their *thoughts dwelling exclusively upon the divine greatness.* Is it possible to peer long into the vast abyss of Infinity and not to fear? Can the mind yield itself up to the thought of the Eternal, Self-existent, Infinite One without being filled, first with awe and then with dread? What am I? An aphis creeping upon a rosebud is a more considerable creature in relation to the universe of beings than I can be in comparison with God. What am I? A grain of dust, that does not turn the scale of the most delicate balance[,] is a greater thing to man than a man is to Jehovah. At best[,] we are less than nothing and vanity. But there is more to abase us than this. We have had the impertinence to be disobedient to the will of this great One; and now the goodness and greatness of his nature are as a current against which sinful humanity struggles in vain, for the irresistible torrent must run its course, and overwhelm every opponent. What does the great God seem to us out of Christ but a stupendous rock, threatening to crush us, or a fathomless sea, hastening to swallow us up? The contemplation of the divine greatness may of itself fill man with horror, and cast him into unutterable misery! Dwell long upon such themes, and like Job, you will tremble before Jehovah, who shaketh the

earth out of her place, and the pillars thereof tremble" (*MTP* 12:712, italics in the original). See also, "Faith Working by Love" (*MTP* 26, Sermon 1553); "What the Farm Labourers Can Do and What They Cannot Do" (*MTP* 27, Sermon 1603); "The Great Birthday and Our Coming of Age" (*MTP* 30, Sermon 1815); and "The Right Kind of Fear" (*MTP* 52, Sermon 2971).

18. It is likely Charles is referring to the fact that Birmingham was known as the "City of a Thousand Trades" and was the "main European producer of buckles, buttons, and a range of small boxes" (http://visitbirmingham.com/what-to-do/heritage/the-history-of-birmingham [accessed October 12, 2018]).

19. The word "one" is written over by "the."

20. Cf. Matt 13:46.

21. Charles later preached a sermon on Jer 24:7 that he titled "Heart-Knowledge of God" (*MTP* 20, Sermon 1206) to describe the foretelling of the new-covenant internal knowledge of God by the indwelling of the Holy Spirit.

22. "2. Generally received, uncontradicted; authoritative" (Johnson's *Dictionary*, s.v. "current").

23. An example from this time of determination in mining "was commenced at Wearmouth colliery, near Sunderland, in 1826. At the depth of three hundred feet a spring was reached, which poured water into the shaft at the rate of three thousand gallons per minute. Having conquered this difficulty, and sunk to the depth of one thousand feet, another spring was encountered, but the obstacle being overcome, the sinking was continued several hundred feet lower, when valuable seams of coal were reached, to reward the perseverance of the proprietors. Ten years passed away, and not less than £100,000 were expended before they had any returns" (*Mines and Mining* [London: Religious Tract Society, 1851], 57).

24. Charles struck through the word "gold."

25. "1. To stop; to withhold; to repress. 2. to delay; to obstruct; to hinder from progression" (Johnson's *Dictionary*, s.v. "to stay").

26. "The broad consensus was that the rates of mortality between the ages of 40 and 50 years were twice as high as the rate for non-miners of a similar age" (Catherine Mills, *Regulating Health and Safety in the British Mining Industries, 1800–1914* [Surrey, UK: Ashgate, 2010], n.p.).

27. Charles's note on not trusting a rope of one's own spinning figures prominently within the growing rope manufacturing industry in Britain. In 1854, the Great Seal Patent Office, under Bennet Woodcroft, published that from 1784 to 1851 there were seventy-two patents granted for the making and coiling of rope, showing the ongoing discovery of the unreliable nature of self-invented rope (*Subject-Matter Index (Made from Titles Only) of Patents of Invention, from March 2, 1617 (14 James I.) to October 1, 1852 (16 Victoriae). Part II. (N. to W.)* [London, 1857], 645–48).

28. "The action of a pick is to penetrate, chip, or break up by rending the mineral substance on which it is used . . . The force of the blow, which is regulated by the blow used by the miner, expends itself in making the point of the pick penetrate the ground, and thus loosen it" (Robert Hunt, *British Mining: A Treatise on the History, Discovery, Practical Development and Future Prospects of Metalliferous Mines in the United Kingdom*, 2nd ed. [London: Crosby Lockwood, 1887], 655).

29. "There are two or three causes existing in metallic mines which tend to render the air injurious to the miners. The burning of candles, the explosions of gunpowder, and the natural processes of respiration, each tend to deprive the air of some of its oxygen, and thus deteriorate it; and, by the processes of combustion and respiration, a considerable proportion of carbonic acid is constantly being added to the air" (Hunt, 607).

30. "The history of the safety-lamp may be said to commence in 1813, for in that year the Society in Sunderland for Preventing Accidents in Coal Mines was formed, which led directly to Sir Humphry Davy's experiments and to the invention of the Davy safety-lamp. In the same year Dr. William Reid Clanny invented his first safety-lamp." (*Transactions of the Institution of Mining Engineers*, vol. 51, *1915–1916*. [London: Published at the Offices of the Institution, Albany Buildings, 39, Victoria Street, Westminster, S.W., 1916], 558).

31. Cf. Matt 7:7–8.   32. Cf. Luke 11:10.

33. "3. To note; to take notice of. 4. To heed; to regard as valid or important" (Johnson's *Dictionary*, s.v. "to mark").

34. "This is to grow in grace: to root downward, to shoot upward, to extend your influences like far-reaching branches, and to bring forth fruit unto the Lord's glory" (*MTP* 8:4).

35. Cf. Matt 13:44.

36. Charles is referencing his use of allegory as an illustration to persuade. Later, he would warn his students to do this with care by reminding them they were not John Bunyan: "Mr. Bunyan is the chief, and head, and lord of all allegorists, and is not to be followed by us into the deep places of typical and symbolical utterance. He was a swimmer, we are but mere waders, and must not go beyond our depth" (*Lectures* 1:114).

37. Charles uses the word "lose," but clearly implies the more familiar "leave no stone unturned."

38. Charles is recording that this is the 299th occasion on which he has preached. Although he had written 190 sermons up to this point, he had used them to preach 299 times. This means that he preached 1.57 sermons per outline written. There is also evidence that Charles was not finished with Notebook 3 before he began writing Notebook 4. The final sermon in Notebook 3 (Sermon 187) was not preached until the 357th occasion, whereas the second-to-last sermon (Sermon 186) was preached last on the 302nd occasion. Notebook 4's first sermon, 188, was preached on the 299th time. While reusing outlines, there does also seem to be some overlap in the timing of the writing of outlines.

Isa. XL. 26.   God's care of the stars.   189

The stars have ever been objects attracting notice & attention & that too naturally for he must be blind indeed who regarded not these wonders.—

Their number was to Abraham the sign of his seed. Gen. XV.5
Their height amazed Job.   Job. XXII. 12.
David wondered that God should regard man when the moon & stars were his servants.   Ps. VIII
Daniel in vision compares the godly to stars.   Dan. XII.3.

To the Christian the stars are quite as full of beauty the star of Bethlehem — one star differeth from another star. the morning star — the stars held in his right hand. Let us lift up our eyes now, & try to meditate as the text would have us.

I. Let us be carried by a contemplation of the stars to consider what their creator must be.
      The universal voice of man as if by instinct cries out "there is a God". Some few there are who deny it but what are their characters? what the influence of such philosophy? these are the fools among men — who rather than believe as their fellow creatures, will laugh at our credulity & become a thousand times more credulous. Their own fears belie them, a storm converts them from their unbelief, death chills their raving madness & lets their soul feel the plain truth.
      The earth is a volume full of proofs of a Deity & sublimest of her pages, stands the sky, studded with golden letters plainly writ.—

GOD'S CARE *of the* STARS
Isaiah 40:26

"Lift up your eyes on high, and behold who hath created these things, that bringeth out their host by number; he calleth them all by names by the greatness of his might, for that he is strong in power; not one faileth."

The stars have ever been objects attracting notice and attention[,] and that too naturally for he must be blind indeed who regarded not these wonders[1] . . .

Their number was to Abraham the sign of his seed. Gen. XV.5[2]
Their height amazed Job. Job XXII.12.[3]
David wondered that God should regard man when the moon and stars were his servants. Ps. VIII.[4]
Daniel in vision compares the godly to stars. Dan XII.3.[5]

To the Christian, the stars are quite as full of beauty the star of Bethlehem[6]—one star differeth from another star—the morning star[7]—the stars held in his right hand.[8]

Let us lift up our eyes now and try to meditate as the text would have us.

I. LET US BE CARRIED BY A CONTEMPLATION OF THE STARS TO CONSIDER WHAT THEIR CREATOR MUST BE.[9]

The universal voice of man[10] as if by instinct cries out "there is a God."[11] Some few there are who deny it, but what are their characters? What [is] the influence of such philosophy?[12] These are the fools among men who[,] rather than believe as their fellow creatures, will laugh at our credulity and become a thousand times more credulous. Their own fears belie[13] them, a storm converts them from their unbelief, death chills their raving madness and lets their soul[s] feel the plain truth.

The earth is a volume full of proofs of a Deity and sublimest of her pages stands the sky, studded with golden letters plainly writ.[14]

Look yonder infidel & blush at your own
impudent folly in refusing to receive the
testimony of those ten thousand witnesses.
   The eye of faith however reads in these stars & moon
something more than the bare being of a God.
   1. It sees therein his immensity – the sun a
vast, inconceivably distant body – the stars vaster
still & immeasurably distant – space infinite
in extent & beyond all human thought – what
must the God be who filleth all in all.
   2. It regards him as inconceivable & unapproachable
seeing the stars are so far beyond us – the sun's
rays too bright for our eye – the motions of the
heavenly bodies wondrously intricate, their
size immense &c – low grand is palace. if heaven be its floor.
surely their maker is inconceivable
   3. It marvels at the power displayed in turning
this solid earth – yon moon & myriad stars –
a comet shoots across us we think of him
who wings it & hangeth the universe on nothing.
   4. It sees divine mercy & benevolence these
the sun shines with due heat – were he
nearer or remoter we must perish.
the darkness comes & retires by good degrees.
Meteors, red comets, thunder bolts hurt us not.
The moon & stars cheer our night – while
the sun is the parent of comfort, the nurse

Look yonder[,] infidel[,] and blush at your own impudent folly in refusing to receive the testimony of those ten thousand witnesses.

The eye of faith[,] however[,] reads in these stars and moon something more than the bare being of a God.

1. It sees therein his immensity—the sun a vast, inconceivably distant body—the stars [are] vaster still and immeasurably distant. Space [is] infinite in extent and beyond all human thought. What must the God be who filleth all in all[?][15]

2. It regards him as inconceivable and unapproachable[16] seeing the stars are so far beyond us—the sun's rays [are] too bright[17] for our eye. The motions of the heavenly bodies [are] wondrously intricate,[18] their size immense, etc. [H]ow grand his palace if heaven be its floor—surely their maker is inconceivable.[19]

3. It marvels at the power displayed in turning this solid earth[20]—you moon and myriad stars. A comet shoots across [as][21] we think of him who wings it and hangeth the universe on nothing.[22]

4 It sees divine mercy and benevolence therein. The sun shines with due heat[23]—were he nearer or remoter, we must perish. The darkness comes and retires by good degrees. Meteors, red comets, thunder bolts hurt us not. The moon and stars cheer our night—while the sun is the parent of comfort, the nurse

of life — What then must God be in grace.

<u>II</u>. Let us consider their number & remember that God knows them all.

God's knowledge of all his creatures is immense, the fish of the sea & birds of the air he counts — so to the stars he brings out in order & calls every star by its name.

1. Faith here discerns a wondrous providence she says then all my wants & ways are known to him & he will provide. It trusts such knowledge.

2. Faith declares her belief that the names of all the elect are known to their Redeemer God & shall be kept safe unto salvation. Their vast number does not cause one to be forgotten.

<u>III</u>. Let us regard the power which moves the stars along as being in God. —

The stars move not by inherent-force but by power exerted on them, by the divine hand.

1. Our hearts would gratefully own that if we have moved till now it is by grace.

2. When weak in our-selves we would grasp the thought that our strength lies in "his power."

3. We regard with pleasure the fact that not one faileth — because this is an earnest of our Perseverance.

<u>IV</u>. Let us learn to apply this at seasons.

1. When our affairs are troblous we must not distrust the knowledge or power of God.

2. When we feel our weakness & sinfulness we must not distrust on that account

of life—what then must God be in grace?

II. LET US CONSIDER THEIR NUMBER AND REMEMBER THAT GOD KNOWS THEM ALL.

God's knowledge of all his creatures is immense. The fish of the sea and birds of the air he counts[24]—so to[o] the stars he brings out in order and calls every star by its name.[25]

1. Faith here discerns a wondrous providence. She says[,] then all my wants and ways are known to him[26] and he will provide.[27] It trusts such knowledge.

2. Faith declares her belief that the names of all the elect are known to their Redeemer God[28] and shall be kept safe unto salvation.[29] Their vast number does not cause one to be forgotten.

III. LET US REGARD THE POWER WHICH MOVES THE STARS ALONG AS BEING IN GOD.

The stars move not by inherent force but by power exerted on them, by the divine hand.

1. Our hearts would gratefully own that if we have moved till now it is by grace.

2. When weak in our-selves we would grasp the thought that our strength lies in "his power."

3. We regard with pleasure the fact that not one faileth because this is an earnest of our perseverance.[30]

IV.[31] LET US LEARN TO APPLY THIS AT SEASONS.

1. When our affairs are troblous[32] we must not distrust the knowledge or power of God.

2. When we feel our weakness and sinfulness we must not distrust on that account

for the strength lies treasured up in our God.
3. When the church droops & conversions are not
frequent — God knoweth and heareth — the
elect are as numerous as stars and one by one
they shall appear — Christ shall see of the
travail of his soul —
                              Lord, move me, a poor planet.
⫫. 304. 469.

John XVI. 8. Convince the world of sin, righteousness 190.
                Sin.   & judgment.

We cannot too often insist on the need of
the Holy Spirit to work salvation in men.
From conviction down to the last step into
glory, all is of the Comforter who worketh all in us.
  It is the Spirit's office to convince of sin
righteousness & judgment. I pray that he may
use me as is instrument in the work —
I. May he convince the world of sin? The fact—
  The whole world is sinful —
✗ The Heathen dare not exempt themselves, but
stand clearly condemned.
  1. For sinning against their own senses in worshipping
      Gods of wood & stone, of filthy character. —
  2. For unnatural lust, filthiness, even in the
      temples, fornication, adultery. —
  3. For cruelty — revenge — murder — even their

for the strength lies treasured up in our God.

3. When the church droops and conversions are not frequent—[33] God knoweth and heareth—the elect are as numerous as stars, and one by one they shall appear[.] Christ shall see of the travail[34] of his soul[35]—

Lord, move me, a poor planet.[36]

~~189~~. 304. 469.

CONVINCE *the* WORLD *of* SIN, RIGHTEOUSNESS, *and* JUDGMENT[1]
John 16:8[2]

"And when he is come, he will reprove the world of sin, and of righteousness, and of judgement."

We cannot too often insist on the need of the Holy Spirit to work salvation in men.[3] From conviction down to the last step into glory, all is of the Comforter[4] who worketh all in us.

It is the Spirit's office to convince of sin, righteousness, and judgment. I pray that he may use me as [h]is instrument in the work.

I. MAY HE CONVINCE THE WORLD OF SIN.

The Fact: The whole world is sinful.

✗[5] The Heathen dare not exempt themselves, but stand clearly condemned.[6]

1. For sinning against their own senses in worshipping gods[7] of wood and stone,[8] of filthy character.

2. For unnatural lust,[9] filthiness, even in the temples,[10] fornication, adultery.[11]

3. For cruelty, revenge, murder.[12] Even their

own offspring they kill – Suttees, Cannibalism.
4. For dishonesty, lying, theft, drunkenness, & a
hundred other crimes —— —— —
X. The Catholics are but little better.
1. Equally are they idolaters.
2. Lust is tolerated in Roman countries, the priests
indulge in it, novels of filthy character are bred
as the worms in putrid carcases, sins are atoned
for by money or expurgated by fire.
3. Talk of cruelty – is not cruelty the soul of persecution? – The Madai even now
X. Professed Protestants are bad enough.
Let me begin at home
1. Even around us are Hypocrites, who talk fair,
who sit with us, pray & sing with us but away they
plunge into sin & folly – Backsliders too who
have been cut out of our communion & are
still such as we could not safely re-admit –
2. Let me go on have we not S. Breakers here?
some come only once in the day, some come
not all some days – some riot at evening.
Their conversation is worldly and fleshly. –
you laugh & giggle the sermon away or riot in
the road worse than another day. – buy or sell
3. But we have dishonest persons here –
Thieves it may be yet undiscovered – Or men
who overreach in trade, who take advantage

own offspring they kill.[13] Suttees.[14] Cannibalism.[15]

    4. For dishonesty, lying, theft, drunkenness, and a hundred other crimes.[16]

✗. The Catholics are but little better.

    1. Equally are they idolaters.[17]

    2. Lust is tolerated in Roman countries. The priests indulge in it.[18] Novels of filthy character are bred as the worms in putrid carcases [*sic*]. Sins are atoned for by money or expurgated by fire.[19]

    3. Talk of cruelty. Is not cruelty the soul of persecution? The Madiai,[20] even now.

✗. Professed Protestants are bad enough.

Let me begin at home[:]

    1. Even around us are Hypocrites who talk fair, who sit with us, pray and sing with us, but away they plunge into sin and folly. Backsliders too, who have been cut out of our communion and are still such as we could not safely re-admit.[21]

    2. Let me go on. Have we not S[abbath] Breakers here? Some come only once in the day. Some come not [at] all some days. Some riot at evening. Their conversation is worldly and fleshly.[22] You laugh and giggle the sermon away or riot in the road worse than another day. <u>Buy or sell</u>.[23]

    3. But we have dishonest persons here. Thieves, it may be yet undiscovered, or men who overreach in trade, who take advantage[,]

who pilfer by littles — Servants taking small things—
Things laid hold on slyly by those who are not owners.
4, Gambling too is rife in some parts. the
cards are shuffled still, bowls are played,
bets staked — You are some of you guilty here.
5, Lewdness & Lust are not gone. Even
adultery is practised by some. fornication by
many.   Men & women are still ruined,
seduced, seducers —   What is the very gem
of your dancing room is it not lust? What was
your feast for? What did you hear at the
playhouse, the theatre? What is done in
the twilight you know & I need not mention.
What your reading, your conversation, your thoughts—
You call it trouble if you are dis-graced, but
call it much rather, lust, sin, filthiness,
6, Drunkenness is not departed either. we
have secret drinkers — who only fear exposure
& open ones in shoals? Who reeled home late
last night? Who was turned out of the
public-house for shameful conduct. —
Some of you spend all but your last farthing
aye & that too & then go some like hell-fiends
to rend your wives' hearts & terrify your
children. To some of you this is common.
7, Profane swearing is too common.
Some hesitate not to commit perjury
& swear to lies. Many curse God, their

who pilfer by littles.[24] Servants taking small things. Things laid hold on slyly[25] by those who are not owners.

4. Gambling too is rife in some parts.[26] The cards are shuffled still, bowls are played,[27] bets staked.[28] You are, some of you, guilty here.[29]

5. Lewdness and Lust are not gone. Even adultery is practised by some. Fornication by many. Men and women are still ruined, seduced, seducers. What is the very gem of your dancing room? Is it not lust? What was your feast for? What did you hear at the playhouse, the theatre? What is done in the twilight you know, and I need not mention. What you'r[e] reading, your conversation, your songs. You call it trouble if you are disgraced, but[30] call it much rather, lust, sin, filthiness.

6. Drunkenness is not departed either. We have secret drinkers who only fear exposure, and open ones in shoals?[31] Who reeled home late last night? Who was turned out of the public-house for shameful conduct?[32] Some of you spend all but your last farthing, aye and that too, and then go home like hell-fiends to rend your wives' hearts and terrify your children. To some of you this is common.

7. Profane swearing is too common. Some hesitate not to commit perjury and swear to lies.[33] Many curse God, their

fellow creatures, themselves or Blasphemers are
even heard in the street, at our doors —
    Have I not proved the fact —
This fair world is foul, the green sod covers
multitudes of graves & putrid bodies. —
II. Oh Holy Ghost convince them of the folly of sin.
1. Men miss the end they design by sin. What
does a swearer get by oaths? Dishonesty cheats itself.
Temperance has more pleasure than excess.
Chastity more than lewdness. Religion is happier
than sin —   Sinner thou pursuest a shadow
a bubble — a worse than that —
2. Men bring on themselves the indignation
of their fellow men — the prison locks up
dishonesty — rags follow drunkenness. character
lost, no respect — but more.
3. Vice punishes itself. Drunkenness wastes
time & money. Gambling destroys the soul —
Lust & Excess bring on horrible disease, speedy
death — pain, groans. satiety, disgrace —
III. Help me oh great one to speak of the great
fault that lies in sin —
    Let it be measured
1. By the reasonableness of every command
you have broken. It is a command not to
hurt our own-selves
2. By the dignity of the lawgiver — he is your
creator, guardian, provider, Lord,

fellow creatures, themselves. Blasphemers are even heard in the street, at our doors[.][34]

Have I not proved the fact? This fair world is foul. The green sod covers multitudes of graves and putrid bodies.

II. OH HOLY GHOST, CONVINCE THEM OF THE FOLLY OF SIN.

1. Men miss the end they design by sin.[35] What does a swearer get by oaths? Dishonesty cheats itself. Temperance has more pleasure than excess. Chastity more than lewdness. Religion is happier than sin. Sinner, thou pursuest a shadow,[36] a bubble, a worse than that.[37]

2. Men bring on themselves the indignation of their fellow men. The prison locks up dishonesty. Rags follow drunkenness.[38] Character lost, no respect. But more.

3. Vice punishes itself. Drunkenness wastes time and money. Gamblings destroys the soul. Lust and Excess bring on horrible disease, speedy death, – pain, groans, satiety,[39] disgrace.

III. HELP ME, OH GREAT ONE, TO SPEAK OF THE GREAT FAULT THAT LIES IN SIN.

Let it be measured:

1. By the reasonableness of every command you have broken. It is a command not to hurt our own-selves.[40]

2. By the dignity of the lawgiver. He is your creator, guardian, provider, Lord.

3 By the nature of the sacrifice necessary
for the atonement — the blood of Jesus.
4. By the pains of Hell —   But then.
IV   Oh my helper — may I warn them of
    the fruit of sin, especially the sin of unbelief.
Sinner none of thy sins can damn thee if
thou believest & any one can if thou wilt not.
Every moment thou delayest thou sinnest more.
Death is coming & then thy pleasure departs.
Then comes Hell — the fruit of thy life
Thy Fortune to retire on.   Flames, racks
company of devils, the pit, eternal woe.
    Heaven lost, never to be regained,
Time gone, Hope gone, Jesus gone.
Oh man, I pray God show thee the
way thou are going & the end thereof.
    So that thou mayest escape.

                        Oh. my God — do help —
No. 305.   For Jesus sake
                            amen

I record with gratitude the fact that I was very much
helped in preaching this. 305 & look for fruit from it.

3. By the nature of the sacrifice necessary for the atonement—the blood of Jesus.[41]

4. By the pains of hell—But then.

IV. OH MY HELPER, MAY I WARN THEM OF THE FRUIT OF SIN, ESPECIALLY THE SIN OF UNBELIEF.

Sinner, none of thy sins can damn thee if thou believest, and any one [of them] can if thou wilt not.[42]

Every moment thou delayest, thou sinnest more. Death is coming, and then thy pleasure departs. Then comes Hell, the fruit of thy life, thy Fortune to retire on. Flames, racks, company of devils, the pit, eternal woe.

Heaven lost, never to be regained. Time gone, Hope gone. Jesus gone.

Oh man, I pray God show thee the way thou are going and the end thereof.

So that thou mayest escape.

Oh my God, do help.
For Jesus['s] sake.
Amen.

~~190~~. 305.

I record with gratitude the fact that I was very much helped in preaching this 305 and look for fruit from it.[43]

1. In his lecture "The Sciences as Sources of Illustration," Charles instructed, "It seems to me that every student for the Christian Ministry ought to know at least something of every science; he should intermeddle with every form of knowledge that may be useful in his life's work. God has made all things that are in the world to be our teachers, and there is something to be learned from every one of them; and as he would never be a thorough student who did not attend all classes at which he was expected to be present, so he who does not learn from all things that God has made will never gather all the food that his soul needs, nor will he be likely to attain to that perfection of mental manhood which will enable him to be a fully-equipped teacher of others" (*Lectures* 3:144). Charles advocated for the study of astronomy as a "special delight of ministers of the gospel," for "the science which tends to bring men to bow in humility before the Lord should always be a favourite study with us whose business it is to inculcate reverence for God" (*Lectures* 3:145).

2. Genesis 15:5, "And he brought him forth abroad, and said, Look now toward heaven, and tell the stars, if thou be able to number them: and he said unto him, So shall thy seed be."

3. Job 22:12, "Is not God in the height of heaven? and behold the height of the stars, how high they are!"

4. Psalm 8:3–4, "When I consider thy heavens, the work of thy fingers, the moon and the stars, which thou hast ordained; what is man, that thou art mindful of him? and the son of man, that thou visitest him?"

5. Daniel 12:3, "And they that be wise shall shine as the brightness of the firmament; and they that turn many to righteousness as the stars for ever and ever."

6. Cf. Matt 2:2. 7. Cf. 2 Pet 1:19; Rev 22:16.

8. Cf. Rev 1:20.

9. Charles appears to have used or been influenced by John Gill's notes on this verse in his commentary (John Gill, *An Exposition of the Books of the Prophets of the Old Testament, Both Larger and Lesser, in Two Volumes*, vol. 1 [London: printed for the author and sold by G. Keith at the Bible and Crown in Grace-church-street; and by J. Robinson at Dock-head, Southwark, 1757, The Spurgeon Library], 213).

10.   Charles begins a word, then scratches out its first letter.

11.   The instinct of man to know there is a God is something Charles referenced in later sermons. As one example, see "The Carnal Mind Enmity Against God" (*NPSP* 1, Sermon 20).

12.   Charles recounted how the character and influence of those who deny the existence of God often is in contrast to the fruit of theism. As one example, he refers to his work with the orphanage: "'This whole Orphanage is an argument for God. I say often to infidels, "Will you take this and carry it on for a month?"' The three motives leading Mr. Spurgeon to undertake the Orphanage were, desire to relieve suffering; a hope of enlisting the lads and girls in the service of God; and a zeal for the honor of God whose power and faithfulness would be signally manifest in the success of a work begun and carried on in trust in him. Modifying the language of the brave old prophet of Jehovah, he has often proposed the test, 'The God that answereth by orphanages, let him be God!'" (H. L. Wayland, *Charles H. Spurgeon: His Faith and Works* [Philadelphia: American Baptist Publication Society, 1892], 171–72).

13.   "1. To counterfeit; to feign; to mimick. 2. To give the lie to; to charge with falsehood. 3. To calumniate; to raise false reports of any man. 4. To give a false representation of anything. 5. To fill with lies" (Johnson's *Dictionary*, s.v. "belie").

14.   Charles referred to the stars as "golden letters" in at least four other sermons. "Do not the stars exalt him, when they write his name upon the azure of heaven in their golden letters?" (*NPSP* 4:27; and similar wording in *"Good Tiding of Great Joy." Christ's Incarnation the Foundation of Christianity: Central Truth Series*, vol. 1 [London: Passmore and Alabaster, 1901, The Spurgeon Library], 5). "The first question, 'Who made all these things?' is one which is easily answered by a man who has a honest conscience and a sane mind; for when he lifts his eyes up yonder to read the stars, he will see those stars spell out in golden letters this word – *God*" (*NPSP* 3:65, italics in the original). "No, sirs, the man's perception of God is all gone, and is all that is gone; his power to realise spiritual things has failed, or else his ears would hear the voice of God in the sounding tops of the pines; his eyes would see the name of God written in golden letters athwart the midnight sky" (*MTP* 60:27).

15. Cf. Eph 1:23; Col 3:11.   16. Cf. 1 Tim 6:16.

17. Charles misjudged the first two letters of this word and corrected the "b" while mistakenly placing a loop on the second letter "r."

18. Dionysius Lardner's *Handbook of Astronomy* gives some context to a Victorian understanding of planetary rotation: "Mere visual observation, however, can at most only supply grounds for probable conjecture, either as to the rotation of the sphere, or the position of its pole, if such rotation take place. To verify this conjecture, to determine with certainty whether the motion of the sphere be one of rotation, and if so, to ascertain with precision the direction of the axis round which this rotation takes place, its velocity, and, in fine, whether it be uniform or variable—are problems of the highest importance, but which are altogether beyond the powers of mere visual observation unaided by instruments of precision" (Dionysius Lardner, *Handbook of Astronomy,* ed. Edwin Dunkin [London: Spottiswoode, 1875], 70).

19. The superscripted "How grand his palace if heaven be its floor" is incorporated in the text.

20. Lardner's *Handbook* provides a Victorian understanding of the Earth's rotation: "A few hours' attentive contemplation of the firmament at night will enable any common observer to perceive, that although the stars are, relatively to each other, fixed, the hemisphere, *as a whole,* is in motion. Looking at the zenith, constellation after constellation will appear to pass across it, having risen in an oblique direction from the horizon at one side, and, after passing the zenith, descending on the other side to the horizon, in a direction similarly oblique. Still more careful and longer continued observation, and a comparison, so far as can be made by the eye, of the different directions successively assumed by the same object, creates a suspicion, which every additional observation strengthens, that the celestial vault has a motion of slow and uniform rotation round a certain diameter as an axis, carrying with it all the objects visible upon it, without in the least deranging their relative positions or disturbing their arrangement" (Lardner, *Handbook of Astronomy,* 69–70, italics in the original).

21. Context would make it seem this is "as" not "us," and Charles simply did not complete the crown of the "a."

22. Cf. Job 26:7.   23. Cf. Ps 19:6.

24. Cf. Gen 1:26.   25. Cf. Ps 147:4.

26. Cf. Ps 139:3.   27. Cf. Phil 4:19.

28. Cf. John 10:14; 2 Tim 2:19.

29. Cf. 1 Pet 1:5.

30. "Earnest" here is a noun meaning "pledge; handful; first fruits; token of something of the same kind in futurity" (Johnson's *Dictionary*, s.v. "earnest").

31. Originally, Charles wrote "4" beneath "IV." The character is smudged.

32. Troubled, or troublesome.

33. "When I began to preach in the little thatched chapel at Waterbeach, my first concern was, Would God save any souls through me? They called me a ragged-headed boy, and I think I was just that; I know I wore a jacket. After I had preached for some time, I thought, 'This gospel has saved me, but then somebody else preached it; will it save anybody else now that I preach it?' Some Sundays went over, and I used to say to the deacons, 'Have you heard of anybody finding the Lord under my ministry? Do you know of anyone brought to Christ through my preaching?' My good old friend and deacon said, 'I am sure somebody must have received the Saviour; I am quite certain it is so.' 'Oh!' I answered, 'but I want to know it, I want to prove that it is so.' How my heart leaped for joy when I heard tidings of my first convert!" (*Autobiography* 1:232).

34. "Labour; toil; fatigue" (Johnson's *Dictionary*, s.v. "travail").

35. Cf. Isa 53:11.

36. As noted throughout many of these early sermons, Charles concludes with a personal prayer.

1. Interestingly, even in Charles's lifetime, the "e" was dropped in dictionaries and other official communications (Johnson's *Dictionary*, s.v. "judgment").

2. This sermon has a few similarities to Charles's later sermon "The Holy Spirit's Threefold Conviction of Men" (*MTP* 29, Sermon 1708). Regarding the first Roman numeral of the later sermon, Charles said, "First, we believe that a promise is here made to the servants of Christ, that when they go forth to preach the gospel the Holy Ghost will be with them to reprove men. By this is meant, not so much to save them as to silence them. When the minister of Christ stands up to plead his Master's cause, another advocate appears in court, whose pleadings would make it hard for men to resist the truth. Observe how this reproof was given with regard to *sin*" (*MTP* 29:122, italics in the original).

3. "One week-night, when I was sitting in the house of God, I was not thinking much about the preacher's sermon, for I did not believe it. The thought struck me, '*How did you come to be a Christian?*' I sought the Lord. '*But how did you come to seek the Lord?*' The truth flashed across my mind in a moment,—I should not have sought him unless there had been some previous influence in my mind to make me seek him. I prayed, thought I; but then I asked myself, *How came I to pray?* I was induced to pray by reading the Scriptures. *How came I to read the Scriptures?* I did read them; but what lead [*sic*] me to do so? Then, in a moment, I saw that God was at the bottom of it all, and that he was the Author of my faith; and so the whole doctrine of grace opened up to me, and from that doctrine I have not departed to this day, and I desire to make this my constant confession, 'I ascribe my change wholly to God'" (*Autobiography* 1:168–69, italics in the original).

4. Cf. John 14:16; 15:26; 16:7.

5. "X" is used as an emphatic device at the beginning of this sentence.

6. Cf. Rom 1:18–32.

7. Charles mistakenly placed an apostrophe in "god's," making it a singular possessive when he intended it to be a plural genitive "gods of."

8. Cf. Deut 4:28; Isa 37:19; 44:14–17.

9. Cf. 1 John 2:16.

10. Cf. 1 Kgs 15:12; 2 Kgs 23:4–14.

11. Cf. Lev 20:10; Matt 5:32; Acts 15:19–20.

12. Cf. Exod 20:13; Ps 74:20; Rom 12:19.

13. Cf. Lev 18:21; 20:2–3; Deut 12:31; 18:10; 2 Kgs 16:2–3; 17:16–17; 21:6; 2 Chr 28:1–3; 33:6; Ps 106:37–38; Jer 7:30–31; and Ezek 23:37–39.

14. Plural of "sati," a practice in India where a widow would throw herself on her husband's funeral pyre. One clergyman notes the plight of women in India (especially widows): "We interfere with suttees, and humanely save the widow from burning. . . . In India a widow is not permitted to marry again but must be supported by her late husband's relations; and it is said that many of these poor women are sent down to Pooree [Puri] in the hope of getting rid of them, and no doubt this purpose frequently succeeds" ("Literature," *London Daily News,* December 25, 1847).

15. In Charles's library is this account, published later, of missionaries in New Guinea encountering cannibalistic tribes: "The cannibal feast was held. Some of our friends appeared with pieces of human flesh dangling from their neck and arms. The child [who was to be included in the feast] was spared for a future time, it being considered too small" (James Chalmers and W. Wyatt Gill, *Work and Adventure in New Guinea 1877 to 1885* [London: The Religious Tract Society, 56; Paternoster Row: 1885, The Spurgeon Library], 62).

16. Cf. Gal 5:19–21.

17. "After all, our reformers acted well, and after a scriptural model, when they poured contempt upon the idols of Rome, and made a mockery of her saints, relics, images, masses, and priests. They were more than justified in exposing the idolatries of Popery, and subjecting the objects formerly reverenced to the utmost contempt. There was a deep meaning in their breaking of crosses, and the burning of holy roods. . . . The iconoclasts of that age did not go one bit too far. I could wish they had been even less lenient than they were, and that not a single thing ever worshiped by man had been spared for a moment" (*MTP* 16:626–27).

18. One example of the reputation of priests that the leaders of Yorkshire sought to protect their women from was recorded on May 9, 1840: "Resolved, 'That on comparing the ritual of the priests and the code of moral theology produced by Mr. Billington, according to which priests are to direct the tribunal of confession, with the books produced by Mr. McGhee, and those sold in the shops for the use of females in York, it is the opinion of this meeting that the system by which Romish priests examine their female penitents in the confessional, is cruel, tyrannical, immoral—not only totally unauthorised by the word of God, but in plain opposition to it; that it is such a system as no father, husband, or brother ought to submit to for his daughter, his wife, or his sister—that the bulls of popes and the secret statutes of the popish bishops prove that they know how their priests abuse their power to licentiousness and vice, while they impose this as a holy tribunal on the people; and that the Roman Catholics in this meeting determine to teach their wives and daughters in future to confess their sins to the Lord Jesus Christ, who is our great high priest, the hope and refuge of our souls, and that they will not allow the females of their families ever to go to confession to a popish priest again'" ("To the Rev. T. Billington," *Yorkshire Gazette*, May 9, 1840).

19. In Charles's library is this account: "The people of Germany were soon after in a state of great excitement. A monk, named Tetzel, went from place to place, with a splendid retinue, selling indulgences, which he declared to be 'the most precious and noble of God's gifts.' Pointing from his pulpit to a red cross that was reared, he profanely declared that it had as much efficacy as the very cross of Christ. 'Come,' he said, 'and I will give you letters, all properly sealed, by which even the sins you intend to commit may be pardoned. There is no sin so great, that an indulgence cannot remit it; and even if any one (which is doubtless impossible) had offered violence to the blessed virgin Mary, mother of God, let him pay—only let him pay well, and all will be forgiven him.' Crowds gathered about this impious pretender; men, women, and children, and even the poor who lived on alms—all found money" (*Characters, Scenes, and Incidents of the Reformation* [London: The Religious Tract Society, 1849, The Spurgeon Library], 142–43).

20. Franceso and Rosa Madiai were imprisoned for their proselytization of Italians to Protestantism. This was a major news story of the time which Charles and his people would have followed closely: "The reading of the Bible has become

a crime in Florence, punishable as an offence against the State. The following official document, issued by the Judge Instructor against two individuals accused of this crime requires, we think, no comment: —Whereas the accused Francesco and Rosa Madiai, have in the depositions confessed to have made themselves apostates from the Catholic religion, and to profess an heterodox confession, which they call by the name of evangelical confession, and of the pure gospel, the which does not recognise the authority and the traditions of the Catholic Church, but subjects the interpretation of the gospel and of the sacred Scriptures to private judgment" ("State Prosecution of Protestants in Florence," *The Elgin and Morayshire Courier and General Advertiser for the North of Scotland*, December 5, 1851).

21. In his *Autobiography* Charles recounts that while pastor at Waterbeach, he "had often to battle with Antinomians,---that is, people who held that, because they believed themselves to be elect, they might live as they liked" (*Autobiography* 1:258).

22. Cf. 1 Cor 3:1–3.

23. Charles's reference here implies attitudes and activities in violation of the Sabbath rest. See further the 1689 London Baptist Confession of Faith: "The Sabbath is then kept holy unto the Lord, when men, after a due preparation of their hearts, and ordering their common affairs aforehand, do not only observe an holy (Isa. lviii. 13; Neh. xiii. 15–23) rest all the day, from their own works, words, and thoughts, about their worldly employment, and recreations, but also are taken up the whole time in the public and private exercises of his worship, and in the duties (Matt. xii. 1–13) of necessity and mercy" (*A Confession of Faith, Put Forth by the Elders and Brethren of Many Congregations of Christians (Baptized upon Profession of Their Faith) In London and the Country. With an Appendix Concerning Baptism* [London: printed for John Harris at the Harrow against the Church in the Poultry, 1688], Chp. XXII:8. Contained in Edward Bean Underhill, ed., *Confessions of Faith, and Other Public Documents, Illustrative of the History of the Baptist Churches of England in the 17th Century* [London: printed for the Hanserd Knollys Society by Haddon, Brothers, and Co., 1854, The Spurgeon Library], 216).

24. Charles uses the phrase "by littles" akin to "little by little." In discussion of Judas Iscariot, he said, "It was true he had been filching for months, but then he did it by littles, and covered his defalcations so well by financial manipulations that he

ran no risk of detection from the honest unsuspecting fishermen with whom he associated" (*MTP* 9:91).

25. Charles used the phrase "on the sly" many times throughout his preaching, referring to those who hide their misdeeds behind a facade. For an example of this usage, see *MTP* 29:512. One of Charles's books gives the meaning of "on the sly" as "secretly" (James M. Dixon, *Dictionary of Idiomatic English Phrases* [London: T. Nelson and Sons, The Spurgeon Library, 1891], 304).

26. Minutes from the House of Commons taken on February 13, 1845, detail that betting occurred in the stock market speculation of railway contracts: The English "[g]overnment will only allow one company to undertake one line, yet half-a-dozen possible companies spring into existence to compete for the line, and long before it is determined which company shall have it, the possible shares of a possible company are in the market and selling at a premium, and the base propensity of gambling is rife in regard to every one of them. All this ought to be checked by authority. There ought to be a penalty upon selling or dealing in any way in the shares of a company which has not been recognised by authority as a real company, by which real business is to be done. The speculating shams ought to be treated as criminal devices, so that sober honesty might have some chance in the world, instead of being abashed, as it is now, by the bold swagger of successful scheming, which is nurtured into life and vivacity by the unrestricted principle of competition" ("London," *Morning Post*, February 13, 1845).

27. Here Charles is likely referencing the game of "bowls," which had a notorious reputation (James M. Pretsell, *The Game of Bowls: Past and Present* [Edinburgh; London: Oliver and Boyd, 1908], 19–21).

28. While horse races were some of the most popular events on which to bet, there were many other forms and occasions for betting, such as timing a horse's journey from Ennis to Limerick and back again ("The Army," *Cork Examiner*, March 16, 1849), cock-fighting ("Illegal Amusements," *Belfast Protestant Journal*, June 14, 1845), and fights among men ("Fight for Tuesday," *Bell's Life in London and Sporting Chronicle*, December 19, 1847).

29. Spurgeon described Waterbeach as "a village notorious for its drunkenness and profanity" (*Autobiography* 1:227–28).

30. In Spurgeon's handwritten text, this line is superscripted: "What your [*sic*] reading, your conversation, your songs."

31. The meaning of "shoals" here is most likely "a crowd; a great multitude; a throng" (Johnson's *Dictionary*, s.v. "shoal").

32. In a specific example of church discipline, Charles recalls an instance in which one "inconsistent professor of religion" was thrown out of a local public-house on Friday night. He was subsequently removed from the Waterbeach Chapel membership roll on Sunday morning (*Autobiography* 1:260).

33. Samuel Johnson defined "perjury" simply as a "False oath" (Johnson's *Dictionary*, s.v. "perjury").

34. In the year before Charles's birth, a letter to the editor published in the *Londonderry Sentinel* noted, "On passing through Fleet-street Saturday morning last, I was much shocked to see a man exhibiting a large printed placard on a board, a glance which sufficed to show me that it was a blasphemous attack upon the name and character of our Lord Jesus Christ. I especially noticed the words *Dagon Jesus*, in very large letters. I feel very deeply, Sir, and I am sure is in common with yourself and all sincere Christians, the continuance with impunity of this wicked abomination.—That in the public streets of this Christian city, in broad daylight, men should be suffered to hold up the *One Great Name* in heaven and earth to ridicule; that that blessed Saviour who died for us all, and by whom, as a nation, we have all been cherished, instructed, and exalted above other people, should be held up to insult and scorn in our public ways, this is enough to make us hide our heads with shame indeed!" ("Awful Blasphemy in the Public Streets of London," *Londonderry Sentinel and North-West Advertiser*, November 9, 1833, italics in the original).

35. "Yet, so is it; God will honour his ministers, he will prove the utter futility of man's brag and boast. You may be careless, sir, while you are well, you may neglect this great salvation, but a little sickness shall make thee tremble, and thy knees shall shake, and thou shalt be convulsed with agony, and find that this is not handling the matter wisely. You are something like a bankrupt who knows that his accounts are going wrong, and fears that he is insolvent; he does not look at his books, he does not like to look at them, for there is no very pleasant

reading there; there may be a few assets, but the entries are mostly on the other side, and so at last he does not keep any book, it would be troublesome to him to know where he was. So is it with you. It is because things are not right, you do not like to sift them and try them, lest you should find out the black reality. Be wise, I pray you, and look a little beyond you. Why shut your eyes and perish?" (*MTP* 7:358).

36. Cf. Eccl 1:14.   37. Cf. Rom 6:23.

38. Cf. Prov 23:21.

39. Defined as "fullness beyond desire or pleasure; more than enough; wearisomeness of plenty; state of being palled or glutted" (Johnson's *Dictionary*, s.v. "satiety").

40. "There have been other men besides Christians who have longed to die. There is the suicide who, mad, from life's history longs to be hurled, even though hell receive him. Tired of all life's troubles he thinks he sees a way to escape from his toil and from his sorrow through the grim gate of death. He stains his hand with his own blood, and red with his own gore appears before his Maker. Ah fool, to leap from *one* evil to a myriad! Ah madman, to plunge from little streams of woe into an unfathomable gulf of agony! There can be no more absurd, revolting, and insensible act, than for a man to take away his life. Setting aside the horrors of crime that surround it, how foolish is the attempt to escape by rushing into the very midst of danger! The ostrich who buries her head in the sand, and when she cannot see the hunter thinks the hunter cannot see her, is sensible and wise compared with such a man, who rushing into the very thick of the battle hopes in this way to escape from his enemy. How can it be thou foolish man? Is the stream too deep for thee already, and instead of seeking to find a shore by faith in God dost thou seek the centre of the stream that thou mayest get a firmer footing there? Oh foolish generation and unwise, 'Put up thy sword into thy scabbard and do thyself no harm,' for harm thou wilt do if thou rush into a greater evil to escape the less" (*NPSP* 5:398, italics in the original).

41. Cf. Rom 5:11; 1 John 1:7.

42. Cf. Mark 16:16; Acts 16:31. Charles made reference to Mark 16:16 in at least one sermon in fifty-two volumes (out of sixty-three) of the *MTP*.

43. This sermon was preached in the fall of 1852, likely in late October. Charles tells us he preached Sermon 128 on August 2, 1852 (the 218th occasion he preached) and Sermon 207 on Christmas Day of 1852 (the 338th occasion he preached). This sermon (190) is recorded as the 305th occasion he preached. It is interesting to note that there are 145 days between 8/2 and 12/25, and Charles recorded 106 occasions that he preached a sermon.

1 John. II. 12 ……… Sermon to Children. 191

Jesus Christ said "preach the gospel to every creature"
this of course means children too. now teachers
are childrens preachers & so would I be now.

I. This verse says children have sins.
  Now this is very true for even little children
have sins & many bad ones too —
1. Some children disobey their parents - this is
very wicked — a curse rests on those who do not obey.
  This is the beginning of evils.
2. Some children quarrel & fight — Some have killed
  each other — how shocking. tale - eye for a pin.
3. Some children steal - shocking indeed. Steal
not at all. little leads to great.
4. Some play in God's house or break the
  Sabbath when at home.
5. Some tell lies. 6. Some use bad words.

II This verse says their sins may be forgiven.
  Little children can serve God —
1. They can pray,   Rev. T. Reader.
2. They can repent.
3. They can believe in Jesus.
4. They can love Jesus.
5. They can die happily —
III And all for Jesus sake. our sins are forgiven
306.

SERMON *to* CHILDREN[1]

1 John 2:12

"I write unto you, little children, because your sins are forgiven you for his name's sake."

Jesus Christ said[,] "Preach the gospel to every creature."[2] This, of course, means children too. Now, teachers are children's preachers,[3] and so would I be now.

I.   THIS VERSE SAYS CHILDREN HAVE SINS.

Now, this is very true, for even little children have sins, and many bad ones too.

1.   Some children disobey their parents.[4] This is very wicked. A curse rests on those who do not obey.[5] This is the beginning of evils.

2.   Some children quarrel and fight. Some have killed each other. How shocking. Tale: eye for a pin.[6]

3.   Some children steal. Shocking, indeed. Steal not at all. Little leads to great.

4.   Some play in God's house or break the Sabbath when at home.[7]

5.   Some tell lies.

6.   Some use bad words.

II.   THIS VERSE SAYS THEIR SINS MAY BE FORGIVEN.

Little children can serve God.

1.   They can pray. Rev. T. Reader.[8]

2.   They can repent.

3.   They can believe in Jesus.

4.   They can love Jesus.[9]

5.   They can die happily.

III. AND ALL FOR JESUS['S] SAKE. OUR SINS ARE FORGIVEN.[10]

306.

1. Charles preached one later sermon on the text of 1 John 2:12–13. It was titled "A Sermon to the Lord's Little Children" (*MTP* 29, Sermon 1711–12), and there is a recorded instance where he preached a "sermon to children" early in his ministry in London. "After I had begun for some little time to preach in London, Dr. Alexander Fletcher was engaged to deliver the annual sermon to children in Surrey Chapel; but as he was taken ill, I was asked in a hurry to preach to the children in his stead" (*Autobiography* 1:34).

2. Cf. Mark 16:15.

3. "Do not think of waiting until you can do some great thing for God; do little things and then the Master will bid you go up higher. Eleven years ago, I was addressing Sunday-school children, and these alone. Ten—nine years ago, I was preaching in little insignificant rooms here and there, generally going out and coming back on foot, and occasionally getting a lift in a cart" (*Autobiography* 3:49).

4. Cf. Exod 20:12; Rom 1:30; Eph 6:1; Col 3:20.

5. Cf. Deut 11:26–32.

6. Charles seems to refer to a story recorded in a book titled *A Kiss for a Blow*: "Two boys, named Abel and George, were at the same school in New York. Each was about ten years old; they were not brothers, but school-mates and class-mates. Both of them had irritable tempers, and had been taught to think that they must resent injuries, and defend their rights at all hazards. Playing *pin* was a common amusement in the school. They played in this way: two boys would take a hat, and set it down between them, crown upward. Each boy would lay a pin on the crown of the hat, and push it—first one boy would push the pin, and then the other. He who could push the pins so as to make them lie across each other, became entitled to them both. One day, during play hour, Abel and George were playing pin. They pushed the pins about for some time. Both became much excited by the game. At last, Abel pushed the pins so that, as he said, one lay across the point of the other. George denied it. Abel declared they did, and snatched up both pins. George's anger broke forth in a moment, and he struck Abel in the face with his fist. This excited Abel's wrath. They began to fight—the other boys clustering around, not to part them but to urge them on. Some cried, 'Hit him, Abel!' and some, 'Give it to him, George!' thus stimulating them to quarrel. The boys seized each other,

and finally came tumbling to the ground, Abel uppermost. Then Abel, in his fury, beat George in the face, till the blood spouted from his nose and mouth, and he lay like one dead. Then the boys pulled Abel off. But George could not get up. The boys now began to be alarmed. They were afraid Abel had killed him. The teacher was called. He carried George in, and washed the blood from his face and head, which he found bruised in a shocking manner[.] One of his eyes was so hurt and swollen that he could not open it. And from that day the sight of it grew more and more dim, till it became blind. *An eye for a pin!* It was a dear bargain. Yet there was as much sense in their fighting, and putting out each other's eyes, for a pin, as there would have been in doing the same thing for a kingdom. It is just as displeasing to our Heavenly Father, to see human beings fighting for a kingdom as for a pin. Two nations may as well go to war for a pin as for an empire. It is wrong to fight for either" (Henry C. Wright, *A Kiss for a Blow: or, A Collection of Stories for Children, Showing Them How to Prevent Quarrelling* [London: Thomas H. Keble, n. d.], 22–23, italics in the original).

7. "There was another evidence of an hypocrite which was equally good, namely, that *he strained at a gnat and swallowed a camel.* Hypocrites in these days do not find fault with us for eating with unwashen hands, but they still fix upon some ceremonial omission. Sabbatarianism has furnished hypocrisy with an extremely convenient refuge. Acts of necessity done by the Christian, are the objects of the sanctimonious horror of Pharisees, and labours of mercy and smiles of joy, are damning sins in the esteem of hypocrites, if done upon a Sunday. Though our Father worked hitherto, and Christ worked, and though works of kindness, and mercy, and charity, are the duty of the Sabbath: yet if the Christian be employed in these, he is thought to be offending against God's holy law" (*NPSP* 5:99, italics in the original).

8. Charles most likely refers to an anecdote concerning Rev. Thomas Reader, of Taunton, who died in 1794: "The examples of early piety have also been rendered very useful. The late Rev. T. Reader, when a child, was deeply impressed with divine truth. A stranger visiting the family, observed that he did not fail to shut himself up alone for prayer. He was powerfully struck with a sense of his own negligence, and said, 'What, shall a little child be so anxious for a place of retirement to pray, and I never prayed in my life!' From that time he began to be serious, and not only became a Christian, but a very valuable minister of Christ"

(Charles Buck, *The Works of Charles Buck, Late Minister of the Gospel. In Six Volumes. Vol. IV. Contains: The Practical Expositor; Or, Scripture Illustrated by Facts, and Arranged for Every Day in the Year* [Philadelphia: McCarty & Davis, 1822], 293).

9. "I used to notice that a good deal of Sunday-school teaching to the children was, 'Dear child, love Jesus.' That is not the way of salvation. The way of salvation is to trust Jesus. The fruit of salvation is that the dear child does love Jesus; but that is not the way of salvation. The way of salvation is to take Christ, to trust Christ" (*MTP* 38:484).

10. Charles may have decided, since he was at the end of the page, to end the sermon here without further content, or he may not have intended to include any content, as the final portion of the verse ends with the same affirmation.

192.   Philippians IV. 5.   Christian Moderation.

There are some other matters in this chapter worth noticing which we must remark upon.

Verse. 2. The dissension between two women Euodias & Syntyche Saul mentions, because he desired perfect unanimity, he felt that even the disunion of two was a serious matter, & he knew that the spark kindles the whole mass. Therefore he gives a "beseech" to each. that they would be one.

Verse. 3. The women are said to labour with him in the gospel — — this was not by preaching — which is most strictly forbidden in I. Tim. II. 2. but in many ways. as Dorcas, by bringing up children well, as Phœbe the messenger, as nurses, deaconesses &c — The yokefellow mentioned was not Paul's wife, for the noun is masculine & likely he had none.

Verse. 3. How did Paul know that the names of persons were in the book of life? He could by apostolic power discern spirits — or he wrote as he thought & judged from their conduct.

But now to the text — the moderation here commended is not moderation in religion not moderation in love or zeal! was Paul so. Not moderation in faith! Trust him with all not moderation in holiness That were sin indeed. In all commendable things we must covet earnestly & strive mightily. Moderation will be damned. if it be any such moderation as afore mentioned. —

CHRISTIAN MODERATION [1]
Philippians 4:5

"Let your moderation be known unto all men. The Lord is at hand."

There are some other matters in this chapter worth noticing which we must remark upon.

Verse. 2.[2] The dissension between two women[,] Euodias and Syntyche[,] Saul mentions because he desired perfect unanimity, he felt that even the disunion of two was a serious matter, and he knew that the spark kindles the whole mass.[3] Therefore, he gives a "<u>beseech</u>"[4] to each that they would be one.

Verse. 3.[5] The women are said to labour with him in the gospel. This was not by preaching, which is most strictly forbidden in I. Tim. II.2,[6] but in many ways. As Dorcas,[7] by bringing up children well.[8] As Phoebe, the messenger,[9] as nurses,[10] deaconesses[11] etc. The yokefellow[12] mentioned was not Paul's wife, for the noun is masculine and likely he had none.[13]

Verse 3. How did Paul know that the names of persons were in the book of life?[14] He could, by apostolic power, discern spirits. Or he wrote as he thought, and judged from their conduct.

But now to the text—the moderation[15] here commended is not moderation in religion.

Not moderation in love or zeal! Was Paul so[?]
Not moderation in faith! Trust him with all.
Not moderation in holiness. That were sin indeed.

In all commendable things we must covet[16] earnestly and strive mightily. Moderation will be damned if it be any such moderation as afore mentioned.

I.   What then is Christian moderation.

1. A moderate use of the allowed enjoyments of this world. is the idea a common reader would lay hold on.   This is good.   We may enjoy all the mercies of God up to a certain point but not beyond —   in them moderation must be practised.

2, In our desires after this world's good. In the pursuit of its business, in our cares for our temporal welfare ; in our struggles & anxieties we must hear the words "Let your moderation &c.

3. When enemies attack us — when we are vexed troubled, & even angry. If we go far we trespass. Forgive & Forget — in your tempers cultivate mod—eration

4. In our views & opinions we never shall all agree, this text binds the hands of bigotry. We must not cut off, or feel any bad feeling towards any but if they err, still let our moderation shine.

II. What does he mean by "let it be known unto all men". we are not to tell of it, nor talk about it. but let men see it for themselves. it means.

1. Apparent Moderation not secret — some say I am not inwardly ruffled here the outward is touched we must not forgive in secret alone but confess to one another —   our pursuit of the world is to be so moderate as to be apparent even to all.

2, Constant Moderation — to all men it must be practised — every where — at all times — There must be nothing too great for it to overcome no offence too great for forgiveness — no object too hotly pursued. —

I. WHAT THEN IS CHRISTIAN MODERATION?

1. A moderate use of the allowed enjoyments of this world is the idea a common reader would lay hold on. This is good we may enjoy all the mercies of God up to a certain point, but not beyond. In them, moderation must be practised.

2. In our desires after this world's good. In the pursuit of its business, in our cares for our temporal welfare; in our struggles and anxieties we must hear the words, "Let your moderation etc."

3. When enemies attack us. When we are vexed, troubled, and even angry. If we go far, we trespass, Forgive and Forget.[17] In your tempers, cultivate moderation.

4. In our views and opinions, we never shall all agree. This text binds the hands of bigotry.[18] We must not cut off or feel any bad feeling towards any. But if they err, still let our moderation shine.[19]

II. WHAT DOES HE MEAN BY *"Let it be known unto all men"*?

We are not to tell of it, nor talk about it[,] but let men see it for themselves. It means:

1. Apparent Moderation, not secret. Some say I am not inwardly ruffled here. The outward is touched. We must not forgive in secret alone, but confess to one another.[20] Our pursuit of the world is to be so moderate as to be apparent even to all.

2. Constant Moderation — to all men it must be practiced — everywhere — at all times. There must be nothing too great for it to overcome. No offence too great for forgiveness. No object too hotly pursued.

III. We must notice the argument.
"The Lord is at hand."

1. Go not to excess for the Judge, the Lord is nigh
+ then your sins will appear hideous.

2. Love not the world too much — a dissolving day
is near, and the earth must pass away.

3. Avenge not yourself on an enemy — the avenger
comes + then he will repay thy persecutions —

4. Dismiss excessive care, trouble, anxiety,
the Lord is at hand —

How close he brings the last day "at hand"; so
it is for it may come at any moment & must
come soon. either in our death or the world's
judgment.   This is the solace + meditation
of God's elect, but to the wicked it is pregnant
with terror. "The Lord is at hand".
If I may but feel those 5 words with power I
fear not to preach,   a dying man to dying men,
sinners — hear! hear! hear! Is it not solemn
what can be more terrible to the swearer,
+ neglecter of God's word. Oh great one turn them
          + bless me much —
                    Even so.

311

III. WE MUST NOTICE THE ARGUMENT.

"The Lord is at hand."

1. Go not to excess, for the Judge, the Lord, is nigh, and then your sins will appear hideous.[21]

2. Love not the world too much[.][22] A dissolving day is near and the earth must pass away.[23]

3. Avenge not yourself on an enemy. The avenger comes, and then he will repay thy persecutions.[24]

4. Dismiss excessive care, trouble, anxiety.[25] The Lord is at hand.

How close he brings the last day "at hand", so it is for it may come at any moment and must come soon, either in our death or the world's judgment.

This is the solace and meditation of God's elect. But to the wicked it is pregnant with terror. "The Lord is at hand."

If I may but feel those 5 words with power, I fear not to preach, a dying man to dying men.[26]

Sinners, hear! hear! hear! Is it not solemn? What can be more terrible to the swearer and neglecter of God's word?

Oh Great One, turn them.[27]

and bless me much.

Even so.

311

1. Charles preached this verse in later sermons: "Prayer, the Cure for Care" (*MTP* 40, Sermon 2351) and "Joy, a Duty" (*MTP* 41, Sermon 2405).

2. Cf. Phil 4:2.   3. Cf. Jas 3:5.

4. In later sermons, Charles emphasized the same point: Paul could have said, "I beseech Euodias and Syntyche"; instead, he reserves a "beseech" for each of them. See *MTP* 40:118; 41:142.

5. Cf. Phil 4:3.   6. Cf. 1 Tim 2:12 instead of 1 Tim 2:2.

7. Cf. Acts 9:36–42.   8. Cf. Deut 11:19; Prov 22:6.

9. Cf. Rom 16:1–2. "There are sixteen girls coming from the Orphanage to join the church, and I am rejoicing in my heart over sixteen women who will, I trust, during a long life glorify Christ; sixteen matrons in the church who shall be Deborahs, Dorcasses, and Phoebes, or whoever else you may like to think of among holy women" (*MTP* 38:342).

10. Cf. 1 Thess 2:7.

11. Cf. Rom 16:1–2. Interestingly, Charles here assumes a distinction between nurses and deaconesses, but conflates the two in later years. "A mission would also find great strength in imitating Jesus by combining medical aid with religious teaching. . . . It may one day be thought possible to have deaconesses whose self-denying nursing of the sick poor shall introduce the gospel into the meanest hovels" (*MTP* 16:257); "So [Phoebe] shall have her name inscribed in this golden book of Christ's nobility, because she is the servant of the church, and because, in being such, she succoured the poor and needy. I doubt not she was a nurse among the poorer Christians, or as some call them, a deaconess, for, in the olden time, it was so, that the elder women who had need were maintained by the church, and in return occupied themselves with the nursing of sick believers; and it were well if such were the case again, and if the old office could be revived" (*MTP* 19:295–96).

12. From the Greek σύζυγος, "a yoke-fellow, an associate or companion in labour . . . [or] an assistant in the ministerial labour." See John Parkhurst, *A Greek and English Lexicon to the New Testament* (London: printed for William Baynes and Son, 1822, The Spurgeon Library), 529.

13. "Not his wife, as some think; for he had none, as appears from 1 Cor. vii. 7, 8. at the writing of which Epistle he was at Ephesus, where he paid some little time, and then went to Jerusalem; where he was quickly apprehended, and sent a prisoner to Rome, and where he now was as such; and therefore it is not likely that he should marry a wife within this compass of time, and much less that he should have one at Philippi; besides, the word used is of the masculine gender, and designs a man and not a women [*sic*]" (Gill, *An Exposition of the New Testament* [London, 1748, The Spurgeon Library], 3:147).

14. Cf. Rev 3:5; 13:8; 17:8; 20:12, 15; 21:27; 22:19.

15. Charles later commented, "The word 'moderation', in the Greek, is a very difficult word to translate into English. It does not mean moderation in the sense in which some people use the word, for they make it, as I think, almost an accursed one. 'Let your moderation' — your gentleness, your willingness, your forbearance — 'be known unto all men.' That is what it means. Do not push your own rights too far; stop short of what you might fairly demand and when you feel, at any time, a little vehement in temper, check yourself, hold yourself in, bear and forbear. Go not as far as you may, nor even as far as some think that you ought, in defending your own rights; let your gentleness, your yieldingness, be known unto all men" (*MTP* 40:118).

16. "2. To be eagerly desirous of; to long for; -- in a good sense" (Worcester, *Dictionary*, s.v. "to covet").

17. Charles used this phrase several times throughout his ministry (*MTP* 20:719; 33:501).

18. "1. Blind zeal; prejudice; *unreasonable warmth in favour of party or opinions*" (Johnson's *Dictionary*, s.v. "bigotry," italics in the original). Despite their diametrically opposite positions on soteriology, Charles and Dwight L. Moody shared a lifelong friendship that was tied together at the common foundation of a love for Jesus Christ. Susannah, in editing Charles's *Autobiography*, presented a list of correspondences between the two men, describing the "mutual esteem and love which [Mr. Moody] and Mr. Spurgeon cherished for each other" (*Autobiography* 4:169).

19. Charles embodied this principle later in life when he became involved in several controversies, most notably the Downgrade Controversy that, by Charles's own

estimation, would eventually claim his life: "Good bye, Ellis [a friend of his]; you will never see me again, *this fight is killing me*" (*Autobiography* 3:152, italics in the original).

20. Cf. Jas 5:16.

21. Cf. Matt 3:2; Jas 5:8.

22. Cf. 1 John 2:15.

23. Cf. 2 Pet 3:10.

24. Cf. Rom 12:19.

25. Cf. Matt 6:25–34.

26. This expression is original to Nonconformist preacher Richard Baxter (1615–1691): "The face of death, and nearness of eternity, did much convince me what books to read, what studies to prefer and prosecute, what company and conversation to choose. It drove me early into the vineyard of the Lord, and taught me to preach as a dying man to dying men" (Richard Baxter, *The Practical Works of the Rev. Richard Baxter, Vol. XVIII* [London: James Duncan, 1830, The Spurgeon Library], 409).

27. Cf. 2 Tim 2:25.

Is. I. 18. Come & let us reason together.   193

The more Justification by grace through faith is held prominent, the more good usually through the Spirit attends the preacher's labours.

Having but a little ago laboured to convince of sin I now would speak of righteousness for sinners

God, the blessed & infinitely gracious invites his rebellious subjects to a conference with him.

I. Let us look at the invitation — To whom. — To all sinners, backsliders, rebels. —

He goes to the extremes of sin & excepts none at all.

1. Though you be deeply dyed through & through.
2. Though you have sinned long —
3. Though you have gone back.
4. Though you have sinned conspicuously.
5. Though you have sinned proud scarlet sins.

Black. Long. Backslider. Glaringly. Proudly.

        Scarlet, Crimson, sinners come.

None are excluded hence but those who do themselves exclude. — Come. <u>Now</u>

II. Let us reason with God. Help me to reason in thy name Oh thou God of Grace.

Sinners ask any question you please.

1. How can God be just & yet forgive.

We must have firm foundation here. We see that future obedience cannot satisfy justice for old offences. God cannot forgive without

COME *and* LET US REASON TOGETHER [1]

Isaiah 1:18

*"Come now, and let us reason together, saith the L*ord*: though your sins be as scarlet, they shall be as white as snow; though they be red like crimson, they shall be as wool."*

The more justification by grace through faith is held prominent, the more good usually through the Spirit attends the preacher's labours. [2]

Having but a little ago laboured to convince of sin, [3] I now would speak of righteousness for sinners.

God, the blessed and infinitely gracious, invites his rebellious subjects to a conference with him.

I. LET US LOOK AT THE INVITATION: TO WHOM.

To all sinners, backsliders, rebels. He goes to the extremes of sin and excepts none at all.

1. Though you be deeply dyed through and through.

2. Though you have sinned long.

3. Though you have gone back.

4. Though you have sinned conspicuously.

5. Though you have sinned proud scarlet sins.

Black. [4] Song. [5] Backslider. Glaringly. Proudly.
Scarlet, Crimson, Sinners come.
None are excluded hence but those who do themselves exclude. [6] Come. <u>Now</u>.

II. LET US REASON WITH GOD.

Help me to reason in thy name Oh thou God of Grace. Sinners ask any question you please. [7]

1. How can God be just and yet forgive?

    We must have firm foundation here. We see that future obedience cannot satisfy justice for old offences. God cannot forgive without finding for his law a fulfiller — his oath he may not alter. "the soul that sinneth it shall die" well poor soul thy answer is easy — the Lord remits not the sworn penalty but executes it on thy substitute even his son. Blood for blood & stripe for stripe he received & thus the law is silenced & forgiveness is just on God's part —

2. But the law not only threatens punishment to the offender —— but also demands a perfect righteousness — So that even if my debts are paid, a tribute is due such as I cannot render. I am sure I cannot fulfil the law for it is so spiritual, perfect & strict. Again then to Jesus cast thine eye — the law fulfiller as well as sufferer of its penalties. His righteousness imputed will make thee spotless as the driven snow —

3. But the faith required in order to the enjoyment of these mercies is something so mysterious & hard that I am afraid I shall perish with all my knowledge. Repentance & other acts are too contrary to my nature for me to effect them. Doubting one — there is a verse which sets thee at rest — "he is exalted to give repentance & remission" — faith too is "not of ourselves but the gift of God". Prayer will get them "he that asketh receiveth" — Go then to Jesus.

finding for his law a fulfiller.[8] His oath he may not alter. "<u>The soul that sinneth, it shall die.</u>"[9]

Well, poor soul, thy answer is easy. The Lord remits not the sworn penalty, but executes it on thy substitute, even his son. Blood for blood and stripe for stripe he received, and thus the law is silenced and forgiveness is just on God's part.[10]

2. But the law not only threatens punishment to the offender, but also demands a perfect righteousness. So that even if my debts are paid, a tribute is due such as I cannot render. I am sure I cannot fulfill the law, for it is so spiritual,[11] perfect, and strict.

   Again then to Jesus cast thine eye, the law fulfiller as well as sufferer[12] of its penalties. His righteousness imputed will make thee spotless as the driven snow.[13]

3. But the faith required in order to[14] the enjoyment of these mercies is something so mysterious and hard that I am afraid I shall perish with all my knowledge. Repentance and other acts are too contrary to my nature for me to effect them.[15]

   Doubting one, there is a verse which sets thee at rest: "he is exalted to give repentance and remission." Faith too is "not of ourselves but the gift of God." Prayer will get them. "He that asketh receiveth."—Go then to Jesus.[16]

4. But then I must be holy as an evidence of faith
how can I leave off my old habits which are
become like bars of brass or triple steel.
not by thy might — yet thou must. He giveth power to the faint
Thou shalt have a new heart & divine aid & thou
shalt be more than a conqueror.
5. But I must persevere to the end & I am
afraid I shall go back. Many have turned
aside to crooked ways & so shall I.
Again to the cross sinner — "hear Jesus." they shall
never perish — nor be plucked from my hand. —

<u>III</u>. Let God reason with us.
1. Have I deserved that ye should rebel. Am not I kind,
gracious & generous — why dost thou rebel.
2. What profit has thy rebellion been, art thou
happy — hast thou reaped a crop in Satan's field.
3. How can I prove my willingness to save — more than
I have. I have given my Son — & have saved multitudes.
4. What wilt thou do at death without me?
5. To whom wilt thou lay the blame of thy damnation.
6. Hast thou sought & found not. — Have any?
Have not some of thy friends found me? Come
now into mine arms by my Son who is the
way —   Oh. great one assist. —

312. 342. 358. 579

4. But then I must be holy as an evidence of faith.[17] How can I leave off my old habits which are become like bars of brass or triple steel?[18]

   Not by thy might. Yet thou must. He giveth power to the faint. Thou shalt have a new heart[19] *and divine aid, and thou shalt be more than a conqueror.*[20]

5. But I must persevere to the end and I am afraid I shall go back. Many have turned aside to crooked ways, and so shall I.[21]

   Again to the cross[,] sinner. Hear Jesus. "They shall never perish nor be plucked from my hand."[22]

III. LET GOD REASON WITH US.[23]

1. Have I deserved that ye should rebel? Am not I kind, gracious, and generous? Why dost thou rebel?

2. What profit has thy rebellion been? Art thou happy? Hast thou reaped a crop in Satan's field?

3. How can I prove my willingness to save more than I have? I have given my Son and have saved multitudes.

4. What wilt thou do at death without me?

5. To whom wilt thou lay the blame of thy damnation?

6. Hast thou sought and found not? Have any? Have not some of thy friends found me? Come now into mine arms by my Son who is the way.

   Oh Great One, assist.[24]

312. 342. 358. 579

1. Charles preached four more sermons on the text of Isa 1:18: "The Silver Trumpet" (*MTP* 7, Sermon 366); "Reasons for Parting with Sin" (*MTP* 22, Sermon 1278); "Scarlet Sinners Pardoned and Purified" (*MTP* 40, Sermon 2354); and "Invitation to a Conference" (*MTP* 49, Sermon 2816). This one appears to have influenced or, at least, overlapped themes with his later sermon, "The Silver Trumpet."

2. Charles held a high view of the doctrine of justification by faith from the very beginning of his ministry. Later in life, he continued this emphasis: "This is the very doctrine of the Reformation,—justification by faith, or rather the very basis doctrine upon which it rests; and I am persuaded the more plainly it is preached the better, for it is the gospel of salvation to a lost and ruined world" (*MTP* 56:306).

3. See the conclusion of the previous sermon ("Christian Moderation," Sermon 192). Charles preached these sequentially on his 311th and 312th preaching occasions—sometime in the fall of 1852.

4. It is not clear why Charles uses the term "black" here other than, perhaps, to describe the darkness of sin. In a later sermon on Jer 3:12–13, "A Proclamation from the King of Kings" (*MTP* 31, Sermon 1833), Charles referred to sinners as "hell-black" and "jet-black backsliders."

5. It is unclear why Charles wrote "Song" here in this list.

6. Charles rejected the doctrine of unconditional reprobation: "[W]e are next met by some who tell us that we preach the wicked and horrible doctrine of *sovereign and unmerited reprobation.* . . . Brethren, this is an unfair charge again. Election does not involved [*sic*] reprobation. There may be some who hold unconditional reprobation. I stand not here as their defender, let them defend themselves as best they can; I hold God's election, but I testify just as clearly that if any man be lost he is lost for sin" (*MTP* 7:301, italics in the original). Charles also spoke of the "madness of many who hear the gospel, and know that there is mercy provided for sinners, that unless the Holy Spirit interferes they will perish, not through ignorance, but because of some cause or other, like the Jews of old, they judge themselves 'unworthy of everlasting life,' and exclude themselves from the gospel, refusing to be comforted" (*MTP* 15:64).

7. Charles writes the following dialogue in noticeably different script, transcribed in italics to indicate each response.

8. "When despair hovers over a man like a black cloud charged with lightning he must run to Jesus. 'How can you be justified?' says the wounded conscience: the answer must be found in Jesus. When we fly to Christ, the fulfiller of the law, despair vanishes at once, for we see that we are righteous in the righteousness of Christ and accepted in the Beloved" (*MTP* 23:259).

9. Cf. Ezek 18:20.

10. This section is written in a different script than Charles usually used and alludes to biblical texts.

11. Cf. Rom 7:14.

12. Charles misspelled this word by adding an extra "r."

13. This section is written in a different script than Charles usually used and alludes to biblical texts.

14. There seems to be a word missing in this sentence that would provide clarity, perhaps "afford."

15. Cf. Rom 3:11–12; Eph 2:1, 4; Titus 3:5.

16. This section is written in a different script than Charles usually used and alludes to biblical texts.

17. "I have known some who have learned election to their soul's destruction; they have learned it, so that they said they were of the elect, whereas they had no marks, no evidences . . . in their souls" (*NPSP* 1:34). "I know you must be regenerate, but the man who trusts Christ is regenerate. You must repent, you must be holy, but the man who trusts Christ shall repent and shall be made holy; the germs of repentance and holiness are in him already" (*MTP* 10:340).

18. In Sir Walter Scott's "The Lady of the Lake" (1822), he wrote, "That desperate grasp thy frame might feel, Through bars of brass and triple steel!—They tug, they strain!—down, down, they go, The Gael above, Fitz-James below" (*The*

Poetical Works of Sir Walter Scott. With Memoir and Critical Dissertation, By The Rev. George Gilfillan [Edinburgh: James Nichol, vol. 1; London: James Nisbet; Dublin: W. Robertson, The Spurgeon Library, 1857], 286).

19. Cf. Ezekiel 36.

20. Cf. Rom 8:37. This section is written in a different script than Charles usually used and alludes to biblical texts.

21. "You know how many passages there are in which it is positively asserted that if a child of God did deliberately and totally apostatize, his restoration would be utterly impossible—not difficult, but impossible. This is one of the greatest proofs of the doctrine of the final perseverance of the saints, since there is no man in a condition in which it is impossible to save him, and yet any man would be in such a state if he apostatized. Therefore true believers shall not apostatize, but shall stand fast, and shall be kept even to the end" (*MTP* 23:129).

22. Cf. John 10:28–29. This section is written in a different script than Charles usually used and alludes to biblical texts.

23. Charles uses the device of speaking for God in the first person in a similar way in "Neither Forsaken Nor Forgotten" (*MTP* 46, Sermon 2672).

24. Charles used the term "Great One" on occasion to describe God. A few examples include *MTP* 11:194; 12:387; 19:322; 33:63; and 62:372.

194. Gen. __XXVIII__. Jacob's dream. —
Jacob sets out with his mother's & father's blessing this
was his only guard & that a good one.   He walked
about 40 miles & then found a certain place where
on the bare earth — with a stone for a pillow & heaven
for his curtain — he being weary, slept & dreamed
(Dreams now matter not, are generally of no consequence
but this was a very valuable one indeed. —
I. It was a picture of Jacob's life — how from
the earth of degradation & sin, he should rise to
heaven where God is — here are many "beholds" but
it is a wonder that any should mount heaven.
The angels stood on the staves to show that God keepeth
his saints in all times. & God was the top. God is heaven
                God "stood" to show his activity for Jacob.
II. It was a type of Jesus.
His humanity touches earth, his godhead heaven.
He is the only means of communication with heaven.
angels carry up our prayers & praises & bring down all
mercies only by means of this ladder. — There is none
other way,   Are you on the ladder?
Note. In trouble this dream came not on a down bed.
Note. Jacob by the act of lying on the ground was
actually taking possession though it was a hard case.
No train lest Esau should injure him. —
Mark.   His vow — 'Tis good to vow & pay —
Sinner up thy Saviour's ladder — not thy own.
313.316

JACOB'S DREAM
Genesis 28[1]

Jacob sets out with his mother's and father's blessing.[2] This was his only guard, and that, a good one. He walked about 40 miles,[3] and then found a certain place where, on the bare earth with a stone for a pillow and heaven for his curtain, he, being weary, slept and dreamed.

Dreams now matter not. [They] are generally of no consequence. But this was a very valuable one indeed.[4]

I. IT WAS A PICTURE OF JACOB'S LIFE[.][5]

How from the earth of degradation and sin, he should rise to heaven where God is. Here are many "beholds,"[6] but it is a wonder that any should mount heaven. The angels stood on the staves[7] to show that God keepeth his saints in all times.[8] And God was the top. God is heaven. God "stood" to show his activity for Jacob.[9]

II. IT WAS A TYPE OF JESUS.

His humanity touches earth, his godhead heaven.[10] He is the only means of communication with heaven.[11] Angels carry up our prayers and praises and bring down all mercies only by means of this ladder.[12] There is none other way.[13]

Are you on the ladder?

Note: In trouble, this dream came not on a down bed.

Note: Jacob, by the act of lying on the ground, was actually taking possession, though it was a hard case. No train lest Esau should injure him.[14]

Mark. His vow—'Tis good to vow and pay.[15]

Sinner, up thy Saviour's ladder, not thy own.

313. 316.

1. This is the only time Charles preached the entire chapter in a single sermon. Later, he did preach on individual events within the chapter. See "Jacob's Waking Exclamation" (*MTP* 7, Sermon 401) and "Four Choice Sentences" (*MTP* 27, Sermon 1630).

2. This is a reference to Gen 28:1–5.

3. Charles likely gathered this information from Gill: "Without any design to take up there, but as it were casually to him, though very providentially, after he had travelled 48 miles; for so far it seems it was from *Beer-sheba* to *Luz* or *Bethel*, as this place was called: *and tarried there all night, because the sun was set*" (John Gill, *An Exposition of the Old Testament*, vol. I [London: printed for the author and sold by George Keith at the Bible and Crown in Grace-church-street, 1763, The Spurgeon Library], 176 , italics in the original).

4. "True, there were in old time dreams in which God spake to men prophetically; but ordinarily they are the carnival of thought, a maze of mental states, a dance of disorder. . . . Dreams ordinarily are the most disorderly of phenomena, and yet it seems that they are ordered of the Lord" (*MTP* 28:123).

5. Charles appears to have developed his outline from Gill's commentary. (Gill, *An Exposition of the Old Testament*, 1:176).

6. Charles appears to be referencing the term "behold," used multiple times in the text. Cf. Gen 28:12–15.

7. This is the plural form of the word "staff." "Round or step of a ladder" (Johnson's *Dictionary*, s.v. "staff").

8. Cf. 1 Sam 2:9.

9. "Ordering, directing, and over-ruling all things in providence, for the glory of his name and the good of his people; and may signify, as the ladder may be a figure of Christ, that Jehovah, the father, is above him, as a man and mediator, and makes himself known in and by him, and delivers out all his blessings and promises through him, both temporal and spiritual" (Gill, *An Exposition of the Old Testament*, 1:176).

10. "[O]r else the incarnation and mediation of Christ, who in his human nature was to be in the fulness [*sic*] of time on earth, there to live a while, obey, suffer, and die, and so was the ladder set on earth; and his divine nature was the top of it, which reached heaven" (Gill, 1:176).

11. "He may be fitly represented hereby as the mediator, who has reconciled things in heaven and things on earth, and has as it were joined and united heaven and earth together. . . . Moreover this may point out to us Christ as the way to his father, of access unto him, and acceptance with him, by which he communicates the blessings of his grace to men, and by which they ascend to God with their prayers and praises to him" (Gill, 1:176).

12. On the role of angels specifically, Gill notes, "*[B]ehold, the angels of God ascending and descending on it;* which may be expressive of the employment of angels in the affairs of providence, who receive their commission from heaven, and execute it on earth, in which they are diligent, faithful, and constant; and of the ministry of them, both to Christ personal, and to his church and people, even to every particular believer" (Gill, 1:176, italics in the original).

13. Cf. John 14:6.   14. Cf. Gen 32:3–8.

15. Cf. Eccl 5:4–5.

Mic. VII. 18 He delighteth in mercy. — 195

Since on the character of our God depends our welfare we cannot but be interested in any account of him.

I. Who are the only objects of mercy?
Beings not alone miserable but also sinful.
angels are not — Devils might be but are not.
Saints redeemed — & lost souls are out of the pale.
Pharisees, righteous, moral people cannot receive mercy for they do not allow that they need it —
But sinners, publicans, prodigals are fit objects.

II. What is the nature of mercy in which he delights.
Mercy strictly just. Wholly unmerited. Sovereign.
Free. Tender, Great. Manifold — Rich. Eternal
Infinite knowing no diminution. —

III. How does God prove his delight in mercy —
He set it on foot. He now manages it.
He spares no expens. His heart is in the work.
He is ever busy at it. He seeks out objects —

IV. Why is mercy his darling.
1. He is the most godlike —
2. This is the attribute which costs most.
3. It glorifies him most
4. It is the youngest born or exercised —

V. Diminish not your sin. Fear not to come.
Trust in him — help. Help. Help

317. 323.

HE DELIGHTETH *in* MERCY
Micah 7:18

"Who is a God like unto thee, that pardoneth iniquity, and passeth by the transgression of the remnant of his heritage? he retaineth not his anger forever, because he delighteth in mercy."

Since on the character of our God depends our welfare, we cannot but be interested in any account of him.[1]

I. WHO ARE THE ONLY OBJECTS OF MERCY?

Beings, not alone miserable but also sinful. Angels are not. Devils might be, but are not.[2] Saints redeemed and lost souls are out of the pale.[3] Pharisees, righteous, moral people cannot receive mercy, for they do not allow that they need it. But sinners, publicans, prodigals are fit objects.[4]

II. WHAT IS THE NATURE OF MERCY IN WHICH HE DELIGHTS?

Mercy, strictly just. Wholly unmerited. Sovereign. Free. Tender. Great. Manifold. Rich. Eternal. Infinite. Knowing no diminution.[5]

III. HOW DOES GOD PROVE HIS DELIGHT IN MERCY?

He set it on foot. He now manages it.

He spares no expense. His heart is in the work.

He is ever busy at it. He seeks out objects.[6]

IV. WHY IS MERCY HIS DARLING?

1. He is the most Godlike.[7]

2. This is the attribute which costs most.[8]

3. So glorifies him most.[9]

4. So is the youngest born or exercised.[10]

V. DIMINISH NOT YOUR SIN.[11]

Fear not to come. Trust in him.

Help. Help. Help.

317. 323.

1. "Remember again, that *the Lord is the very model of health.* All perfections meet in him. In God's nature no single attribute ever intrudes upon another" (*MTP* 21:185–86, italics in the original). Charles preached this text again in his sermon, "A Sweet Salaam" (*MTP* 58, Sermon 3317).

2. "The mercy of God differs, in some respects, both from the love and grace of God; from the love of God in its object, and order of operation . . . mercy supposes its objects miserable, and so fallen . . . yet all grace is not mercy: grace and favour are shewn to the elect angels . . . but not mercy; since they never were miserable" (John Gill, *Gill's Complete Body of Practical and Doctrinal Divinity: Being a System of Evangelical Truths, Deduced from the Sacred Scriptures* [Philadelphia: printed for Delaplaine and Hellings, 1810, The Spurgeon Library], 1:152).

3. "2. Any inclosure. 3. Any district or territory" (Johnson's *Dictionary*, s.v. "pale").

4. Cf. Luke 5:31–32.

5. Charles often recited these kinds of lists as a rhetorical device. See, for example, "Necessity of Purity for an Entrance to Heaven" (Notebook 1, Sermon 2); "Count the Cost" (Notebook 2, Sermon 83); and "Christ the Power of God" (Notebook 3, Sermon 169).

6. Cf. Luke 15; Rom 5:6–8.

7. "The Eternal God has thrown his whole soul into the business of redeeming men. If you desire to see God most Godlike, it is in the pardon of sin, and the saving of men" (*MTP* 32:350).

8. "[Believers] are saved in the price of salvation. All that was necessary to save them from the result of sin has been endured by the Lord Jesus Christ. He has ransomed them by his death upon the cross. He has stood in their stead, and borne their sin in his own body on the tree, and suffered the full penalty for it. He has finished the transgression, and made an end of sin, and made reconciliation for iniquity, and brought in for them everlasting righteousness; so that they are saved. The great work of their salvation was completed by Christ upon the cross when he laid down his life for them, and now they are 'bought with a price,' even 'the precious blood of Christ, as of a lamb without blemish and without spot'" (*MTP* 48:123).

9. "It is for God's glory that a sinner should be saved. When we seek pardon, we are not asking God to do that which will stain his banner, or put a blot on his escutcheon. He delighteth in mercy. It is his peculiar, darling attribute. Mercy honours God. Do not we ourselves say, 'Mercy blesseth him that gives, and him that takes?' And surely, in some diviner sense, this is true of God, who, when he gives mercy, glorifies himself" (*TD* 1:64).

10. "We are quite sure that whenever an attribute of God comes into action it will be sufficiently revealed to make its glory manifest. There could be no mercy exercised by God until there was sin" (*MTP* 20:542).

11. "2. To impair; to lessen; to degrade" (Johnson's *Dictionary*, s.v. "to diminish").

196.   Ps. 112. 4.   Light to the godly.

A Sermon given in an hour of extremity. —
How full the Bible is with promise for every season.
1.   Note the character.
Upright.   Cured of nature's crook. not worldly, carnal &c.
Gracious.   Saved by grace, & adorned with the graces. faith &c &c.
Full of Compassion.   to his brethren fellow sinners – the world.
Righteous.   by Imputation & the work of the Spirit. —
2.   Note the darkness they endure.
(Darkness in the first step.   conviction.
In circumstances.   In soul trouble,   desertion.
But certain light arises,   deliverance.   help to bear.
3.   Note the light —
a.   The morning star. comforts the sin mourner.
b.   The lamp of the word.   guides in all doubtful places.
c.   The Blessed Sun of the Spirit illuminates
d.   The tiny stars – ministers do cheer oftimes —
only be upright & our all is secured —
I had in this light in darkness. Praise him —
            By faith —
314. 315.

LIGHT *to the* GODLY
Psalms 112:4

"Unto the upright there ariseth light in the darkness: he is gracious, and full of compassion, and righteous."

A Sermon[1] given in an hour of extremity.
How full the Bible is with promise for every season.

1. NOTE THE CHARACTER.

Upright. Cured of nature's crook.[2] Not worldly, carnal, etc.

Gracious. Saved by grace and adorned with the graces, faith, etc., etc.

Full of Compassion. to his brethren fellow sinners, the world.

Righteous. by Imputation and the work of the Spirit.[3]

2. NOTE THE DARKNESS THEY ENDURE.

Darkness in the first step. Conviction.

In circumstances. In soul trouble, desertion.

But certain light arises. Deliverance. Help to bear.[4]

3. NOTE THE LIGHT.

    a.   The morning star[5] comforts the sin mourner.[6]

    b.   The lamp of the word[7] guides in all doubtful places.[8]

    c.   The Blessed lamp[9] of the Spirit illuminates.

    d.   The tiny stars. Ministers do cheer ofttimes.

         Only be upright and our all is secured.

         I had in this[,] light in darkness.[10] Praise him.

           By faith.

314. 315.

1. Charles never preached on this text again, but he expounded on it in *The Treasury of David* (5:226).

2. Charles engages in wordplay by contrasting the term "upright" with a metaphor for sin, "nature's crook."

3. Charles is likely combining two functions of the Holy Spirit into one: the imputation of righteousness to the justified sinner (cf. Rom 5:1–2) and the continual work of the Holy Spirit in sanctifying the believer's life (cf. Rom 6:22).

4. Cf. 1 Cor 10:13.

5. Cf. Rev 22:16.

6. Cf. Matt 5:4.

7. Cf. Ps 119:105.

8. Cf. Isa 58:11.

9. Cf. Rev 4:5.

10. Cf. John 1:5.

Ex. XXV. 21. The ark of the covenant. 197.

The types of the old testament form a complete museum of theology, a series of picture lessons on the wondrous truth of revalation. A mere child can learn much & the most erudite will have abundant room for the exercise of his talents

The ark or sacred chest was one of the most sacred things in the Jewish tabernacle, it was kept in the most Holy place. — for it the tabernacle was made, it was not so much a part of the furniture of the tabernacle, as the chief article — the dwelling of the master — the very owner of the whole. — May God instruct us in looking within the vail so that we may see much to profit by.

I. The ark itself a type of Christ. & here we must come to particulars ... .

1. The ark itself - made of shittim wood, overlaid with plates of gold - sets out Jesus in his nature both human & divine, united together forming one. The shittim wood was (light) incorruptible, lasting. So the human nature of Jesus is no subject to sin. This was completely overlaid with gold - so is the human nature of Jesus completely covered with a blaze of glory, through his divine golden nature within & without this golden glory covers him. In mind as well as actions, he is ever godlike.

2. The crown of gold. the carving upon the edge is to represent the kingly office of Jesus. The crown

THE ARK *of the* COVENANT[1]
Exodus 25:21

*"And thou shalt put the mercy seat above upon the ark; and in the
ark thou shalt put the testimony that I shall give thee."*

The types of the old testament form a complete museum of theology,[2] a series of picture lessons on the wondrous truth of revelation.

A mere child can learn much, and the most erudite will have abundant room for the exercise of his talents.[3]

The ark, or sacred chest, was one of the most sacred things in the Jewish tabernacle. It was kept in the most Holy place.[4] For it, the tabernacle was made.[5] It was not so much a part of the furniture of the tabernacle as the chief article,[6] the dwelling of the master,[7] the very owner of the whole.

May God instruct us in looking within the vail[8] so that we may see much to profit by.

I. THE ARK ITSELF A TYPE OF CHRIST.[9]

And here, we must come to particulars.

1. The ark itself, made of shittim wood[10] overlaid with plates of gold,[11] sets out Jesus in his nature, both human and divine, united together, forming one.[12] The shittim wood was (light) incorruptible, lasting.

    So the human nature of Jesus is not subject to sin.[13] This was completely overlaid with gold. So is the human nature of Jesus completely covered with a blaze of glory through his divine golden nature.[14] Within and without, this golden glory covers him. In mind as well as actions, he is ever godlike.

2. The crown of gold. The carving upon the edge is to represent the kingly office of Jesus.[15] The crown

of pure gold the gift of his Father. the crowns of his Saints which they place on his head alone.

3. The 4 cast rings of pure gold may picture the doctrines of the gospel by which the ark - Jesus is to be carried from one country to another. The doctrines are all pure & golden as well as round that is harmonious —— There needs no more than the ordained number & no less. Neither add nor take away

These are all cast - not beaten out by man but cast in the mould god has ordained, moreover like cast metal they cannot be melted in our fires so as to be welded into our own shapes.

By these rings alone is Christ conveyed to sinners.

4. The staves of shittim wood overlaid with gold are (or I think represent) ministers of the gospel who bear the ark as the staves did. They are men — wood — but good & faithful men of the lasting unrotting shittim wood — They are overlaid with gold by god — they derive gifts, grace & help from him, though still they are but wood overlaid. These are put in the rings, and are to keep there that is the doctrines of truth they must ever maintain & never leave. They should be wholly devoted to the work, never out of it. Married to the work & wearing two rings of double obligation to serve as bearers in the work. The Saints too are bearers in a great measure.

of pure gold the gift of his Father.[16] The crowns of his saints, which they place on his head alone.[17]

3. The 4 cast rings of pure gold[18] may picture the doctrines of the gospel by which the ark, Jesus, is to be carried from one country to another.[19] The doctrines are all pure and golden as well as round. That is harmonious. There needs no more than the ordained number, and no less. Neither add nor take away.

   These are all cast. Not beaten out by man, but cast in the mould God has ordained. Moreover, like cast metal, they cannot be melted in our fires[20] so as to be welded into our own shapes.[21] By these rings alone is Christ conveyed to sinners.

4. The staves of shittim wood overlaid with gold are (or I think represent) ministers of the gospel who bear the ark as the staves did.[22] They are men, wood, but good and faithful men of the lasting, unrotting shittim wood.

   They are overlaid with gold by God. They derive gifts, grace, and help from him. Though still, they are but wood overlaid. These are put in the rings and are to keep there. That is the doctrines of truth they must ever maintain and never leave.[23] They should be wholly devoted to the work, never out of it. Married to the work and wearing two rings of double obligation to serve as bearers in the work. The Saints too are bearers in a great measure.

their lives should be devoted to God & the bearing of the cross.
5. The mercy seat - resting on the ark within the crown, represents the glorious atonement of Jesus, which is the top of all his works. Jesus as the atonement for such is he. The mercy seat was its name, and is not Jesus the seat of mercy? God sits there when he dispenses mercy & truly mercy is enthroned in Jesus agony, death & sufferings for us — The mercy seat was all gold. So God's mercy is far above man there is no wood, no human in it It is godlike & only godlike — This mercy seat was a complete covering for the ark. Jesus was wholly covered by his mediatorial work, his whole soul was engrossed in it — There was no chink, the law within was wholly concealed, So Jesus held the whole law within in him here & thus for ever frees his people from it as a law of condemnation. There God communed with man & only there or by its means So Jesus is the sole mediator & there is no other way. God used this as his footstool the law was thus separated from him by this lid of Gold — Of beaten gold. Ah! Jesus was beaten indeed.
6. The Cherubim with outstretched wings represent the angelic hosts whose glory it was to guard the symbol of the covenant — These were not minister for. 1. Pet. 1. 12 seems to allude to angels as bending over the ark to view its mysteries.
These cherubs were made of gold to shew their excellence, & purity — They were made of the same lump as the mercy seat, not joined on it but

Their lives should be devoted to God and the bearing of the cross.[24]

5. The mercy seat, resting on the ark within the crowns,[25] represents the glorious atonement of Jesus, which is the top of all his works.[26] Jesus as the atonement. For such is he.[27] The mercy seat was its name. And is not Jesus the seat of mercy? God sits there when he dispenses mercy, and truly, mercy is enthroned in Jesus['s] agony, death, and sufferings for us.

    The mercy seat was all gold. So God's mercy is far above man. There is no wood, no human in it.[28] It is godlike, and only godlike. This mercy seat was a complete covering for the ark. Jesus was wholly covered by his mediatorial work. His whole soul was engrossed in it.

    There was no chink. The law within was wholly concealed. So Jesus held the whole law within in him here, and thus for ever frees his people from it as a law of condemnation.[29] There God communed with man, and only there, or by its means. So Jesus is the sole mediator, and there is no other way. God used this as his footstool. The law was thus separated from him by this lid of gold. Of beaten gold. Ah! Jesus was beaten indeed.

6. The Cherubim with outstretched wings represent the angelic hosts whose glory it was to guard the symbol of the covenant. These were not ministers, for 1 Pet. 1.12[30] seems to allude to angels as bending over the ark to view its mysteries.

    These cherubs were made of gold to shew their excellence and purity. They were made of the same lump as the mercy seat. Not joined on it, but

of the same mass & lump - so angels join in the one
great design of mercy, they are not beings put in
after the commencements of the scheme to help
at a stress but they are part of the grand whole.
— They are joined to Jesus, he is their head
they stand on his grace & immoveably are they
knit to him so as to be like the saints infallibly
secure.   Their wings are outstretched to show
their readiness for service — "Upwards - to show
that their strength comes from God & that they
long to bear a prayer or tear on high from
contrite worshippers. —   While tarrying
they wish not to waste time but to employ
it in looking at mercy & its golden plans.
Devoutly waiting till more mysteries be revealed.
They look to one another to show their love
& unity —   They love this we may say
after the manner of men better than guarding
the tree of life as comrades with the flaming sword.
Between their wings the Shecinah appeared
as if angelic wings must be a vail for our poor
mortal sight — their wings too have to cover
their own eyes & faces for the sight is too sublime.
At the last day, Jesus in all the glory of his
Father will come, attended by hosts of flaming
ones in splendid dread array —

of the same mass and lump.[31] So angels join in the one great design of mercy. They are not beings put in after the commencements of the scheme to help at a stress, but they are part of the grand whole.

They are joined to Jesus. He is their head. They stand on his grace and immoveably are they knit to him so as to be like the saints, infallibly secure.[32]

Their wings are outstretched to show their readiness for service.[33] "Upwards"[34] to show that their strength comes from God and that they long to bear a prayer or hear on high from contrite worshippers.[35]

While tarrying, they wish not to waste time, but to employ it in looking at mercy and its golden plans.[36] Devoutly waiting till more mysteries be revealed.

They look to one another to show their love and unity.[37]

They love this, we may say, after the manner of men better than guarding the tree of life as comrades with the flaming sword.

Between their wings, the Shecinah[38] [*sic*] appeared, as if angelic wings must be a vail[39] for our poor mortal sight. Their wings too have to cover their own eyes and faces, for the sight is too sublime.[40]

At the last day, Jesus in all the glory of his Father will come attended by hosts of flaming ones in splendid, dread, array.[41] _

II. The history of the ark still further shewing its nature as typical of Jesus. —

1. Numbers. X. 33. The ark always had the cloud over it — it was carried before the armies of Israel & thus became their great guide. So Jesus is the captain of our salvation, our guard, our forerunner. God's presence was near those who dwelt near the mercy seat — Enemies were scattered at its presence.

2. Josh. IV. 11. By means of the ark the people passed over Jordan dry shod — this made the way. So seas of sin, rivers of sorrow, & Jordan death are dried up by the passage of the ark. This stood in Jordan till every one was over & then up it came. How the waters roared & dashing ran into their accustomed channels. Now the floods of wrath are dry till the last Israelite shall land in Canaan then wrath shall come even to the uttermost.

3. Josh. VI. 13. Jericho tottered when at the appointed time the ark stood before her walls. So Jesus & his gospel shall make all the kingdoms of this world bow their necks & mighty ones shall yield to his dominion ~

4. Judges. XX. 27. When the Israelites asked of God before the ark they received a good answer & help whereas before they were beaten. Benjamin soon failed when the ark was consulted & so is it nothing can give us victory over our own selves but the ark, the mercy seat, Jesus sought by earnest prayer. —

II. THE HISTORY OF THE ARK STILL FURTHER SHEWING ITS NATURE AS TYPICAL OF JESUS.

1. Numbers X.33.[42] The ark always had the cloud over it.[43] It was carried before the armies of Israel[44] and thus became their great guide. So Jesus is the captain of our salvation,[45] our guard,[46] our forerunner.[47] God's presence was near those who dwelt near the mercy seat. Enemies were scattered at its presence.[48]

2. Josh. IV.11.[49] By means of the ark, the people passed over Jordan dry shod.[50] This made the way. So seas of sin, rivers of sorrow, and Jordan's death are dried up by the passage of the ark.[51] This stood in Jordan till every one was over, and then up it came. How the waters roared, and dashing, ran into their accustomed channels. Now the floods of wrath are dry till the last Israelite shall land in Canaan. Then wrath shall come, even to the uttermost.

3. Josh. VI.13.[52] Jericho tottered when, at the appointed time, the ark stood before her walls.[53] So Jesus and his gospel shall make all the kingdoms of this world bow their necks, and mighty ones shall yield to his dominion.[54]

4. Judges XX.27.[55] When the Israelites asked of God before the ark, they received a good answer and help. Whereas before, they were beaten. Benjamin soon failed when the ark was consulted.[56] And so is it nothing can give us victory over our own selves but the ark, the mercy seat, Jesus sought by earnest prayer.

5, 1 Sam. V. Dagon owned the mighty power of the
sacred symbol & fell shattered by its might.
Emerods seized its enemies, they were glad to be
rid of it — So shall Christs enemies seek to escape
the vengeance of Jesus. but they cannot.
6. 1 Sam. VI. 19. The men of Bethshemesh take
off the mercy seat & look within. The law thus
uncovered smote 50070 men & caused slaughter.
    The Law cannot be endured out of the covenant
it is death to the whole world. Pharisees &
work-trusters beware — ye will find not life but
death anywhere out of Jesus Christ. —
7. II Sam II. 6. Uzzah touched it & died.
It ought not to have been on a cart but even
there it was save though Uzzah thought not.
He touched irreverently — & died.   Christ ought
not be dragged by hirelings on a state-church
waggon — & those who try to set the ark right
will find certain death.
8. II Sam. VII. 11. Obededom prospered because
of the ark. He prospers who has the ark in his
house — yea & his household too — soul prosp—
surely goes where Jesus goes.
    The ark rested in Solomons temple so will
9 Jesus in heaven remain settled for ever the
chief glory & beauty of the golden streets.

5. I Sam. V.[57] Dagon owned the mighty power of the sacred symbol and fell shattered by its might.[58] Emerods seized its enemies.[59] They were glad to be rid of it.[60] So shall Christ's enemies seek to escape the vengeance of Jesus. But they cannot.[61]

6. I Sam. VI.19.[62] The men of Beshemesh [*sic*] take off the mercy seat and look within. The Law thus uncovered smote 50,070 men and caused slaughter. The Law cannot be endured out of the covenant. It is death to the whole world. Pharisees and work-trusters beware. Ye will find not life but death anywhere out of Jesus Christ.[63]

7. II Sam. VI.6.[64] Uzzah touched it and died. It ought not to have been on a cart, but even there it was save, though Uzzah thought not. He touched irreverently[65] and died. Christ ought not be dragged by hirelings on a state-church wagon,[66] and those who try to set the ark right will find certain death.

8. II. Sam. VII.11.[67] Obededom prospered because of the ark. He prospers who has the ark in his house. Yea, and his household too. Soul prospering[68] surely goes where Jesus goes.

9. The ark rested in Solomon's temple.[69] So will Jesus in heaven remain settled for ever, the chief glory and beauty of the golden streets.[70]

III   Let us now learn a little from the whole subject — — Great one teach us aright!

1. Here we discern the true refuge of sinners. This is a sanctuary for all offenders. The mercy seat & ark need only to be looked at that we may live.

2. Here we discern the true place for the law in the ark & only there can it be borne at all. We must see it fulfilled in Jesus & endeavour to follow its precepts if we are in him.

3. The Cherubim teach us unity, zeal, attention, humility — & give us hope that with such guards we shall be kept by God.

4. Here we learn what is wanted in every house of prayer, in every church. Jesus & prayer.   My friends let us go oftener to this mercy seat, let us carry the ark with us.   Cease not to pray for me. Agonize in your prayers. & he that dwelleth between the cherubim will soon shine forth — Come boldly to the throne — 'tis a throne of grace & may I too learn the lesson I would teach

Amen

318. & 320. 474.

III. LET US NOW LEARN A LITTLE FROM THE WHOLE SUBJECT. GREAT ONE[,] TEACH US ARIGHT!

1. Here we discern the true refuge of sinners. This is a sanctuary for all offenders. The mercy seat and ark need only to be looked at that we may live.

2. Here we discern the true place for the law: in the ark, and only there can it be borne at all.

    We must see it fulfilled in Jesus and endeavour to follow its precepts if we are in him.

3. The Cherubim teach us unity, zeal, attention, humility, and give us hope that with such guards we shall be kept by God.

4. Here we learn what is wanted in every house of prayer, in every church. Jesus and prayer.[71] My friends[,] let us go oftener to this mercy seat. Let us carry the ark with us. Cease not to pray for me. Agonize in your prayers and he that dwelleth between the cherubim will soon shine forth.[72]

Come boldly to the throne—'tis a throne of grace, and may I too learn the lesson I would teach.

Amen.

318 and 320. 474.

1. Charles took the greater portion of his material in his first point from John Gill's commentary on Exod 25:10–22 (John Gill, *An Exposition of the New Testament* [London: printed for the author, 1746, The Spurgeon Library], 1:428–31). Charles did not preach on this text again, but he did include it in the "Exposition" section of his sermon "God's Glory in Hiding Sin" (*MTP* 49, Sermon 2838). He used significant elements of the present outline in composing the later exposition.

2. Later commentator James Comper Gray would call his commentary on the Scriptures *The Biblical Museum*. Charles owned the New Testament collection (James Comper Gray, *The Biblical Museum: A Collection of Notes Explanatory, Homiletic, and Illustrative, on the Holy Scriptures*, 5 vols. [London: Elliot Stock, 1871, The Spurgeon Library]), but it was published after his Waterbeach Ministry ended. Additionally, it does appear that Charles uses this phrase elsewhere in his works. As for Gray's work, he said, "[I]t is surpassingly useful, sententious and sensible. Buy the work at once" (C. H. Spurgeon, *Commenting and Commentaries: Two Lectures Addressed to the Students of The Pastors' College, Metropolitan Tabernacle, Together with a Catalogue of Biblical Commentaries and Expositions* [London: Passmore and Alabaster, 1890, The Spurgeon Library], 36).

3. "All the types, promises, and prophecies were now fully accomplished in [Christ] . . . when he said, 'It is finished,' the whole book, from the first to the last, in both the law and the prophets, was finished in him. There is not a single jewel of promise, from that first emerald which fell on the threshold of Eden, to that last sapphire-stone of Malachi, which was not set in the breast-plate of the true High Priest. Nay, there is not a type, from the red heifer downward to the turtle-dove, from the hyssop upwards to Solomon's temple itself, which was not fulfilled in him; and not a prophecy, whether spoken on Chebar's bank, or on the shores of Jordan, not a dream of wise men, whether they had received it in Babylon, or in Samaria, or in Judea, which was not now fully wrought out in Christ Jesus" (*MTP* 7:586).

4. Cf. Exod 26:31–33; 40:21; 2 Chr 3:8.   5. Cf. Exod 25:8.

6. "The first thing which is here ordered to be made is the ark with its appurtenances, the furniture of the most holy place, and the special token of God's presence; the tabernacle was· erected to be the receptacle of that. . . . This ark was the chief token of God's presence. . . . God dwells where that rules."

(Matthew Henry, *An Exposition of the Old and New Testament*, vol. I [London: W. and J. Stratford, 1793, The Spurgeon Library], "Exodus 25:10–22").

7.   Cf. Exod 25:8; 29:45.

8.   For more on the "vail" (veil) and the tabernacle from Spurgeon's early sermons, see "The Tranquility, Security, and Supplies Afforded to the Gospel Church" (Notebook 2, Sermon 97) and "The Tabernacle of Jacob and Mount Zion Blessed of God" (Notebook 3, Sermon 145).

9.   "This was a very eminent type of Christ, with whom the name of an ark, chest, or coffer, where treasure lies, agrees; for the treasures of wisdom and knowledge, and the riches of grace, even all the fulness of it, lie in him" (John Gill, *An Exposition of the Old Testament* [London: printed for the author and sold by G. Keith at the Bible and Crown in Grace-church-street; and by J. Robinson at Dockhead, Southwark, 1757, The Spurgeon Library], 1:428). Additionally, for more of Charles's references to typology in this volume, see "Jacob's Dream" (Sermon 194). In other volumes, see "The Peculiar People" (Notebook 1, Sermon 25); "King of Righteousness and Peace" (Notebook 1, Sermon 42); "David in the Cave with Adullam" (Notebook 2, Sermon 116).

10.   "[A]cacia, the *spina Aegyptiaca* of the ancients, *Mimosa Nilotica* of Linn. It is a large tree growing in Egypt and Arabia, from which is obtained the Gummi Arabicum; its bark is covered with large black thorns; the wood is exceedingly hard, and when old resembles ebony" (William Gesenius, *A Hebrew and English Lexicon of the Old Testament, Including the Biblical Chaldee. Translated from the Latin of William Gesenius, Doct. and Prof. of Theology in the University of Halle-Wittenberg. By Edward Robinson, D.D. Late Prof. Extraord. of Sac. Lit. in the Theol. Sem. Andover* [Boston: Crocker and Brewster, 1836, The Spurgeon Library], 1003–4, italics in the original).

11.   Cf. Exod 25:11.

12.   "[I]ts being made of *shittim*-wood, which is an incorruptible wood, a wood that rots not, by which the *Septuagint* version here, and in v.5. And elsewhere render it, may denote the duration of Christ in his person, and the natures united in it; in his divine nature from everlasting to everlasting, he is God; in his human nature, he saw no corruption, though he died and lived again, and lives for evermore"

(Gill, *An Exposition of the Old Testament*, 1:428, italics in the original). In his later sermon Charles said, "Yet the ark, though made of wood, did not appear to be so, for it was completely overlaid with pure gold; so everywhere, the Deity, or, if you will, the perfect righteousness of Jesus Christ could be seen. The ark was of shittim wood, yet it was an ark of gold; and he, who was truly man, was just as truly God, blessed be his holy name" (*MTP* 49:322).

13. "[H]e saw no corruption" (Gill, *An Exposition of the Old Testament*, 1:428). In his later sermon Charles said, "The ark was made of wood, perhaps to typify the human nature of our blessed Lord; but it was of unrotting wood, acacia, which resists the worm; and, truly, in him there was no corruption in life by way of sin, and no corruption sullied him in death when he slept for a while in the grave" (*MTP* 49:322).

14. "*And thou shalt overlay it with pure gold, &c. Not gild it, but a plate of pure gold over it: within and without shalt thou overlay it*; so that nothing of the wood could be seen: this may denote the glory of Christ in both his natures, divine and human, the riches of his person and office, which are unsearchable and durable, and his preciousness to them that believe" (Gill, *An Exposition of the Old Testament*, 1:429, italics in the original).

15. "*[A]nd shalt make upon it a crown of pure gold round about*; or a cornish of pure gold upon it, every way, which was a square on which the mercy seat was set; which may point at the honour and glory of Christ, especially in his kingly office, who has indeed on his head many crowns" (Gill, 1:429, italics in the original). In his later exposition Charles said, "Round about the top of this ark there was a crown of gold. How glorious is Christ, in his mediation, as covering the law, and preserving it within himself! He is King, glorious in holiness, and honoured in the midst of his people" (*MTP* 49:322).

16. "[O]ne a crown of pure gold, his divine Father has set upon him" (Gill, 1:429).

17. "[A]nother [crown] which the church has crowned him with, and indeed both angels and saints cast their crowns at his feet, and set the crown on his head, or give him the glory of all they have and are" (Gill, 1:429). Cf. Rev 4:10.

18. Cf. Exod 25:12.

19. "[T]hose gold rings in the ark may signify the churches of Christ, which are instrumental to bear his name, and spread his truth in the world" (Gill, *An Exposition of the Old Testament*, 1:429). In his later sermon Charles said, "The rings were, of course, for the staves to pass through, and the staves were for the priests to carry the ark as it moved from place to place. It went with the children of Israel in all their journeys; and our Lord Jesus is always with us. He goes with us wherever we go, and tarries with us wherever we abide" (*MTP* 49:323).

20. Cast iron was used in abundance in Victorian England. It is strong, but not easily malleable; that is why it must be cast into specific shapes and not molded. It also has a high resistance to fire and heat, so it is not easily welded and retains its shape unless heated in superior furnaces. For more, see Quentin R. Skrabec, Jr., *The Metallurgic Age: The Victorian Flowering of Invention and Industrial Science* (London: Mcfarland, 2005), 51–52; and Paul Dobraszczyk, *Iron, Ornament and Architecture in Victorian Britain: Myth and Modernity, Excess and Enchantment* (Surrey, UK: Ashgate, 2014), 6–7.

21. "What does an idolater do? He says, 'I cannot believe in an unseen God; I must have a golden calf or an image, that I can see with my eyes and touch with my hand.' You say just the same. You cannot believe God's naked word, you demand something you can feel, something you can see. Sheer idolatry. Do you not see it? You make your own feelings and emotions, or strange impressions, to be more worthy of trust than even God himself: you make them idols, and put them into God's place. You, so far as you can, undeify the Deity. O tremble at such a crime as this!" (*MTP* 14:610).

22. "[W]hich staves overlaid with gold, and put into golden rings, figured the ministers of Christ, enriched with the gifts and graces of his Spirit, and possessed of the truths of the gospel, more precious than gold and silver; who bear the name of Christ, and carry his gospel into the several parts of the world" (Gill, *An Exposition of the Old Testament*, 1:429).

23. "Not only put into them, but remain in them, yea, always" (Gill, 1:429).

24. Cf. Matt 16:24–26.

25. "*[A]nd shalt make upon it a crown of gold round about*; or a cornish of pure gold upon it, every way, which was a square on which the mercy-seat was set" (Gill, *An Exposition of the Old Testament*, 1:429, italics in the original). Cf. Exod 25:21, 26.

26. "[It] was typical of Christ; he is *the seat of mercy*, or, as it is in the new testament expressed, *the throne of grace*; whereon, or, in whom God shews himself to be gracious and merciful to the children of men; all the stores of mercy are in him, and all the vessels of mercy are put into his hands; the mercy of God is displayed in the mission of him as saviour, and is glorified by him in a way consistent with justice and holiness; thro' him only special mercy is communicated to sinful men, to whom God is only merciful in Christ: and Christ himself is all mercy to his people; his ways of old were mercy and truth, and all his works, especially his great work of redemption, are done in mercy and pity to them" (Gill, 1:429, italics in the original).

27. "[A]nd he is the *propitiation* or *propitiatory*, who has made atonement and reconciliation for sin; and in and through whom God shews himself propitious to his people, he being pacified, his wrath appeased, and his justice satisfied by his obedience and sufferings" (Gill, 1:430, italics in the original). Cf. Rom 5:11.

28. "*[P]ure gold*, without any allay or mixture in it, may denote the purity of Christ's obedience, righteousness and sacrifice in the compleatness *[sic]* of salvation by him" (Gill, 1:430, italics in the original). Charles later said, "It was the meetingplace of God and men, where the law was covered with a solid plate of gold; so is Jesus the meetingplace between God and sinners, where the law is covered with his perfect righteousness" (*MTP* 49:323).

29. ["*And thou shalt put into the ark the testimony I shall give thee.*] Which was the principal use of it. . . . which may signify that the law was in the heart of Christ, and which he undertook to fulfill, and with pleasure did it; that he is become the fulfilling end of the law for righteousness to them that believe in him" (Gill, *An Exposition of the Old Testament*, 1:429, italics in the original). Cf. Rom 8:1–4; Heb 7:12, 18–19, 28.

30. Charles's assertion here diverts from Gill's commentary. Gill views the cherubim as "the ministers of the word in particular," specifically denoting the prophets of the Old Testament and the apostles of the New Testament (Gill 1:430).

31. "[T]hey were made not only out of the same kind of metal with that, but out of the same mass of gold or lump" (Gill, 1:430). Cf. Exod 25:19.

32. Charles departs from Gill's treatment, who rendered them as "prophets, apostles," and later used them as an image of the union of Christ and his church (Gill, 1:430, s.v. "Exodus 25:18"). See also "He Took Not Up Angels" (Notebook 1, Sermon 52).

33. "[T]heir wings did not hang down by them, or on the side of them, but were stretched out upwards towards the heaven above their heads; denoting the readiness, agility, and swiftness of the ministers of the word to do the work and will of Christ" (Gill, *An Exposition of the Old Testament*, 1:430).

34. Cf. Exod 25:20.

35. Charles diverts from Gill's exposition, which says, "[A]s before observed, it may denote their directing souls to Christ as the only way of salvation, keeping always in their ministrations this great truth in view" (Gill, *An Exposition of the Old Testament*, 1:430). Charles is likely envisioning the kind of ministry described in his prior sermon, "Jacob's Dream" (Sermon 194).

36. Cf. 1 Pet 1:12.

37. "[A]nd their faces shall look one to another; and which is expressive of the harmony, concord and agreement of the true and faithful ministers of Christ one with another" (Gill, *An Exposition of the Old Testament*, 1:431, italics in the original).

38. The "Shekinah" glory of God comes from the Hebrew word שכינה (Shekinah), literally meaning "the dwelling." It does not appear in the Old Testament text, but in other Jewish literature. "Nothing is more frequently mentioned in the writings of the Jews, than the Shekinah, by which they understand the presence of the Holy Spirit" (Charles Taylor, Calmet's *Dictionary of the Holy Bible, with the Biblical Fragments* [London: Samuel Holdsworth, Amen Corner, Paternoster Row, 1838, The Spurgeon Library], 2:584).

39. "[T]his may signify that the way to communion with God lies through Christ, the mercy seat and propitiation, through his blood and righteousness, through the veil" (Gill, *An Exposition of the Old Testament*, 1:431).

40. Cf. Isa 6:2.

41. Cf. Isa 29:6; 66:15; 2 Thess 1:7.

42. Numbers 10:33: "And they departed from the mount of the LORD three days' journey: and the ark of the covenant of the LORD went before them in the three days' journey, to search out a resting place for them."

43. Cf. Exod 40:38; Lev 16:2.   44. Cf. Deut 10:8; 1 Sam 4:3.

45. Cf. Heb 2:10. For Charles's work on Jesus as captain, see "The Fight" (Notebook 1, Sermon 37b); "In the World Ye Shall Have Tribulation" (Notebook 3, Sermon 187); "All Fullness in Jesus" (Notebook 5, Sermon 254); and "The Mind of Christ" (Notebook 7, Sermon 330).

46. Cf. Ps 121:8; Phil 4:7.   47. Cf. Heb 6:20.

48. Cf. Num 10:35.

49. Joshua 4:11: "And it came to pass, when all the people were clean passed over, that the ark of the LORD passed over, and the priests, in the presence of the people."

50. Cf. Josh 3:17.

51. "At the presence of the Ark the waters of Jordan stood still till Israel, the ransomed of the Lord, passed over from the wilderness to Canaan; and it is by the power and presence of Christ that we pass over death, Jordan's antitype, from the wilderness of this world to heaven" (John Bunyan, *The Whole Works of John Bunyan* [Glasgow: Blackie & Son, 1862], 3:501).

52. Joshua 6:13: "And seven priests bearing seven trumpets of rams' horns before the ark of the LORD went on continually, and blew with the trumpets: and the armed men went before them; but the rereward came after the ark of the LORD, the priests going on, and blowing with the trumpets."

53. Cf. Josh 6:20.   54. Cf. Ps 2:7–12; Phil 2:9–11; Rev 2:27; 19.

55. Judges 20:27, "And the children of Israel enquired of the LORD, (for the ark of the covenant of God was there in those days)."

56. Cf. Judg 20:35.

57. 1 Samuel 5:2–5: "When the Philistines took the ark of God, they brought it into the house of Dagon, and set it by Dagon. And when they of Ashdod arose early on the morrow, behold, Dagon was fallen upon his face to the earth before the ark of the LORD. And they took Dagon, and set him in his place again. And when they arose early on the morrow morning, behold, Dagon was fallen upon his face to the ground before the ark of the LORD; and the head of Dagon and both the palms of his hands were cut off upon the threshold; only the stump of Dagon was left to him. Therefore neither the priests of Dagon, nor any that come into Dagon's house, tread on the threshold of Dagon in Ashdod unto this day."

58. Cf. 1 Sam 5:4.

59. Cf. 1 Sam 5:9. "Emerods" is an archaic term for hemorrhoids.

60. Cf. 1 Sam 5:11.

61. "Those that fight against God will soon have enough of it, and, first or last, will be made to know that none ever hardened their hearts against him and prospered" (Matthew Henry, *An Exposition of the Old and New Testament*, vol. 1, see "1 Samuel Chap. V").

62. 1 Samuel 6:19: "And he smote the men of Bethshemesh, because they had looked into the ark of the Lord, even he smote of the people fifty thousand and three-score and ten men: and the people lamented, because the Lord had smitten many of the people with a great slaughter."

63. Cf. John 14:6; Acts 4:12.

64. 2 Samuel 6:6: "And when they came to Nachon's thrashingfloor, Uzzah put forth his hand to the ark of God, and took hold of it; for the oxen shook it."

65. "When Uzzah put forth his hand to stay the ark when the oxen shook it, as despairing of God's protection of it without a human help, he died before the Lord; even so will all those do (without repentance) who use unlawful means to promote Christ's religion and to support it in the world" (Bunyan, *The Whole Works of John Bunyan*, 3:502).

66. "Hence sprang the monster of a State-church, a conjunction ill-assorted, and fraught with untold ills. This incongruous thing is half human, half divine: as a theory it fascinates, as a fact it betrays; it promises to advance the truth, and is itself a negation of it. Under its influences a system of religion was fashioned, which beyond all false religions, and beyond even Atheism itself, is the greatest hindrance to the true gospel of Jesus Christ" (*MTP* 26:262).

67. The transcript reads, "II. Sam. VII.11," but Charles is actually referring to 2 Sam 6:11: "And the ark of the LORD continued in the house of Obededom the Gittite three months: and the LORD blessed Obededom, and all his household."

68. Cf. 3 John 1:2.   69. Cf. 1 Kgs 8:6; 2 Chr 35:3.

70. Cf. Heb 8:1; Rev 21:21.

71. "A prayerless soul is a Christless soul. Prayer is the lisping of the believing infant, the shout of the fighting believer, the requiem of the dying saint falling asleep in Jesus. It is the breath, the watchword, the comfort, the strength, the honour of a Christian. If thou be a child of God, thou wilt seek thy Father's face, and live in thy Father's love" (C.H. Spurgeon, *Morning by Morning; or Daily Readings for The Family or the Closet* [New York: Sheldon and Company, 1866, The Spurgeon Library], 2).

72. Cf. Isa 58:8.

198   Heb. XIII . 11. 12. 13,   Going out of the camp. —

Here are in my text two verse about Jesus & one about our duty to him. Truly the best spur to a Christian is to remind him of what his Lord has done for him & ask what wilt thou do for thy friend? Gospel will get a larger revenue by voluntary offerings than law can by taxes enforced with thunders & lightnings.

I. What Christ did. —

1. He suffered — the beast was burned, hair, flesh, fat, skin, dung & all — so Jesus suffered in his whole soul & bodily frame. Suffered.

2. He suffered without the gate. He bade farewell to all friends, relinquished all the rites of the Jewish temple & in doleful style made a journey bearing his cross to Calvary. They reviled him as not fit to be in the city, they fetched him to bloody Golgotha & slew him.

3. He did this to sanctify his people — by pardon through his atonement & cleansing by his spirit. His people, His darlings — For me. For me. Unworthy, vile, proud, wicked yet his own blood as water ran. for our sin. Not for those to whom he owed, but for his debtors.

GOING OUT *of the* CAMP[1]

Hebrews 13:11–13

"For the bodies of those beasts, whose blood is brought into the high sanctuary by
the high priest for sin, are burned without the camp. Wherefore Jesus also, that
he might sanctify the people with his own blood, suffered without the gate. Let
us go forth therefore unto him without the camp, bearing his reproach."

Here are in my text two verse[s] about Jesus and one about our duty to him. Truly the best spur to a Christian is to remind him of what his Lord has done for him and ask, what wilt thou do for thy friend?[2] [The] Gospel will get a larger revenue by voluntary offerings than [the] law can by taxes enforced with thunders and lightnings.[3]

I.   WHAT CHRIST DID.

1.   He suffered. The beast was burned: hair, flesh, fat, skin, dung and all.[4] So Jesus suffered in his whole soul and bodily frame. **Suffered**.

2.   He suffered without the gate. He bade farewell to all friends, relinquished all the rites of the Jewish temple, and in doleful style made a journey bearing his cross to Calvary. They reviled him as not fit to be in the city. They fetched him to bloody Golgotha and slew him.

3.   He did this to sanctify his people[5] by pardon through his atonement and cleansing by his Spirit.[6] His people. His darlings. For me. For me. Unworthy, vile, proud, wicked. Yet his own blood as water ran. For our sins.

    Not for those to whom he owed, but for his debtors.[7]

II. What we ought to do. —

B. To leave the camp, follow him & bear his reproach.

1, The camp. is the world, Satan's camp.
It is a camp ever moving, unstable as tents are.
It is full of enemies, warriors, hostile to goodness.
It is a noisy, troublesome, sinful place.
The place where the multitudes herd.

2. We go out of the camp. when we repent.
when the house of God is our choice - when
we make an open profession or practise the
ordinances -   & by a life different from others.
Christ is not in the camp, he left it, let us go
to seek him & follow his steps.

3. To bear his reproach - means for his sake
one undeserved, one he sympathizes with.
He bore a ponderous cross, bear thou thy light one.
He was reproached as mad - as a deceiver -
as not being what he professed to be - as helpless -
So let us go out boldly & bear the same,

III, Camp of Satan - we dare ye to your worst.
Triumph will one day be ours! we fear not.
Come soldiers of the devil, desert & enlist with
us - Comrades fear not, some shall come,
Even so

819.

II. WHAT WE OUGHT TO DO.

~~I.~~ To leave the camp, follow him and bear his reproach.[8]

1. The camp is the world. Satan's camp.[9]

   It is a camp ever moving, unstable as tents are.

   It is full of enemies, warriors, hostile to goodness.

   It is a noisy, troublesome, sinful place. The place where the multitudes herd.

2. We go out of the camp. When we repent.[10] When the house of God is our choice.[11] When we make an open profession or practise the ordinances.[12] And by a life different from others.[13] Christ is not in the camp. He left it. Let us go to seek him and follow his steps.[14]

3. To bear his reproach means for his sake, one undeserved, one he sympathizes with.[15]

   He bore a ponderous[16] cross. Bear thou thy light one.

   He was reproached as mad.[17] As a deceiver,[18] as not being what he professed to be,[19] as helpless.[20]

   So let us go out boldly and bear the same.

III. CAMP OF SATAN—WE DARE YE TO YOUR WORST[.]

Triumph will one day be ours.[21] We fear not.

Come, soldiers of the devil. Desert and enlist with us.

Comrades[,] fear not, some shall come.

<u>Even so</u>[.]

319.

1.   Charles preached two additional sermons on this text: "'Let Us Go Forth'" (*MTP* 10, Sermon 577) and "Suffering Without the Camp" (*MTP* 46, Sermon 2660).

2.   Cf. John 15:12–14.

3.   "God loves his people's services, because they do them voluntarily. Voluntaryism is the essence of the gospel. Willing people are those whom God delights to have as his servants" (*NPSP* 2:165). "I believe in the might of the voluntary principle. I believe it to be perfectly irresistible in proportion to the power of God's Spirit in the hearts of those who exercise it. When the Spirit of God is absent, and the Church is at a low ebb, the voluntary principle has no power whatever, and then it becomes a question with many carnal wise men, whether they shall not look to Egypt for help and stay themselves on horses. But, when the Spirit of God is shed abroad, and men's hearts are in the right state, we find the voluntary principle equal to every design of the Church" (*NPSP* 6:359–60).

4.   Cf. Exod 29:13; Lev 8:17.   5.   Cf. Heb 10:10; 1 Pet 1:2.

6.   "We know that, when our Saviour died, His sacrifice had a double objective; one objective was pardon, the other was cleansing; and both the blood and the water flowed from the same source, to show us that justification and sanctification both spring from the same divine fountain; and, though sanctification is the work of the Spirit in us, yet, to accomplish this purpose, the Holy Spirit uses the sacrificial blood of Jesus, and the sacred water of His atonement applied to our heart, sprinkling us from dead works, and purging us from an evil conscience, that we may serve God without let or hindrance" (*MTP* 46:50). Cf. 1 Cor 6:11.

7.   Cf. Rom 8:12.   8.   Cf. Matt 16:24; Mark 8:34.

9.   "[T]his world, which may be compared to a 'camp'; for its instability, a camp not being always in one place; and for its hostility, the world being full of enemies to Christ and his people; and for the noise and fatigue of it, it being a troublesome and wearisome place to the saints, abounding with sins and wickedness" (John Gill, *An Exposition of the New Testament* [London, 1748, The Spurgeon Library], 3:458). William Gouge also compares the camp to "the world": "[C]amp is here metaphorically put for the world. . . . The world is as a camp of enemies, to saints especially" (William Gouge, *A Commentary on the Whole Epistle to the Hebrews,*

Being the Substance of Thirty Years' Wednesday's Lectures at Blackfriars, London, vol. 3 [Edinburgh: James Nichol, 1867, The Spurgeon Library], 337).

10. "[T]here must be a quitting of the world, in some sense, or there is no true coming to Christ, and enjoyment of him. . . . Now to go forth to him is to believe in him; to hope in him; to love him; to make a profession of him, and follow him" (Gill, *An Exposition of the New Testament*, 3:458).

11. "[R]equired of every member of Christ's Church is attendance upon the means of grace. I do not mean merely Sunday attendance. Any hypocrite comes on a Sunday, but they do not, to my knowledge, all of them, come on Monday to the prayer meeting, nor all to the weeknight service on a Thursday. . . . Take care that you do not become lax in that respect" (*MTP* 60:294).

12. See also "Baptismal Regeneration" (*MTP* 10, Sermon 573); "Baptism—A Burial" (*MTP* 27, Sermon 1627); "Baptism Essential to Obedience" (*MTP* 39, Sermon 2339); "The Lord's Supper: A Remembrance of Jesus" (*MTP* 34, Sermon 2038); "The Right Observance of the Lord's Supper" (*MTP* 45, Sermon 2638); "Fencing the Table" (*MTP* 50, Sermon 2865); and "The Object of the Lord's Supper" (*MTP* 51, Sermon 2942).

13. "When effectual grace separates men from the world by conversion and regeneration, then they become, in another sense, the sanctified; they are set apart even as Christ set apart himself, dedicated to God's service, and separated from sinners" (*MTP* 18:79).

14. Cf. John 17:15–18. See "The Character of Christ's People" (*NPSP* 2, Sermon 78).

15. "[T]he reproach, which saints meet with, for the sake of Christ, and a profession of him, is called his, because of the union there is between them, and the sympathy and fellow feeling he has with them in it; he reckons what is said and done to them as said and done to himself; and besides, there is a likeness between the reproach, which Christ personally bore, and that, which is cast upon his followers" (Gill, *An Exposition of the New Testament*, 3:458, italics in the original).

16. "Heavy; weighty" (Johnson's *Dictionary*, s.v. "ponderous").

17. Cf. Mark 3:21.   18. Cf. Luke 7:39; John 8:52–53.

19. Cf. Matt 21:23; 26:60, 63–65; Luke 20:2; John 2:18–20; 10:33; 19:7.

20. Cf. Matt 27:27–31.

21. Cf. 1 Cor 15:57; 2 Cor 2:14; Col 2:15; Rev 20:7–10.

199.   1. Pet. 2 – 1. 2. 3.   Milk of the word.

I, What is to be laid aside.
"all malice" – the dog of hell. Brother of Satan.
"all guile" – craft, tricks in trade &c –
"hypocrisies" – in word, action – formalism
"Envies" of the rich, great, or good –
"evil speakings"; even if true spread not evil.

II. New born babes desire sincere milk.
Babes – for weakness & need of attention.
Milk – pure, unadulterated doctrine.   Milk
Contains every substance necessary to support life
growth. not comfort is our dearest aim.
they care not for fine words, nor man but truth.

III. If so be ye have tasted &c –
Heard all of us have. But tasted is a different
thing. something within. the heart ~
                              Thanks for help – ~
322. 328

MILK *of the* WORD [1]
1 Peter 2:1–3

*"Wherefore, laying aside all malice, and all guile, and hypocrisies, and envies,
and all evil speakings, as newborn babes, desire the sincere milk of the word, that
ye may grow thereby: if so be ye have tasted that the Lord is gracious."*

I.   WHAT IS TO BE LAID ASIDE.

"All malice."   The dog of hell.[2] Brother of Satan.[3]

"All guile."   Craft, tricks in trade, etc.[4]

"Hypocrisies."   In word, action, formalism.[5]

"Envies."   Of the rich, great, or good.[6]

"Evil speaking."   Even if true, spread not evil.[7]

II.   NEW BORN BABES DESIRE SINCERE MILK.

Babes.[8]   For weakness and need of attention.

Milk.[9]   Pure, unadulterated doctrine. Milk contains every substance
necessary to support life.

Growth, not comfort[,] is our dearest aim. They care not for fine words, nor
man, but truth.

III. IF SO, BE YE HAVE TASTED, ETC. —

Heard, all of us have. But tasted is a different thing.[10] Something within the
heart.

Thanks for help.

322. 328

1. Charles preached two additional sermons on this text: "A Sermon for Men of Taste" (*MTP* 8, Sermons 459–60) and "The Test of Taste" (*MTP* 36, Sermon 2168).

2. A popular image of Satan during Charles's time was Cerberus, the Greek mythological "Hound of Hades," a fifty-headed dog that guards the domain of the dead (Hesiod, *The Works of Hesiod Translated from the Greek by Mr. Cooke* [London: printed by J. Wilson for J. Wood and C. Woodward, 1740, The Spurgeon Library], 161–62). See Charles's usage in "Gratitude from Deliverance from the Grave" (*MTP* 38, Sermon 2237).

3. Charles never again called malice the "Brother of Satan," but he did have harsh words for this vice, referring to it as "cruel as a wolf" (*TD* 2:67), "hellish" (*MTP* 24:468), and "fiendish" (*MTP* 44:129).

4. "Brethren, if we profess to be Christians, we must have done with all craft, policy, double-dealing, and the like" (*MTP* 39:425).

5. See the note on formalism in Notebook 1, Sermon 32, "The Wrong Roads" (*LS* 1:228).

6. "That green-eyed monster envy, lives in London as well as elsewhere, and he creeps into God's church" (*NPSP* 1:127).

7. "You certainly cannot expect to have fellowship with Christ if you mar the fellowship of Christ's Church by talking the one against the other" (*MTP* 8:393).

8. Cf. Matt 11:25; Luke 10:21; 1 Cor 3:1.

9. "The only way to be sure of having milk, was to keep a cow; and I recommend everybody to ensure getting the unadulterated milk of the Word by keeping his own cow, that is, by reading the Bible for himself" (*MTP* 48:323). Cf. Heb 5:12–13.

10. Cf. Heb 6:4–5.

Isa II. 11.   The downfall of pride.   200.

Pride was the means of Satan's fall, God could not
endure it among angels and chased it from his presence
it sought a refuge among us — it bears a wide
dominion here now — but rejoice! one day it shall be
rooted up — — See the man proud of wealth &
dress he shall lie as low as we. The man vain & sneering
sneering at our religion, the hireling gowned priest — the
infidel, these shall be as things of nought — —

I. Pride in her glory is full of lofty looks —
  1. She looks over others heads, she is somewhat
superior, not so bad as some she knows — —
  2. She looks for reward, or at least thinks she
ought to have grace — for her works.
  3. Should she indeed be found as poor as others
she trusteth that she has abundant strength of
her own to seek God with — without any assistance.
  4. She disdains the mercy-seat & the Bible she
looks not so low as this — —
     She is a fine dressed lady though the dress be
mere patchwork. She wears a veil & never suffers
her skin to be seen. She married Mr. Pharisee. She
cannot bear harlots & sinners. nor vulgarity — she has
things in good, rich style. Goes to church, mostly.

II. Pride's great enemies. Law & Gospel.
These keep up continual war with her
two mighty champions they are & do great
things. — —
Law was the first to attack her. She at

THE DOWNFALL *of* PRIDE [1]
Isaiah 2:11

"The lofty looks of man shall be humbled, and the haughtiness of men shall be bowed down, and the LORD *alone shall be exalted in that day."*

Pride was the means of Satan's fall.[2] God could not endure it among angels and chased it from his presence.[3] It sought a refuge among us. It bears a wide dominion here now. But rejoice! One day it shall be rooted up.[4]

See the man proud of wealth and dress. He shall lie as low as we.[5] The man vain of wisdom sneering at our religion, the hireling gowned priest,[6] the infidel.[7] These shall be as things of nought.

I.   PRIDE IN HER GLORY IS FULL OF LOFTY LOOKS.

1.   She looks over others['] heads. She is somewhat superior, not so bad as some she knows.[8]

2.   She looks for reward, or at least thinks she ought to have grace for her works.

3.   Should she indeed be found as poor as others, she trusteth that she has abundant strength of her own to seek God with without [*sic*] any assistance.[9]

4.   She disdains the mercy-seat[10] and the Bible. She looks not so low as this. She is a fine dressed lady[,] though the dress be mere patchwork. She wears a veil and never suffers her skin to be seen. She married M[r] Pharisee.[11] She cannot bear harlots and sinners. Nor vulgarity. She has things in good, rich style. Goes to Church, mostly.

II. PRIDE'S GREAT ENEMIES: LAW AND GOSPEL.

These keep up continual war with her. Two mighty champions they are, and do great things.[12]

Law was the first to attack her. She at

first thought to get him on her side but it is of no
use — Bad Law helps pride but not good law,
^{To} bring Mrs Pride down.
1. Law drew up a bill of charges against the lady,
such as she could no how pay at all.
2. Law refuses any compromise — no money, no bullock
no sincere half-obedience, no future holiness.
3. Law declares that he will shut her up in
the same dungeon as drunkards & harlots.
If moralists would hear the Law, they would fear the law
Then the Gospel comes in — Pride thought to make
it out between the two but no Law was inexorable
& Gospel refused to help unless all works were
thrown away. Then the Gospel erected a battery
of 5 great guns to destroy pride utterly. their names.
Gun. 1. Natural depravity. Man fallen, inclined
to evil, only evil — averse to good, unable to do good.
Gun. 2. Election. God a sovereign, having right
& power to do as he liked with his own. choosing some.
Gun 3. Justification by faith on Jesus Christ
not of works but by grace alone.
Gun 4. Effectual Calling — by the mighty grace of
the Spirit, man's inability & unwillingness to come.
Gun. 5. Continual grace. We never having any
but ever receiving from above, all of pure grace
& Thus Pride gets a warm reception from
the Gospel, in fact she has no where to go, unless
it be to the Church of England where there is neither law nor
gospel.

first thought to get him on her side. But it is of no use. Bad Law helps pride, but not good law.[13]

To bring Mrs Pride down:

1. Law drew up a bill of charges against the lady such as she could no how pay at all.[14]

2. Law refuses any compromise. No money, no bullock,[15] no sincere half-obedience, no future holiness.

3. Law declares that he will shut her up in the same dungeon as drunkards and harlots.

If moralists would hear the Law, they would fear the law. Then the Gospel comes in. Pride thought to make it out between the two, but no Law was inexorable, and Gospel refused to help unless all works were thrown away. Then the Gospel erected a battery of 5 great guns to destroy pride utterly. Their names:

Gun. 1. Natural depravity. Man fallen, enclined [*sic*] to evil, only evil, averse to good, unable to do good.

Gun. 2. Election. God [is] a sovereign, having right and power to do as he liked with his own. Choosing some.

Gun 3. Justification by faith on Jesus Christ not of works but by grace alone.

Gun 4. Effectual Calling by the mighty grace of the Spirit. Man's inability and unwillingness to come.

Gun 5. Continual Grace. We never having any but ever receiving from above, all of pure grace[.] Thus Pride gets a warm reception from the Gospel. In fact, she has no where [*sic*] to go, unless it be to the Church of England where there is neither law nor Gospel.[16]

III. Pride's battle & defeat in the Christian. —

Pride is a native of man's heart & it goes hard to root her out, moreover she returns often to the spot

Conviction first shakes her out of her nest,

Faith turns her altogether out of doors. —

A View of our own heart kills pride for the time.

A Slip, the mis-carriages in our duty all show us that pride ought not to be with us.

Dulness, coldness in prayer, famine of soul, sickness, want of God's presence these start pride of it.

The glories of the cross - she cannot bear.

Starve her, put her in your dark cellar, hold her eyes to the sun, drown her in tears, crucify her, —— —

IV. Defeat of Pride in the Ungodly. —

Pride may not have a dwelling even in the damned & therefore God humbles them.

How humbling for great & little to be in one hell.

To be in the hand of the despised one.

To be tried by the Nazarene & his poor disciples

To reflect on their own folly in not escaping hell

To see the glories of the poor disciples of Jesus.

To be utterly unable to escape. to be without hope.

Pride cannot endure hell-fire - she leaves man when he leaves the earth, Oh that it were before. Father. May it leave us all Amen

I desire to record thanks for this second 100 may God receive glory from them as well as for them.

III. PRIDE'S BATTLE AND DEFEAT IN THE CHRISTIAN.

Pride is a native of man's heart, and it goes hard to root her out. Moreover, she returns often to the spot.

Conviction first shakes her out of her nest.[17]

Faith turns her altogether out of doors.

A view of our own heart kills pride for the time.

A slip, the miscarriages in our duty, all show us that pride ought not to be with us.

Dulness [*sic*], coldness in prayer, famine of soul, sickness, want of God's presence, these start pride off.[18]

The glories of the cross she cannot bear.

Starve her. Put her in your dark cellar. Hold her eyes to the sun. Drown her in tears. Crucify her.[19]

IV. DEFEAT OF PRIDE IN THE UNGODLY.

Pride may not have a dwelling even in the damned, and therefore God humbles them.

How humbling for great and little to be in one hell.

> To be in the hand of the despised one.[20]

> To be tried by the Nazarene and his poor disciples.[21]

> To reflect on their own folly in not escaping hell.[22]

> To see the glories of the poor disciples of Jesus.

> To be utterly unable to escape. To be without hope.

Pride cannot endure hell-fire. She leaves man when he leaves the earth. Oh, that it were before.

Father, May it leave us all.

Amen.

I desire to record thanks for this second 100.

May God receive glory from them as well as for them.

324.

1. Charles preached on this text again in his sermon "An Infallible Sign of Revival" (*MTP* 51, Sermon 2922).

2. Cf. Isa 14:12–15 and Ezek 28:13–19.

3. "Take heed of pride, by pride fell the angels—how can men, then, though the image of their Maker, hope to win by it? Shun it, flee from it; for so sure as thou art proud, wilt thou incur the guilt of making light of Christ" (*NPSP* 2:357).

4. "Pride is yet my darling sin, I cannot shake it off" (*Autobiography* 1:146).

5. Cf. Job 14:2; Isa 40:8; Jas 1:10–11.

6. "We know that Catholics pretend that they can get grace without getting it from God directly; for they believe that God puts all his grace into the pope, and then that runs down into smaller pipes, called cardinals and bishops, through which it runs into the priests; and by turning the tap with a shilling you can get as much grace as you like. But it is not so with God's grace. He says, 'I will give them showers.' Grace is the gift of God, and is not to be created by man" (*NPSP* 1:218).

7. "At least, nearly the whole of us bear the professing Christian name; living in England, you would think it a disgrace to you if you were not called Christian. You are not heathen, you are not infidel; you are neither Mahometans nor Jews, you think that the name, Christian, is a creditable one to you, and you have taken it" (*NPSP* 3:186).

8. Cf. Luke 18:9–14.

9. "That which is not in Holy Scripture is not to be received as matter of faith in the Christian church; but that which is there is to be received and held with that stern steadfastness, that incorruptible faith, which no more changes than the unchanging truth which it has grasped. Woe be to the man who is first a Calvinist, then an Arminian, then a Pelagian, then a Unitarian, never finding rest for the sole of his foot; keeping nothing because he has nothing to keep" (*MTP* 30:677).

10. "The doctrine of salvation by works would silence the hallelujahs of heaven. Hush, ye choristers, what meaning is there in your song? You are chanting,

'Unto him that loved us, and washed us from our sins in his own blood.' But why sing ye so? If salvation be by works, your ascriptions of praise are empty flatteries" (*MTP* 26:247–48).

11. For early examples in which Charles personifies a group as an individual, see "Election" (Notebook I, Sermon 10) and "The Dog and Swine" (Notebook 2, Sermon 85).

12. "Self-righteous people are not much inclined to search *the Scriptures*, they do not read them with an understanding heart, so as to get the meaning; they rather make the Bible say their own meaning, and twist it to support their own pleasing dream. Like a battery of ordnance of the strongest kind, both law and gospel fire into the sinner's righteousness and sink it, like a riddled hulk, into the deeps of the sea" (*MTP* 25:559, italics in the original).

13. Cf. Rom 7:21–23.   14. Cf. Rom 6:23.

15. Cf. Isa 1:11.

16. "I am not aware that any Protestant Church in England teaches the doctrine of baptismal regeneration except one, and that happens to be the corporation which with none too much humility calls itself *the* Church of England. This very powerful sect does not teach this doctrine merely through a section of its ministers, who might charitably be considered as evil branches of the vine, but it openly, boldly, and plainly declares this doctrine in her own appointed standard, the Book of Common Prayer, and that in words so express, that while language is the channel of conveying intelligible sense, no process short of violent wresting from their plain meaning can ever make them say anything else" (*MTP* 10:315, italics in the original).

17. "All the members of the body are defiled with it; the tongue is a little member, and is a world of iniquity itself, and defiles the whole body; the several members of it are used as instruments of unrighteousness . . . all employed in the service of sin" (John Gill, *Gill's Complete Body of Practical and Doctrinal Divinity: Being a System of Evangelical Truths, Deduced from the Sacred Scriptures. Abridged by William Staughton, D.D.* [Philadelphia: printed for Delaplaine and Hellings by B. Graves, 1810, The Spurgeon Library], 530).

18. "Lord, keep Thy servant low and humble at Thy feet! How prone am I to pride and vain-glory! Keep me always mindful that I have nothing which I have not received; 'tis grace, free, sovereign grace that has made me to differ. Why should I be chosen an elect vessel? Not that I deserve it, I am sure; but it is rich love" (*Autobiography* 1:144).

19. "I say, then, that the first thing in mortification is the weakening of this habit [fornication], that it shall not impel and tumultuate as formerly; that it shall not entice and draw aside; that it shall not disquiet and perplex the killing of its life, vigour, promptness, and readiness to be stirring. This is called 'crucifying the flesh with the lusts thereof,' Gal. v. 24; that is, taking away its blood and spirits that give it strength and power,—the wasting of the body of death 'day by day,' 2 Cor. iv. 16. As a man nailed to the cross; he first struggles, and strives, and cries out with great strength and might, but, as his blood and spirits waste, his strivings are faint and seldom, his cries low and hoarse, scarce to be heard;—when a man first sets on a lust or distemper, to deal with it, it struggles with great violence to break loose; it cries with earnestness and impatience to be satisfied and relieved; but when by mortification the blood and spirits of it are let out, it moves seldom and faintly, cries sparingly, and is scarce heard in the heart; it may have sometimes a dying pang, that makes an appearance of great vigour and strength, but it is quickly over, especially if it be kept from considerable success. This the apostle describes, as in the whole chapter, so especially, Rom. vi. 6" (John Owen, *The Works of John Owen, D.D.,* vol. 6 [London: Johnstone and Hunter, 1861, The Spurgeon Library], 30).

20. Cf. John 5:21–31.   21. Cf. 1 Cor 6:3.

22. Cf. Luke 16:19–31.

201.   Rev. XXI. 7. 8 —   The Great Promise & Awful Threat.
The threatenings & promises of the Scriptures con-
-stitute a main feature of the natural strength
of the Christian religion.   They are most awful
— most sublime.   Here in these two verses
we have Ebal & Gerizim — the blessing & the curse.

I   The Blessing —

1. To whom. "He that overcometh". This implies an
enemy & surely there are many our hearts, the world,
sin in ten-thousand shapes, the devil &c &c —
It implies a fight with the enemy, no slothful
submission, no mere wish, or prayer but a hearty war
It includes also the idea of continued contest, not a
spasmodic movement, a temporary stir but a war.
& this must be successful — but how — only by divine
aid —   If we wish for salvation we must fight & conquer.

2. The Inheritance. — "Shall inherit all things" —   All things
are in an especial manner the property of a believer
but he comes not in for his inheritance till the fight
is over —   Heaven, Justification, complete pardon.
All good, desirable, conceivable, imaginable things
he shall inherit, not earn for all is of grace.

3. The God — "I will be his God" — all a God can
be God will be to the conqueror. For strength, grace
faithfulness, eternity, wisdom. All the attributes are
by this promise engaged on the conqueror's side —

4. The adoption. "He shall be my son" which is
the greatest honour man can e'er attain. to

THE GREAT PROMISE *and* AWFUL THREAT
Revelation 21:7–8[1]

"He that overcometh shall inherit all things; and I will be his God, and he shall be my son. But the fearful, the unbelieving, and the abominable, and murderers, and whoremongers, and sorcerers, and idolaters, and all liars, shall have their part in the lake of fire which burneth with fire and brimstone: which is the second death."

The threatenings and promises of the Scriptures constitute a main feature of the natural strength of the Christian religion. They are most awful, most sublime. Here in these two verses we have Ebal and Gerizim, the blessing and the curse.[2]

I. THE BLESSING

1. To whom. "*He that overcometh.*" This implies an enemy, and surely there are many: our hearts,[3] the world,[4] sin in ten-thousand shapes,[5] the devil[6] etc. etc. It implies a fight with the enemy. No slothful submission, no mere wish or prayer, but a hearty war.[7] It includes also the idea of continued contest. Not a spasmodic movement, a temporary stir, but a war.[8] And this must be successful. But how? Only by divine aid.[9] If we wish for salvation, we must fight and conquer.[10]

2. The Inheritance. "*Shall inherit all things.*" All things are in an especial manner the property of a believer.[11] But he comes not in for his inheritance till the fight is over. Heaven, Justification, complete pardon, all good, desirable, conceivable, imaginable things he shall inherit, not earn[,] for all is of grace.[12]

3. The God. "*I will be his God.*"[13] All a God can be, God will be to the conqueror. For strength, grace, faithfulness, eternity, wisdom. All the attributes are by this promise engaged on the conqueror's side.

4. The adoption. "*He shall be my son.*" Which is the greatest honour man can e'er attain. To

be a son & heir of the Divine Being, The Creator.

1. How besotted men are to choose to hug their sins & lose the amazing advantages here set out.

2. How careful ought we to be lest we do not overcome, let us try our faith, look to our foundation

3. Let the promise cheer us in any conflict.

II. The Threatening. —

To whom is the Black Letter addressed.

1. The Fearful — not poor timid, fearing souls afraid of being accepted, or afraid of falling — but cowards afraid of persecution, laughter, scorn. Afraid of trouble in the way, afraid of the toil of the journey.

2. Unbelieving. These are among the first, as being the worst, this is the damning sin. To reject the Bible, Jesus, his gospel. to die unconverted.

3. Abominable — such as swearers, drunkards, defilers of themselves these must go to-gether.

4. Murderers — a crime, society cannot endure, but alas how many heart murderers there are.

5. Whoremongers. the abhorred of the Lord fall into this sin, all uncleanness is included.

6. Sorcerers. professing to deal with Spirits tell fortunes, or to be witches &c —

7. Idolaters. Lovers of self, money & so on

8. All liars. To take in trade liars, now & then liars, hypocrites, cheats, tricky men all liars of all sort —

be a son and heir of the Divine Being, the Creator.

1. How besotted[14] men are to choose to hug their sins and lose the amazing advantages here set out.

2. How careful ought we to be, lest we do not overcome. Let us try our faith, look to our foundation.[15]

3. Let the promise cheer us in any conflict.

II. THE THREATENING.

To whom is the Black Letter[16] addressed?

1. The Fearful. Not poor timid, fearing souls afraid of being accepted, or afraid of falling,[17] but cowards afraid of persecution, laughter, scorn.[18] Afraid of trouble in the way, afraid of the toil of the journey.

2. Unbelieving. These are among the first as being the worst. This is the damning sin. To reject the Bible, Jesus, his gospel. To die unconverted.[19]

3. Abominable. Such as swearers, drunkards, defilers of themselves. These must go to-gether [*sic*].[20]

4. Murderers. A crime society cannot endure. But alas, how many heart murderers there are.[21]

5. Whoremongers. The abhorred of the Lord fall into this sin. All uncleanness is included.[22]

6. Sorcerers professing to deal with Spirits, tell fortunes, or to be witches etc.[23]

7. Idolaters. Lovers of self, money, and so on.

8. All liars. To take in trade liars, now and then liars, hypocrites, cheats, tricky men. All liars of all sorts.[24]

The Lake burning with Fire & Brimstone is the portion of this catalogue of transgressors. —

A Lake, not a river that may dry but a lake. Fire & Brimstone will be no delightful bed.

<u>III</u>. Some reflection on the promise & threat.

1. They are most just. Should not the righteous dwell with the righteous — & the wicked go to their own place. Which out of the sinners mentioned could be endured in heaven!

2. Admire the grace, that took us from being just such persons & has washed us & made us white in the blood of the Lamb —

3. Surely the pleasures of the vices named are not commensurate with the pain which is their inevitable consequence. How dare we venture on them with hell-fire for a penalty —

4. How sad to remember what myriads are in hell & on the highway there, for multitudes on multitudes exactly answer one or other of the descriptions.

325. 327. 343.   <u>Oh Lord save men.</u>

The Lake burning with Fire and Brimstone[25] is the portion of this catalogue of transgressors. A Lake, not a river that may dry, but a lake. Fire and Brimstone will be no delightful bed.

III. SOME REFLECTION ON THE PROMISE AND THREAT.

1. They are most just. Should not the righteous dwell with the righteous and the wicked go to their own place[?] Which, out of the sinners mentioned, could be endured in heaven?

2. Admire the grace that took us from being just such persons and has washed us and made us white in the blood of the Lamb.[26]

3. Surely the pleasures of the vices named are not commensurate with the pain which is their inevitable consequence. How dare we venture on them with hell-fire for a penalty.

4. How sad to remember what myriads are in hell and on the highway there, for multitudes on multitudes exactly answer one or other of the descriptions.[27]

Oh Lord[,] save men.

325. 327. 343.

1.   Charles never preached again from this specific passage.

2.   Cf. Deut 11:29.

3.   "The Scripture tells you that your heart is deceitful—see whether it be not so. It tells you that there is a natural inclination in man towards evil—study yourself, and see whether this is not the case" (*MTP* 34:160–61). Cf. Jer 17:9.

4.   "What hast thou, O man of God, to do with society? Christians are to come out from among the ungodly, to take up their cross daily, and follow Christ, to go without the camp, bearing his reproach. The friend of the world is the enemy of Christ. What have you to do with doing as the world does?" (*MTP* 54:65). Cf. Jas 4:4.

5.   "[T]he inbred enmity both against God and man, which appears in ten-thousand shapes; the love of the world, the self will, the foolish and hurtful desires, which cleave to [the] inmost soul (John Wesley, *The Works of the Reverend John Wesley* [New York: J. Emory and B. Waugh, 1831], 1:182).

6.   Cf. Acts 13:8; 1 Pet 5:8.

7.   "Fight on, then. Never think of saying, 'I cannot overcome this sin.' By God's help you must, for no sin can enter heaven with you. You must overcome it. It cannot be permitted that you sit down in peace with any foe to purity. You are never to have peace with any sin. When, first of all, the Lord Jesus made peace with us, he proclaimed war against sin on every side and of every size, and the loyal Christian never dreams of peace, but contemplates only a perpetual fighting against sin, expecting to have perpetual grace bestowed" (*MTP* 61:232).

8.   "The saints, whose souls breathe after deliverance from [sin's] perplexing rebellion, know that there is no safety against [sin] but in a constant warfare . . . Sin will not only be striving, acting, rebelling, troubling, disquieting, but if left alone, if not continually mortified, it will bring forth great, cursed, scandalous, soul-destroying sins" (John Owen, *The Works of John Owen D.D.*, vol. 6 [London: Johnstone and Hunter, 1851, The Spurgeon Library], 12).

9.   "There is no fighting sin except under the leadership of Christ. We must fight sin with his weapons, we must see its sinfulness by the light of his sufferings, see its mischief in the sorrows of his death, see its destruction in the triumphs of his resurrection" (*MTP* 12:535).

10. Cf. Rom 8:37.   11. Cf. Rom 8:17.   12. Cf. Eph 2:8.

13. See "Christ in the Covenant" (*NPSP* 2, Sermon 103). "Here is a great possession —Jesus Christ by the covenant is the property of every believer" (*NPSP* 2:393).

14. "To infatuate; to stupify; to dull; to take away the senses" (Johnson's *Dictionary*, s.v. "to besot").

15. "[Y]ou will be often led to try your foundation, and at times you will tremble as you cling to it" (*MTP* 35:506).

16. "A heavy angular condensed typeface used especially by the earliest European printers and based on handwriting used chiefly in the 13th to 15th centuries" (Merriam-Webster.com, s.v. "Black Letter"). "Let the printer take heed, that his life be set in heavenly type, and not in the black letter of sin" (*NPSP* 4:335).

17. "If you should tell me you were not afraid of falling, I would not have you in the church for the world; you would be no Christian. All Christians, when they are in a right state, are afraid of falling into sin. Holy fear is the proper condition of a child of God" (*NPSP* 3:331).

18. Cf. Matt 10:33; Prov 29:25.   19. Cf. Mark 16:16; John 3:18.

20. Cf. 1 Tim 1:10.   21. Cf. Matt 5:21; 1 John 3:15.

22. Cf. 1 Tim 1:10.

23. "The present existence of demons within the bodies of men I shall neither assert nor deny; but certainly, in our Saviour's day it was very common for devils to take possession of men and torment them greatly" (*MTP* 29:577). Cf. Gal 5:20; Rev 21:8.

24. Cf. Col 3:9.   25. Cf. Rev 20:14.

26. Cf. Rev 7:14.   27. Cf. Matt 7:13.

Luke. *XIV*. 34 35. Salt is good.   202.

How beautifully our Saviour lays hold on common
objects to throw light on subjects otherwise abstruse.
Now this verse contains the same sense as that
passage in Heb. *X*. 26 - "If we sin wilfully" - or *II* Pet. 2. 20. 21.
Heb. *VI*. 4 - "If they shall fall away &c" - - It is a lively,
easy comment on those passages & throws very
much light upon them .. far more than many
earthly writers are able to do - May we be
helped to understand it - - -

I. A substance said to be good - "Salt" -

II. A fearful supposition "if the salt have lost its savour"

III. An unanswerable question "wherewith shall it be seasoned"

IV. A hopeless condition. "neither fit for the land &c"

I. An excellent substance. "Salt."
This does not mean the gospel - for that cannot
lose its savour - its powerful, active effect -
   But by this word the Church is meant as
made up of men & women, members & ministers
who all profess to be heirs of glory.
   The Church - the salt is good.
1. Good in itself - as salt is savoury to us so
are God's people very agreeable to him.
2. Good to with others. as they preserve the
world & keep it from being putrid, rotten
corrupt, abominable & unbearable.

SALT IS GOOD [1]
Luke 14:34–35

"Salt is good: but if the salt have lost his savour, wherewith shall it be seasoned? It is neither fit for the land, nor yet for the dunghill; but men cast it out. He that hath ears to hear, let him hear."

How beautifully our Saviour lays hold on common objects to throw light [2] on subjects otherwise abstruse. [3]

Now, this verse contains the same sense as that passage in Heb. X.26, "If we sin willfully," [4] or II Pet. 2.20.21. [5]

Heb. VI.4, "If they shall fall away etc." [6] It is a lively, easy comment on those passages and throws very much light upon them, far more than many earthly writers are able to do. [7] May we be helped to understand it.

I.   A SUBSTANCE SAID TO BE GOOD. *"salt."*

II. A FEARFUL SUPPOSITION. *"if the salt have lost its savour."*

III. AN UNANSWERABLE QUESTION. *"wherewith shall it be seasoned."*

IV. A HOPELESS CONDITION. *"neither fit for the land, etc."*

I.   AN EXCELLENT SUBSTANCE. *"salt."*

This does not mean the gospel, for that cannot lose its savour, [8] its powerful, active effect. [9] But by this word the Church is meant as made up of men and women, members and ministers who all profess to be heirs of glory.

The Church. The salt is good. [10]

1. Good in itself. As salt is savoury to us, so are God's people very agreeable to him. [11]
    <u>to</u>
2. Good with others, as they preserve the world and keep it from being putrid, rotten, corrupt, abominable, and unbearable. [12]

The Church should season the world by holy conversation & preaching; as also by holy living & godly example.   Though infidels in our day will not allow that the church is useful, God says it is — & experience speaks plainly enough every saying "Salt is good." Look at the countries where it is found & where it is not found.

II. A fearful supposition. "If the Savour be lost" — Some say this is impossible but why then suppose such a thing if it be impossible why not say "if the moon roll on the green".

It is possible — in the other above noticed passages it is pretty plain that the "ifs" may become facts or why speak on them.

The Savour may be lost by the Church.

Those who have come to the knowledge of the truth may sin wilfully.

Those who have tasted the heavenly gift &c may fall away. & the once enlightened may return as a dog to his vomit.

But — The final perseverance of believers is not affected by this in the least degree that is still as sure as God can make it.

The Church should season the world by holy conversation and preaching as also by holy living and godly example. Though infidels in our day will not allow that the church is useful, God says it is, and experience speaks plainly enough ever saying, "salt is good." Look at the countries where it is found and where it is not found.[13]

II. A FEARFUL SUPPOSITION. *"If the savour be lost."*

Some say this is impossible. But why then suppose such a thing if it be impossible? Why not say, "[I]f the moon roll on the green?"[14] It is possible. In the other above noticed passages, it is pretty plain that the "ifs" may become facts or why speak on them[?][15]

The savour may be lost by the Church.

Those who have come to the knowledge of the truth[16] may sin wilfully [*sic*].

Those who have tasted the heavenly gifts etc. may fall away,[17] and the once enlightened may return as a dog to his vomit.[18]

But, the final perseverance of believers is not affected by this in the least degree.[19] That is still as sure as God can make it.

A man may come to the knowledge of the truth & yet not be converted — & the other characters are not believers.

So in this verse by the salt who may lose their savour are not meant true followers of the Lamb but nominal ones — nominal churches.

The Scriptures ever call men by the name they bear outwardly — it is not a system of divinity & we must not look for polemical terms & accurate phrases in it. It is the simple, poor man's book — It speaks of men professing to be a church as a church. Of faith even when false, as faith. It talks to us in our common language, if it were ever putting in salvo's & technical terms it would have to be twice as big. Yet it tells us something in one part to set another part all right.

So that in this passage it speaks of a church from which the savour was gone & alas. there are some such in our day, Let us take heed lest ours prove so too. —

III. An unanswerable question "How can they be seasoned"? A bad world, like meat may have a flavour put into it but what is to be done with bad salt. how can that be seasoned

Jesus cannot help such for they have rejected his gospel as an unholy thing.

A man may come to the knowledge of the truth[20] and yet not be converted.[21] And the other characters are not believers.

So in this verse. By the salt who may lose their savour are not meant true followers of the Lamb, but nominal ones, nominal churches.

The Scriptures ever call men by the name they bear outwardly.[22] It is not a system of divinity, and we must not look for polemical terms and accurate phrases in it.[23] It is the simple, poor man's book. It speaks of men professing to be a church as a church. Of faith even when false, as faith. It talks to us in our common language[;][24] if it were ever putting in salvo's[25] [*sic*] and technical terms it would have to be twice as big.

Yet it tells us something in one part to set another part all right.[26]

So that in this passage it speaks of a church from which the savour was gone. And alas, there are some such in our day.[27] Let us take heed, lest ours prove so too.

III. AN UNANSWERABLE QUESTION. *"How can they be seasoned[?]"*

A bad world, like ~~bad~~ meat, may have a flavour put into it. But what is to be done with bad salt? How can that be seasoned?

Jesus cannot help such, for they have rejected his gospel as an unholy thing.

They, despise the Holy Spirit's operations, they have
grieved him — where else can power come.
There is no other religion that can avail,
no book of any use, no preaching now
can help — he that bursts the bonds of
the gospel — can never be bound at all
    Apostates are mostly hopeless. They who
turn to the beggarly world are seldom brought
out. Let any backslider fear lest he be
found in this condition — for their remain
IV. A hopeless condition. "good for nothing".
    A man who becomes an apostate is good
for nothing. — no use to the Church but
rather a great curse, plague & dis-grace.
No use to moral men, they scout a hypocrite
no use on the dunghill, even the lowest
of the low sneer at Pliable & laugh at him
    He is cast out — the church rejects him
& the very world loathes him though glad
of his fall —
    Give serious consideration to this "earth then
1. Christian behold thy exalted calling.
2. Professor see thy danger.
3. Professor see thy hopeless ruin if thou art
    a mere professor. Great me keep me

330

They despise the Holy Spirit's operations. They have grieved him. Where else can power come[?]

There is no other religion that can avail,[28] no book of any use, no preaching now can help. He that bursts the bonds of the gospel can never be bound at all.

Apostates are mostly hopeless. They who turn to the beggarly world are seldom brought out. Let any backslider fear, lest he be found in this condition, for there remain[s]:

IV. A HOPELESS CONDITION. *"good for nothing."*

A man who becomes an apostate is good for nothing.[29] No use to the Church but rather a great curse, plague, and disgrace.

No use to moral men. They scout[30] a hypocrite.

No use on the dunghill.[31] Even the lowest of the low sneer at Pliable and laugh at him.[32]

He is cast out. The church rejects him and the very world loathes him, though glad of his fall.

Give serious consideration to this. "Ear to hear."[33]

1. Christian, behold thy exalted calling.

2. Professor, see thy danger.

3. Professor, see thy hopeless ruin if thou art a mere professor.

Great one, **keep me**.

330.

1. Charles never preached again from this passage or the parallel passages, Matt 5:13 and Mark 9:50.

2. "A building without windows would be a prison rather than a house, for it would be quite dark, and no one would care to take it upon lease; and, in the same way, a discourse without a parable is prosy and dull, and involves a grievous weariness of the flesh" (*Lectures* 3:2).

3. "Hidden; difficult; remote from conception or apprehension" (Johnson's *Dictionary*, s.v. "abstruse").

4. "[T]here may be a notional knowledge, when there is no experimental knowledge" (John Gill, *An Exposition of the New Testament* [London: printed for the author, 1748, The Spurgeon Library], 3:422).

5. "[R]ather such are meant, who are so enlightened as to see the evil effects of sin, but not the evil that is in sin; to see the good things which come by Christ, but not the goodness that is in Christ; so as to reform externally, but not to be sanctified internally; to have knowledge of the Gospel doctrinally, but not experimentally; yea, to have such light into it, as to be able to preach it to others, and yet be destitute of the grace of God" (Gill, 3:381).

6. "[T]his can be no instance of the final and total apostacy [*sic*] of real saints; external reformation; for the house may be swept, and garnished with an external reformation; persons may be outwardly righteous before men, have a form of godliness and a name to live, and yet be dead in trespasses and sin . . . not a spiritual experimental knowledge of Christ, for that is eternal life, the beginning, the pledge, and earnest of it; but a notional knowledge of Christ, or a profession of knowledge of him" (Gill, 3:566).

7. Although Charles's specific referent cannot be determined, it is possible that he is referring to Adam Clarke. "It appears from this, whatever sentiment may gain or lose by it, that their[s] is a fearful possibility of *falling away from the grace of God;* and if this scripture did not say so, there are many that do say so. And were there no scripture express on this subject, the nature of the present state of man, which is a state of *probation* or *trial*, must necessarily imply it. Let him who most assuredly standeth, take heed lest he fall" (Adam Clarke, *The Holy Bible, Containing the Old and New Testaments: The Text Carefully Printed from the Most Correct*

Copies of the Present Authorised Translation, Including the Marginal Reading and Parallel Texts. With a Commentary and Critical Notes; Designed as a Help to a Better Understanding of the Sacred Writings. In Six Volumes. Volume VI. I Corinthians to Revelation, new ed. (London: William Tegg and Co., 1854, The Spurgeon Library). In his 1854 edition, Charles crossed out the remainder of the title, starting with "Designed . . ." and wrote, "Adapted to blind the eye and prevent the truth in Jesus from shining upon the soul." He also replaced Clarke's educational credentials with the epithet, "Arminian Twister of the Word."

8. "The *savour* here supposed, that it may be lost, cannot mean the savour of grace, of true grace itself, which cannot be lost, being an incorruptible seed" (Gill, *An Exposition of the New Testament*, vol. 1 (London: printed for the author, 1746, The Spurgeon Library), 1:35, cf. Matt 5:13, italics in the original).

9. "I question whether our preaching in unbelief is of much service, but if we preach believing that souls will be saved, then they will be saved. If we preach relying on God's promise that his Word shall not return unto him void, it will not return void, but there shall be fruit for the sower, according to the assurance of our faithful God" (*MTP* 59:595). Cf. Isa 55:11; Heb 4:12.

10. "This is to be understood of the disciples and apostles of Christ. . . . These were the salt *of the earth*; that is, of the inhabitants of the earth, not of the land of *Judea* only, where they first lived and preached; but of the whole world, into which they were afterwards sent to preach the Gospel" (Gill, *An Exposition of the New Testament*, 1:35, italics in the original).

11. "He that believes in God believes in all the words that God speaks, and he surrenders himself to all that God does; and such a man must be pleasing to God. We believe in one God, and in one Mediator between God and man, the man Christ Jesus; and we trust in the Lord as he thus draws near to us: thus are we in the way of pleasing God. By faith we ourselves have become pleasing to God, and our actions performed with a view to his honour are pleasing to him. What a joy is this!" (*MTP* 35:453).

12. "The holy ones are 'the salt of the earth,' the means of the preservation of the wicked. Without the godly as a conserve, the race would be utterly destroyed" (*NPSP* 1:17).

13. "Look at Robespierre, in France, look at the doings of the Reign of Terror, turn to heathen countries, I dare not tell you what abominable vices, what lascivious sins are committed there in public; I point you to Sodom and Gomorrah, and I ask you what man may become; and I say that I do not know but that a man might become as vile as a devil, if God's restraining mercy were taken from him" (*NPSP* 2:294).

14. This appears to be an adage of Charles's own creation, summoning the image of something as impossible and as foolish as imagining the moon rolling on the lawn.

15. "[E]ither gifts qualifying men for the ministry, which may cease; or the savoury doctrines of the Gospel, which may be departed from; or a seeming savoury conversation, which may be neglected; or that seeming savour, zeal, and affection, with which the Gospel is preached, which may be dropped" (Gill, *An Exposition of the New Testament*, 1:35).

16. Cf. 1 Tim 2:4.   17. Cf. Heb 6:4.

18. Cf. Prov 26:11; 2 Pet 2:22.

19. Charles is treating the "savour" of Christians being lost, not salvation itself. Charles mentions salvific perseverance several times in this volume and preceding volumes: see "Final Perseverance" (Notebook 1, Sermon 8); "Final Perseverance Certain" (Notebook 2, Sermon 8); "Linsey-Woolsey Forbidden" (Sermon 210); and "Nonconformity" (Sermon 223).

20. Cf. 1 Tim 2:4.

21. "Moreover, the same persons God would have saved, he would have also come to the knowledge of the truth: of Christ, who is the truth, and to faith in him, and of all the truth of the Gospel, as it is in Jesus; not merely to a notional knowledge of it, which persons may arrive unto, and not be saved, but a spiritual and experiential knowledge of it; and all that are saved are brought to such a knowledge" (Gill, *An Exposition of the New Testament*, 3:266).

22. "[N]ominal Christianity, fostered by a national Church [. . .] has no root nor soul within it. Oh! there are millions of Englishmen who think they are Christians, because they were sprinkled in infancy with holy drops, and because they have

come to the Lord's Table. . . . This is the curse and plague of England, that we have so much profession and so little possession" (*MTP* 7:295). Cf. 1 John 2:29; Matt 7:20.

23. "Now, we are compelled to confess with the greatest sorrow, and I may add also with no little indignation, [that] there have been some men who have never been able to grasp the gospel in its integrity, and present the grace of God to men's minds at once in its sovereignty and in its freeness. Though their sermons sometimes ring with the clear melodious note of grace, they are too often bent on qualifying the extent of its welcome, and inventing explanations of their own, to wrest the simple meaning of Scriptures. Calvinists, such men may call themselves, but, unlike the Reformer whose name they adopt, they bring a system of divinity to the Bible to interpret it, instead of making every system, be its merits what they may, yield, and give place to the pure and unadulterated Word of God" (*NPSP* 6:302).

24. "Oh, that all would tell the gospel out with plain words! . . . The way of salvation is far too important a matter to be the theme of oratorical displays. The cross is far too sacred to be made a pole on which to hoist the flags of our fine language" (*MTP* 32:28).

25. "An exception; a reservation; an excuse" (Johnson's *Dictionary*, s.v. "salvo").

26. "At one level, the claim that Scripture interprets itself was nothing new in the sixteenth century. . . . The idea that in the Bible a clearer place makes known a more difficult one was a staple of both medieval and Reformation exegesis" (Timothy George, *Reading Scripture with the Reformers* [Downers Grove, IL: InterVarsity Press, 2011], 125–26).

27. "It is an awful thing to see a dead church. I have seen such a thing with my own eyes. I recollect very well preaching in a chapel where the church had become exceedingly low, and somehow the very building looked like a sepulchre, though crowded that one night by those who came to hear the preacher. The singers drawled out a dirge, while the members sat like mutes. I found it hard preaching; there was no go in the sermon, I seemed to be driving dead horses . . . The Lord save us from becoming such a ghastly crew" (*MTP* 25:284–85).

28. "Where the Spirit of God comes he creates in the man a new nature, pure, bright, fresh, vigorous, like a fountain, and the fact that this new nature does exist in multitudes of men is a standing evidence that the gospel is true, for no other religion makes men new creatures, no other religion even pretends to do it; they may propose to improve the old nature, but none of them can say, 'Behold, I make all things new.' This is the sole prerogative of Jesus our Lord" (*MTP* 20:451).

29. Cf. Matt 5:13; Jer 13:10.

30. "[T]o Ridicule; to sneer" (Johnson's *Dictionary*, s.v. "to scout").

31. Cf. Luke 14:35.

32. "Pliable is yielding, and easily induced to engage in things of which he understands neither the nature nor the consequences," John Bunyan, *The Pilgrim's Progress* in *Works* ([Glasgow, Edinburgh: Blackie and Son, 1856, the Spurgeon Library], 3:90n4).

33. Cf. Matt 11:15; 13:9; Mark 4:9.

Matt. XVIII. 3.　　　　Conversion　　　　203

To reprove his disciples for the ambitious thoughts he
sets a child before them & bids them not talk of
how high they should be in heaven, but think of
the only way of getting there, by becoming like
that Child. Here is something solemn. Verily, &c.

I. What is it to be converted?

It means simply to be turned
From Sin – all sin is to be left & abhorred
From Self – for this is one very great essential
From Man or the World – no trust in man – no conformity
To Holiness – without this no man can see the Lord
To Christ as our only Refuge & Hope
To Religion – as our delight. He church, believe &c

II. What is it to become as little children?

This is the effect of conversion.
Here is faith in our father. Humility,
teachableness, & a sense of weakness.

III. What is it to enter the Kingdom of heaven.
1. To be a Christian – to be a King unto
God, even on earth.
2. To enter the gates of blessedness –
the Kingdom of the righteous
for this strive so as to enter –
God be praised for a hope

329. 334. 347. 576. 577.

CONVERSION[1]

Matthew 18:3

"Verily I say unto you, Except ye be converted, and become as little children, ye shall not enter into the kingdom of heaven."

To reprove his disciples for the ambitious thoughts[,] he sets a child before them and bids them not talk of how high they should be in heaven, but think of the only way of getting there, by becoming like that Child. Here is something solemn. Verily, I say.

I. WHAT IS IT TO BE CONVERTED?

It means simply to be turned.

From sin. All sin is to be left and abhorred.[2]

From Self. For this is one very great essential.[3]

From Man or the World. No trust in man.[4] No conformity.[5]

To Holiness. Without this, no man can see the Lord.[6]

To Christ. As our only Refuge and Hope.[7]

To Religion. As our delight. The church, bible.[8]

II. WHAT IS IT TO BECOME AS LITTLE CHILDREN?

This is the effect of conversion. Here is faith in our father. Humility, teachableness, and a sense of weakness.[9]

III. WHAT IS IT TO ENTER THE KINGDOM OF HEAVEN?

1. To be a Christian, to be a King unto God, even on earth.[10]

2. To enter the gates of blessedness, the Kingdom of the righteous. For this, strive so as to enter.[11]

God be praised for a hope[.]

329. 334. 347. 576. 577.

1. Charles never again preached from this passage.

2. Cf. Matt 5:48; 1 John 3:6.

3. Cf. Matt 16:24; Mark 8:34; Luke 9:23.

4. Cf. John 2:24–25.   5. Cf. Rom 12:1–2.

6. Cf. Heb 12:14.   7. Cf. Ps 62:5–8.

8. Cf. Ps 133:1; John 17:21; 1 Thess 5:11; Jas 5:16.

9. "Difficulty there is none: only believe and thou art saved. It is not a mystical, obscure thing; it is near and familiar. Believe in Christ as you would believe in your friend: believe that he died for sinners, and trust in him for salvation. If God has made you feel yourself a sinner, then Christ is such a Saviour as you need and you may have him at once: the only difficulty lies in the way being so easy that you can hardly think it can be so. Have done with doings, and feelings, and trust yourself with Christ. 'The word is nigh thee.' It is simple; indeed, so simple that people try to obscure it in order to understand it. It is such milk for babes that I have known people refuse such plain truth because they were not willing to be treated like little children" (*MTP* 29:32-33).

10. Cf. Rev 1:5–6.   11. Cf. Matt 7:13–14; Luke 13:24.

204   Rev. XXI . 27.   The Lamb's book of life .
We have thousands of books on various subjects
& we do well to read some of them — for what
others worked for thus easily becomes ours.
   Let us take a look into God's library & see
the precious volumes there stored up & then
come to look at especially at the book of Life.
1. There stands a book in two parts, written
on stone —   that is the **Book** of the **Law**.
It was written with the finger of God &
shall endure — not one dot or cross of a
letter shall pass away till all be fulfilled,
That book is in black Letter to a sinner
but to the saint it is a lovely volume.
2. The book most known to us is a volume
that contains Vol 1. and much more . **Bible**.
Of this book we have copies in abundance
there are I fear more Bibles than Readers.
We can never prize this too much.
3. The next book is a very ancient one
it is the **Book of the Eternal Council**
"In the volume of the book it is written I
delight to do thy will Oh God." Ps. XL. 7.
This is the secret book of the covenant, on
it all the other volumes depend .

THE LAMB'S BOOK *of* LIFE [1]
Revelation 21:27

"And there shall in no wise enter into it any thing that defileth, neither whatsoever worketh abomination, or maketh a lie; but they which are written in the Lamb's book of life."

We have thousands of books on various subjects, and we do well to read some of them.[2] For what others worked for thus easily becomes ours.

Let us take a look into God's library and see the precious volumes there stored up, and then come to look at, especially at, the book of Life.[3]

1. There stands a book in two parts, written on stone.[4] That is the **Book of the Law.** It was writ with the finger of God[5] and shall endure.[6] Not one dot or cross of a letter shall pass away till all be fulfilled.[7] That book is in black letter[8] to a sinner, but to the saint it is a lovely volume.[9]

2. The book most known to us is a volume that contains Vol. I., and much more. **Bible.** Of this book we have copies in abundance. There are, I fear, more Bibles than Readers. We can never prize this [book] too much.

3. The next book is a very ancient one. It is the **Book of the Eternal Council.** "In the volume of the book it is written[,] 'I delight to do thy will Oh God.'" Ps. XL.7.[10] This is the secret book of the covenant. On it, all the other volumes depend.[11]

4. The Book of Decrees —   Hymn Rip-9 —   In this vol-
David's members were written   Ps. 139. 16 .   The books
of the prophets are but extracts from this complete
book — which is only unfolded in providence .
This book is further described in Rev t. as being
sealed with 7 seals & held in God's right hand.
None of us are worthy to touch the seals — the Lion
of the tribe of Judah alone unfolds & executes the
awful decrees of the Infinite One . —
5. The Book of Remembrance . In this all the
actions of men are recorded . Rev XX. 12 . — by this
we are to be tried — In this book the words of the
saints are recorded. Mal III. 6. Tears – Ps. 56. 8
A Solemnly Important Book this is .
6. The Lamb's Book of Life — the one before
us – may we understand it —

I. Why is Jesus called a Lamb —
1. From his nature — Holy. Harmless. Gentle. Meek.
2. From his use . As the food & clothing of his people
3. From his office . The Sacrafice . The Lamb of
our passover – The Lamb of God —
II. Why is it the Lamb's book .
Not Because the other persons have no hand in
it — for equally are they concerned .
But because —

4. **The Book of Decrees.**[12] Hymn: Rippon 9.[13]—In this vol[ume], David's members were written. Ps. 139.16.[14] The books of the prophets are but extracts from this complete book, which is only unfolded in providence.

   This book is further described in Rev. V. as being sealed with 7 seals and held in God's right hand.[15] None of us are worthy to touch the seals. The Lion of the tribe of Judah alone unfolds and executes the awful decrees of the Infinite One.

5. **The Book of Remembrance.** In this all the actions of men are recorded. Rev XX.12.[16] By this we are to be tried. In this book the words of the saints are recorded. Mal III.6.[17] Tears. Ps. 56.8.[18] A Solemnly Important Book this is.

6. **The Lamb's Book of Life.** The one before us. May we understand it.

I. WHY IS JESUS CALLED A LAMB?

1. From his nature. Holy, Harmless, Gentle, Meek.

2. From his use. As the food and clothing of his people.

3. From his office. The Sacrifice. The Lamb of our Passover.[19] The Lamb of God.

II. WHY IS IT THE LAMB'S BOOK?

Not Because the other persons have no hand in it, for equally are they concerned.

But because—

1. His name stands first in it. "Christ be my first elect he said" ours after it.

2. He purchased all who are written there none would have been saved had he not ransomed them all — the names are all [illegible] paid for.

3. He is responsible for all like Jacob with the sheep — not one must be lost.

III. Why called the Book of Life?

1. Because only those whose names are there shall enjoy — life - grace below — heaven above.

2. Because there is nothing but life for those written therein — nothing but happiness of life — justification - pardon - peace - glory all. all

3. Because the book is eternal & every letter of it — no erasure. Life nothing but Life. No final apostacy, no falling away. but life.

IV. Whose names are in it?

1. Jesus the first elect.

2. All saints gone home.

3. All believers however poor or little.

Oh if my name be there — may it be so —

331 & 332.   335.

1. His name stands first in it. "Christ be my first elect, he said."[20] Ours after it.

2. He purchased all who are written there. None would have been saved had he not ransomed them all. The names are all paid for.[21]

3. He is responsible for all, like Jacob with the sheep. Not one must be lost.[22]

III. WHY CALLED THE BOOK OF LIFE?

1. Because only those whose names are there shall enjoy life,[23] grace below, heaven above.

2. Because there is nothing but life for those written therein. Nothing but happiness of life: justification, pardon, peace, glory. All.[24] All.

3. Because the book is eternal, and every letter of it. No erasure.[25] Life. Nothing but Life. No final apostacy. No falling away. But life.

IV. WHOSE NAMES ARE IN IT?

1. Jesus[,] the first elect.

2. All saints gone home.[26]

3. All believers, however poor or little.

> Oh if my name be there—May it be so[.][27]

331 and 332.   335.

1. Charles preached on this text again in "The Barrier" (*MTP* 27, Sermon 1590).

2. By the time of his death in 1892, Charles had amassed an impressive 12,000 books—about half of which are housed in The Spurgeon Library at Midwestern Baptist Theological Seminary in Kansas City, Missouri. See http://www .spurgeon.org.

3. Cf. Ps 69:27–28; Dan 12:1; Luke 10:20; Phil 4:3; Rev 3:5; 13:8; 20:15.

4. Cf. Exod 31:18.   5. Cf. Exod 31:18.

6. Cf. Matt 5:18.   7. Cf. Matt 5:18.

8. See "The Great Promise and Awful Threat" (Sermon 201).

9. Charles would later say of Psalm 119, "The more one studies it, the fresher it becomes. As those who drink the Nile water like it better every time they take a draught, so does this Psalm become the more full and fascinating the oftener you turn to it" (*TD* 6:1).

10. "*In the volume of the book* it is *written of me*; either in the book of divine predestination, in the purposes and decrees of God, *Psal.* cxxxix. 16. or in the book of the scriptures" (John Gill, *An Exposition of the Old Testament*, vol. 3 [London: printed for the author, 1765, The Spurgeon Library], 650, italics in the original). Cf. Ps 40:7.

11. The term "Book of the Covenant" is synonymous with the "Book of the Eternal Council."

12. "Here we have poor souls [people who will not come to Christ because they cannot understand election] that want to be M.A.'s before they have gone to the penny school. They want to read the tomes before they will read the horn-book. They are not content to spell A, B, C —'I am a sinner, Christ is a saviour,'—but they long to turn over the book of decrees, and find out the deep things of God" (*MTP* 7:215).

13. "Keep silence all created things; / And wait your Maker's nod: / My soul stands trembling while she sings / The honours of her God. / Life, death, and hell, and worlds unknown, / Hang on his firm decree: / He sits on no precarious throne, / Nor borrows leave to be. / Chain'd to his throne, a volume lies, / With all the fates of men, / With every angel's, form and size / Drawn by th' eternal pen. / His providence unfolds the books / And makes his councils shine; / Each

opening leaf, and every stroke, / Fulfils some deep design" (John Rippon, *A Selection of Hymns: from the Best Authors, Including a Great Number of Originals, Intended to Be an Appendix to Dr. Watts' Psalms and Hymns* [London: W. Whittemore; Houlston and Stoneman, 1844, The Spurgeon Library], 10).

14. Cf. Ps 139:16.   15. Cf. Rev 5:1.

16. Cf. Rev 20:12.   17. Charles likely intended to cite Mal 3:16.

18. Cf. Ps 56:8.   19. Cf. 1 Cor 5:7.

20. "[Christ is foreordained]; that is, by God; and which intends, not barely his prescience of Christ, of what he should be, do, and suffer; but such a previous knowledge of him, which is joined with love and affection to him; not merely as his own Son, and the express image of his person, but as mediator; and whom he loved before the world was, and with a love of complacency and delight, and which will last for ever" (John Gill, *An Exposition of the New Testament*, vol. 3 [London: printed for the author, 1748, The Spurgeon Library], 505). Cf. 1 Pet 1:20.

21. "A redemption which pays a price, but does not ensure that which is purchased, a redemption which calls Christ a substitute for the sinner, but yet which allows the person to suffer . . . is altogether unworthy of our apprehensions of Almighty God, it offers no homage to his wisdom, and does despite to his covenant faithfulness" (*MTP* 49:39).

22. Cf. John 10:27–29.   23. Cf. Ps 69:27–28; Rev 20:11–15; 21:22–27.

24. Cf. Rev 20:15; 21:22–27; 22:1–5.

25. Cf. Matt 5:18.

26. "It behoves [*sic*] us, my dear brothers and sisters, to have a firmer faith than Old Testament saints, because we see more clearly our ground of trust. Those who lived in the comparative darkness of the previous dispensation were saved by faith, and among them there were not a few eminent believers, surely we also ought to excel in our confidence in God" (*MTP* 27:257). Cf. Luke 16:19–31.

27. For examples of Charles's closing prayers, see "God's Care of the Stars" (Sermon 189); "Convince the World of Sin, Righteousness, and Judgment" (Sermon 190); "Christian Moderation" (Sermon 192); "Come and Let Us Reason Together" (Sermon 193); and "He Delighteth in Mercy" (Sermon 195).

II. Cor. VI. 1.   Grace received in vain. 205

As I have sometimes done before I would first
notice some points in this chapter needing attention.
   In verse 2 —   perhaps all who think they under-
- stand it are not quite so learned as they fancy.
It is a quotation from Is. 49. 8 — except the last
half which is the apostle's own sentiment. —
In Is. the Father is speaking to the Son & is giving
him an assurance that he had heard him &
would in a time appointed, here called the day
of salvation, give him to see the triumphs of
his gospel. & the salvation of many. —
   Behold! Behold! cries out the apostle this is the
promised time — this is that very season promised
in covenant —   take heed lest in such days.
Ye miss of grace & be encouraged to try for now is
the accepted time when God resolves to save.
      There are other passages, however, which incul-
- cate the doctrine that "now" is the time a sinner
should believe   "To day if ye will hear his voice &c" by
this is meant not that sinners can never be
saved if they are not saved at this moment,
but to show that we have only a time allowed
& no more —   death closes it — or being given
up by God may end our day long 'ere we die.

   Verses. 14. 15 — 18 — Call loudly for a complete
separation from the ungodly.   Be not yoked
with them — be not their intimate friend —

GRACE RECEIVED *in* VAIN [1]

2 Corinthians 6:1

*"We then, as workers together with him, beseech you also
that ye receive not the grace of God in vain."*

As I have sometimes done before, I would first notice some points in this chapter needing attention.

In verse 2.[2] Perhaps all who think they understand it are not quite so learned as they fancy. It is a quotation from Is. 49.8,[3] except the last half which is the apostle's own sentiment.[4]

In Is., the Father is speaking to the Son and is giving him an assurance that he had heard him and would, in a time appointed, here called the day of salvation, give him to see the triumphs of his gospel and the salvation of many.[5]

Behold! Behold! cries out the apostle. This is the promised time. This is that very season promised in covenant.[6] Take heed, lest in such days ye miss of grace and be encouraged to try, for now is the accepted time[7] when God resolves to save.

There are other passages, however, which inculcate the doctrine that "now" is the time a sinner should believe.[8] "To day if ye will hear his voice, etc."[9] By this is meant, not that sinners can never be saved if they are not saved at this moment, but to show that we have only a time allowed and no more. Death closes it. Or, being given up by God, may end our day long 'ere we die.[10]

Verses 14.15—18.[11] Call loudly for a complete separation from the ungodly. Be not yoked with them. Be not their intimate friend.

in your ordinary converse avoid them as much
as in you lies — & especially never intermarry
with them —   It would be like yoking a
lion & a lamb — an ox & an ass.   Much hurt
has come to men through their companions,
more through their friends & most through ungodly
husbands or wives. —   The apostle backs up
his words. How can ye have communion?
Will family devotion be warm? Will your children
be well trained?   How can Christ & Belial
dwell together? The soldier of God & the servant of Satan.
Come ye out therefore & be separate. These things
are so unclean that the touch will defile if not
infect — Only Separatists are Sons of God.

Now return to the text.
& first let us read it without the italics.
"We then, workers together, beseech also
that ye receive not the grace of God in vain—

<u>I</u>. What is intended by the grace of God here
Some will say by this is meant that the
grace of God comes into a man's heart &
finds it so carnal that it can do no
good there whatever.
1. But this dishonour the Holy Spirit.
2. It would much distress believers for they
would feel a doubt lest they (though having

In your ordinary converse,[12] avoid them as much as in you lies. And especially never intermarry with them.[13] It would be like yoking a lion and a lamb,[14] an ox and an ass.

Much hurt has come to men through their companions, more through their friends, and most through ungodly husbands or wives.[15]

The apostle backs up his words. How can ye have communion? Will family devotion be warm? Will your children be well trained? How can Christ and Belial dwell together? The soldier of God and the servant of Satan.

Come ye out therefore, and be separate. These things are so unclean that the touch will defile, if not infect. Only Separatists are Sons of God.

Now return to the text. And first, let us read it without the italics.[16]

"We then, workers together, beseech also that ye receive not the grace of God in vain."[17]

I. WHAT IS INTENDED BY THE GRACE OF GOD HERE[?]

Some will say by this is meant that the grace of God comes into a man's heart and finds it so carnal that it can do no good there whatever.

1. But this dishonour[s] the Holy Spirit.

2. It would much distress believers, for they would feel a doubt lest they (though having

that grace) might yet prove too full of sin to be cured.

3. It would make sinners despair, when they felt their need of a Saviour — lest he could not save. —

Some say again that grace did work a real change but that afterwards man turned from it & so received it in vain. —

1. We answer — this is a doctrine that would lead us to boast, it being purely Arminian — we should say it is I that kept myself & not God kept me. & when in heaven we shall say, if such be true. How good I must have been to hold on so long while many turned back, I am worthy indeed.

2. This is Antinomian as well as Arminian for if men receive divine grace & yet it saves them not or keeps them not from turning back, I may then say. I will sin a while & then get grace again. I may have grace & yet run into sin & then easily run back again.

3. It is most unscriptural —

But by "grace of God", is meant "the gospel" which alas many do indeed hear & receive in vain.

This is meant in Jude. 4 — for surely no other thing called grace can in any way be turned to lasciviousness well may the gospel be called "grace of God" seeing it is full of grace & plenteous mercy.

<u>II</u>. What is it to receive it in vain.

To hear as though you did not hear.

that grace) might yet prove too full of sin to be cured.

3. It would make sinners despair when they felt their need of a Saviour, lest he could not save.

Some say again that grace did work a real change, but that afterwards man turned from it and so received it in vain.[18]

1. We answer: this is a doctrine that would lead us to boast, it being purely Arminian. We should say it is I that kept myself, and not God kept me. And when in heaven we shall say, if such be true, how good I must have been to hold on so long while many turned back. I am worthy indeed.[19]

2. This is Antinomian as well as Arminian, for if men receive divine grace and yet it saves them not or keeps them not from turning back[,] I may then say, I will sin a while and then get grace again. I may have grace and yet run into sin and then easily run back again.[20]

3. It is most unscriptural. But by "grace of God" is meant "the gospel," which, alas, many do indeed hear and receive in vain. This is meant in Jude 4,[21] for surely no other thing called grace can in any way be turned to lasciviousness. Well may the gospel be called "grace of God," seeing it is full of grace and plenteous mercy.

II. WHAT IS IT TO RECEIVE IT IN VAIN[?]

To hear as though you did not hear.[22]

To hear the gospel in vain — is —

1. to receive it, being yourself clad in steel against all its arrows, blows, & sword-thrusts.

2. to receive it — let it wound, but ever to have a false blister, a balm of Satan's mixing close at hand crying Peace, Peace, where there is no peace.

3. to receive it — with hypocritical bows, false smiles & blandly false words. —

4. to receive it — to sit on the ground, or a footstool & not to the very best place. outside not in.

5. to receive it — & keep the old lodger in there.

6. to receive it on Sunday & not on the week.

III. What did Paul do to prevent the evil.

"He was a worker" one who toiled & laboured.
"He was a worker together," he put himself side by side with others as being of one Master.

"He besought" the people most earnestly.

"He besought" God — with cries, groans & petitions.

He felt that if they missed this — all hope was gone — no more sacrafice — no other name — this was the only chance — this recet in vain all would be over.

Help. Help H Veing

339.

To hear the gospel in vain is:

1. To receive it, being yourself clad in steel[23] against all its arrows, blows, and sword-thrusts.[24]

2. To receive it. Let it wound, but ever to have a false blister, a balm of Satan's mixing close at hand, crying, Peace, Peace, where there is no peace.[25]

3. To receive it with hypocritical bows, false smiles and blandly,[26] false words.[27]

4. To receive it. To sit on the ground or a footstool, and not to the very best place.[28] Outside, not in.[29]

5. To receive it, and keep the old lodger sin there.[30]

6. To receive it on Sunday, and not on the week.[31]

III. WHAT DID PAUL DO TO PREVENT THE EVIL[?]

"He was a worker," one who toiled and laboured.

"He was a worker together[.]"[32] He put himself side by side with others as being of one Master.[33]

"He besought"[34] the people most earnestly.

"He besought" God with cries, groans, and petitions.[35]

He felt that if they missed this, all hope was gone. No more sacrifice.[36] No other name.[37] This was the only chance. This reced[38] in vain, all would be over.

Help. Help Oh King[.]

339.

1. Charles exposited this passage in "Christ's Sympathy with His People" (*MTP* 50, Sermon 2885).

2. Cf. 2 Cor 6:2.

3. Cf. Isa 49:8.

4. "*Behold now is the accepted time, behold now is the day of salvation.* These are the words of the Apostle, applying the former to the present Gospel-dispensation" (John Gill, *An Exposition of the New Testament Writings*, vol. 2 [London: printed for the author, 1747, The Spurgeon Library], 733, italics in the original).

5. Cf. Isa 49:8; 2 Cor. 6:1.

6. Cf. Isa 49:8.

7. Cf. 2 Cor 6:2.

8. Cf. Ps 95:6–8.

9. Cf. Heb 3:7–10, 15; 4:7.

10. "*Now* is, and not yesterday was, the day of salvation; and *now*, and that forever, that is, as long as the Gospel-dispensation continues; for it will be always *now* till all the elect of God are gathered in. This day of grace and salvation will never be over till that time comes: 'tis still *now is the day of salvation*; tho' men may have long withstood the ministration of the Gospel, and notwithstanding their manifold sins and transgressions. There's no withstanding the *now* of grace when it comes with the power of the Holy Ghost" (Gill, *An Exposition of the New Testament*, 2:733, italics in the original).

11. Cf. 2 Cor 6:14–18.

12. "1. Conversation; manner of discoursing in familiar life" (Johnson's *Dictionary*, s.v. "converse").

13. Cf. 2 Cor 6:14–16.

14. "'And if by grace, then is it no more of works; otherwise grace is no more grace. But if it be of works, then is it no more grace; otherwise work is no more work.' For if you mix the two together, you spoil them both. Go home, sir, and make yourself a stirabout with fire and water, endeavour to keep in your house a lion and a lamb, and when you have succeeded in doing these, tell me that you have made works and grace agree, and I will tell you, you have told me a lie even then,

for the two things are so essentially opposite, that it cannot be done" (*NPSP* 2:128). Cf. Isa 11:6; Rev 5:5–6.

15. Cf. 1 Kgs 11:4; 2 Kgs 17:15–17, 34–41; Ezek 8:9–16; Gal 4:9–10.

16. The Bible Charles and his congregation used included italicized words not in the original Hebrew and Greek texts to facilitate proper English syntax and clarity. For the present verse, 2 Cor 6:1, one of Charles's personal Bibles reads, "We then, *as* workers together *with him*, beseech *you* also that ye receive not the grace of God in vain," with the italicized words being absent in the Greek (George D'Oyly and Richard Mant, eds., *The Holy Bible, According to the Authorized Version; with Notes, Explanatory and Practical; Taken Principally from the Most Eminent Writers of the United Church of England and Ireland: Together with Appropriate Introductions, Tables, Indexes, Maps, and Plans: Prepared and Arranged by the Rev. George D'Oyly, B.D. and the Rev. Richard Mant, D.D., Domestick Chaplains to His Grace the Lord Archbishop of Canterbury, Under the Direction of the Society for Promoting Christian Knowledge. For the Use of Families.* [vol. II, Oxford: printed for the Society at the Clarendon Press, 1817, The Spurgeon Library]).

17. Cf. 2 Cor 6:1.

18. Charles has in mind those like Adam Clarke, who later would comment on this verse, "By the *grace of God*, την χαριν του θεου, *this grace* or *benefit of God*, the apostle certainly means the *grand sacrificial offering* of Christ for the sin of the world, which he had just before mentioned in speaking of the *ministry of reconciliation*. We learn, therefore, that it was possible to *receive the grace of God* and not ultimately benefit by it; or in other words, to begin in the Spirit and end in the flesh" (Adam Clarke, *The Holy Bible, Containing the Old and New Testaments: Volume VI. 1 Corinthians to Revelation* [London: William Tegg and Co., 1854, The Spurgeon Library], s.v. "2 Cor 6:1"; italics in the original).

19. "Where is boasting then? It is excluded. By what law? the law of works? No, but by the law of grace. Grace puts its hand on their boasting mouth, and shuts it once for all; and then it takes its hand off from the mouth, and that mouth now does not fear to speak to man, though it trembles at the very thought of taking any honour and glory from God. I must say—I am compelled to say—that the doctrine which leaves salvation to the creature, and tells him that it depends

upon himself, is the exaltation of the flesh, and a dishonouring of God. But that which puts in God's hand man, fallen man, and tells man that though he has destroyed himself, yet his salvation must be of God, that doctrine humbles man in the very dust, and then he is just in the right place to receive the grace and mercy of God. It is a humbling doctrine. Again, this doctrine gives the death-blow to all self-sufficiency. What the Arminian wants to do is to arouse man's activity; what we want to do is to kill it once for all, to show him that he is lost and ruined, and that his activities are not now at all equal to the work of conversion; that he must look upward" (*NPSP* 6:258–59).

20. "I have often heard such a remark as yours, my friend [that Calvinism leads to antinomianism], but experience is dead against you. Whenever justification by faith has been uppermost in the preaching, the morals of the people have been purest, and their spirituality has been brightest. But whenever the preachers have extolled the works and ceremonies of the law, or the Arminianism which brings in something of trust in works, or human power, it is most certain that there has been a declension in point of morals, while religion itself has seemed almost ready to expire" (*MTP* 46:170).

21. Cf. Jude 4.

22. Cf. Deut 29:4; Isa 42:20; Jer 5:21; Matt 13:13; Rom 11:8.

23. Cf. Eph 6:10–20.

24. "The Word of God is so sharp a thing, so full of cutting power, that you may be bleeding under its wounds before you have seriously suspected the possibility of such a thing. You cannot come near the gospel without its having a measure of influence over you; and, God blessing you, it may cut down and kill your sins when you have no idea that such a work is being done" (*MTP* 34:115–16).

25. Cf. Jer 6:14; 8:11.

26. "Soft; mild; gentle" (Johnson's *Dictionary*, s.v. "bland").

27. Cf. Matt 15:8; 2 Pet 2:1; 1 John 2:4; Jude 4.

28. Cf. Jas 2:3.

29. Cf. Matt 25:1–13.

30. Cf. Mark 3:27; 1 John 3:6–9.

31. "Step into the next church or chapel, I do not care which, and observe the multitudes of the people going through the worship with mere formality, confessing what they never felt, and professing to believe what they know nothing of. Ah, we might look into the face of each worshipper and say, 'If thou knewest the gift of God, thou wouldst give up this formalism, and worship God in spirit and in truth.' We need not go far; there are many of you here in that state. May you know the gift of God, and forget formalities, and worship God in truth" (*MTP* 13:658).

32. Cf. 2 Cor 6:1.   33. Cf. Eph 4:5.

34. Cf. 2 Cor 6:1.   35. Cf. 2 Cor 5:4.

36. Cf. Heb 10:26. This may indicate that Charles believed Paul to be the author of the Epistle to the Hebrews.

37. Cf. Acts 4:12.

38. Abbreviation of "received."

I Cor. XV. 45.   The two Adams.   206.

Our minds can never revert to the manger without
at the same time running to the garden of Eden.
'Tis there alone we can understand the life of
Christ —   the second Adam is a deep mystery without
the first. —

The Life of Adam I is too well known to need
more than a mere sketch to be given. —

His body is said to have been made of the dust of
the earth & so chemists declare that our bodies are.
His body certainly did not suffer, though we cannot
imagine how it could be preserved, but yet it was.
No doubt in mind & body too he was the very
model of a man.   a man indeed, noble & majestic.
He plucked the fruit but let us not murmur
for we should have done it sooner even than he.
Driven from the garden he begat a son whom
his wife thought was the second Adam but alas
he was Cain — the father of murderers.
After a long life he died — now did he go to
heaven —   It is thought he did — see Bible Class. Mag. for Nov. 52.
1. Sacrafice seems to have been offerred by them.
2. Doubtless contrition & confession attended it for it does not
            appear to have been rejected.
3. The expressions of Eve, seem to be pious.
4. They instructed their households —
I do trust however one day to see our great
progenitor, our sire, safe in the land
of glory. —

THE TWO ADAMS [1]

1 Corinthians 15:45

*"And so it is written, The first man Adam was made a living
soul; the last Adam was made a quickening spirit."*

Our minds can never revert to the manger without at the same time running to the
garden of Eden. 'Tis there alone we can understand the life of Christ. The second
Adam is a deep mystery without the first.

THE LIFE OF ADAM [1] IS TOO WELL KNOWN TO NEED MORE THAN A MERE SKETCH TO BE GIVEN.

His body is said to have been made of the dust of the earth.[2] And so, chemists
declare that our bodies are.[3] His body certainly did not suffer, though we cannot
imagine how it could be preserved. But yet, it was. No doubt in mind and body, too,
he was the very model of a man. A man, indeed, noble and majestic. He plucked the
fruit,[4] but let us not murmur, for we should have done it sooner even than he.

Driven from the garden, he begat a son whom his wife thought was the second
Adam. But alas, he was Cain, the father of murderers.[5] After a long life, he died.
Now, did he go to heaven? It is thought he did. See Bible Class Mag. for Nov. 52.[6]

1. Sacrifice seems to have been offered by them.[7]

2. Doubtless, contrition and confession attended it, for it does not appear to
    have been rejected.[8]

3. The expressions of Eve seem to be pious.[9]

4. They instructed their households.[10] I do trust, however, one day to see our
    great progenitor, our sire, safe in the land of glory.[11]

The life of Adam II. is equally well known
& scarcely can your memories need refreshing.
I think he was not born to day (X'mas) – since
cold snow would almost drive the shepherds
within. — he was born of the royal race
though almost forgotten, their throne usurped &
they earning the bread of the mechanic. He
was a child (I think) of exquisite beauty &
of most commanding mind – early it showed
itself. & when matured in age. like the
first surely he was a man among men, the
highest stile of all men. so eloquent, so
kind, so noble, yet alas so despised. He
had a friend but he died, he had brethren
they rejected him, a country it hated him,
a darling disciple, he too forsook him & fled.
He died & earth groaned at the loss of her
friend, he rose again heaven shouted, he
ascended angels & archangels shouted welcome.
        May I one day behold his face.
I.   The singularities of the two Adams.
1. They were the only two men, not born
by carnal generation, but by God formed.
2. For this reason they were the only two
who were free from the taint of natural

THE LIFE OF ADAM [2] IS EQUALLY WELL KNOWN AND SCAR[C]ELY CAN YOUR MEMORIES NEED REFRESHING.

I think he was not born to day (X'mas)[12] since cold snow would almost drive the shepherds within.

He was born of the royal race, though almost forgotten. Their throne usurped, and they earning the bread of the mechanic.[13]

He was a child (I think) of exquisite beauty and of the most commanding mind. Early it showed itself.[14] And, when matured in age, like the first. Surely, he was a man among men, the highest stile [*sic*] of all men.

So eloquent, so kind, so noble, yet alas, so despised.[15] He had a friend, but he died.[16] He had brethren. They rejected him.[17] A country, it hated him.[18] A darling disciple. He too forsook him and fled.[19]

He died and earth groaned at the loss of her friend.[20] He rose again. Heaven shouted.[21] He ascended. Angels and archangels shouted welcome.

May I one day behold his face.

I.   THE SINGULARITIES OF THE TWO ADAMS.

1.   They were the only two men not born by carnal generation, but by God formed.[22]

2.   For this reason they were the only two who were free from the taint of natural

depravity — the one free but fallable — the other impeccable.

3. They were the only two who life depended on their own will — Adam had life or death at his own choice & Jesus laid it down of himself.

4. They were the only two representative men before God — other men are fools who speak of being sponsors for others — these are the only sponsors who take our places before God.

II. The difference between the two Adams.

1 In their nature — one of the earth—the other heavenly. one a creature — the other Creator & Creature too.

2. In their office. Adam stood for a world who sinned in him — Christ for a world believing in him — Adam for an unfallen race — Jesus for a degraded nation — Adam had only a simple action — Jesus unutterable suffering. Adam had to keep. Jesus to recover. He paid a debt he owed — the other paid what he owed not one farthing of, no obligation at all

3. In their success — Adam was tempted & fell Jesus was tempted & overcame. Adam ruined all his, Jesus saved them. Adam did not affect Jesus — Jesus died for Adam. Adam loved self, Jesus loved us. Adam ceades to do ought for us but Jesus labours on still for ever. — adam brought death & Jesus life.

depravity. The one free but fallable,[23] the other impeccable.[24]

3. They were the only two who[se] life depended on their own will. Adam had life or death at his own choice, and Jesus laid it down of himself.[25]

4. They were the only two representative men before God.[26] Other men are fools who speak of being sponsors for others.[27] These are the only sponsors who take our places before God.

II. THE DIFFERENCE BETWEEN THE TWO ADAMS.

1. In their nature. One of the earth, the other heavenly. One a creature, the other Creator and Creature too.

2. In their office. Adam stood for a world who sinned in him.[28] Christ, for a world believing in him. Adam, for an unfallen race. Jesus, for a degraded nation. Adam had only a simple action. Jesus, unutterable suffering. Adam had to keep. Jesus to recover. He paid a debt he owed. The other paid what he owed not one farthing of, no obligation at all.[29]

3. In their success. Adam was tempted and fell.[30] Jesus was tempted and overcame.[31] Adam ruined all his. Jesus saved them. Adam did not affect Jesus. Jesus died for Adam. Adam loved self. Jesus loved us. Adam ceases to do ought for us, but Jesus labours on still for ever.[32] Adam brought death, and Jesus life.[33]

<u>III</u>. Our relation to the two Adams.
1 In the first Adam we so fell that we are
naturally corrupt — no man is damned
for Adam's sin; infants are not damned
but saved through Jesus. It is not wondered
at that children inherit the parents' diseases
& why not also partake in moral disease.
So they do+, the parents temper seems to flash
out of the child's eyes. See now sinner
thy fall in Adam & hear again of
2. The second Adam has also a relation
to all — for all he purchased mercies unnum-
-bered and even our reprieve from death,
He has a double relation to believers, he is
specially their redeemer. His merit does
save without our works — though Adam's
sin cannot damn without our sin.
Let us rejoice in him, trust in him &
rejoice if our names are in his book.
Father glorify thy son.
Amen
387.

III. OUR RELATION TO THE TWO ADAMS.

1. In the first Adam we so fell that we are naturally corrupt. No man is dammed [*sic*] for Adam's sin.[34] [I]nfants are not damned, but saved through Jesus.[35] It is not wondered at that children inherit the parents' diseases. And why not also partake in moral disease? So they doe. The parents' temper seems to flash out of the child's eyes. See now, sinner, thy fall in Adam and hear again of:

2. The second Adam has also a relation to all—for all he purchased mercies unnumbered, and even our reprieve from death.

   He has a double relation to believers.[36] He is specially their redeemer. His merit does save without our works, though Adam's sin cannot damn without our sin.

   Let us rejoice in him, trust in him and rejoice if our names are in his book.[37]

   Father[,] glorify thy son.

   <u>Amen.</u>

337.

1. Charles never again preached from this passage. From his notes, it is clear he preached this sermon on Christmas Day, 1852.

2. Cf. Gen 2:7.

3. "Such then is that peculiar and most wonderful feature in the constitution of creation—the accomplishment of astonishing variety out of the fewest materials, which at the very onset chemistry presents to our admiration. And such in fact is the universal language of science; it may be called the economy of the creation. The Creator has taken, as it were, a mere handful of elements, and has formed out of them not only the gorgeous structure on which we dwell, but also ourselves, that is our material bodies, and our fellow-occupants of the earth, and the inhabitants of the air and the sea" (Robert Ellis, *The Chemistry of Creation: Being a Sketch of the Chemical Phenomena of the Earth, the Air, the Ocean* [London: printed for the Society for Promoting Christian Knowledge, 1850], 32).

4. "*and [Eve] gave also to her husband with her*; that he might eat as well as she, and partake of the same benefits and advantages she hoped to reap from hence; for no doubt it was of good will, and not ill will, that she gave it to him; and when she offered it to him, it is highly probable she made use of arguments with him, and pressed him hard to it, telling him what delicious food it was, as well as how useful it would be to him and her. The *Jews* infer from hence, that *Adam* was with her all the while, and heard the discourse between the serpent and her, yet did not interpose nor dissuade his wife from eating the fruit, and being prevailed upon by the arguments used; or however thro' a strong affection for his wife, that she might not die alone, he did as she had done: *and he did eat*" (John Gill, *An Exposition of the Old Testament*, vol. 1 [London: printed for the author, 1765, The Spurgeon Library], 22, italics in the original). Cf. Gen 3:6.

5. Cf. Gen 4:1, 8, 24; Jude 10–11.

6. "What evidence is there of the piety of Adam and Eve after the fall?" (*Bible Class Magazine Vol. V* [London: Sunday School Union, 1852], 299).

7. "This was done, apparently, directly after the fall, and that from the skins of animals thus offered their first clothing was formed. Doubtless the divine

Being instructed them in this mode of propitiating guilt a symbolical of the sacrifice ultimately to be offered upon Calvary, in the person of our blessed Lord; and it seems but fair to suppose that their faith, like Abel's afterwards, would hence repose on that adorable sacrifice for pardon and acceptance. If so, we have the same reason to believe in their personal piety as in that of Abel's or any accredited Old Testament saint" (*Bible Class Magazine* 5:299). Cf. Gen 3:21; 4:3–4.

8.   "And as nothing is said in the least degree implying that their act of contrition was rejected, we have reason to hope it found acceptance with the sacrifice they offered" (*Bible Class Magazine* 5:299). Cf. Gen 4:4.

9.   "When Cain was born, she at once exclaimed, 'I have gotten a man from the Lord,' which some commentators render, 'a man, the Lord' and consider it as indicating an idea on her part of her babe being the promised Saviour. However this may be, the expression is one which shows either her acknowledgement of God's hand in all her affairs, or her faith in the promise of an atoning Lord. Either way it is a devout exclamation, and such as, at that unsophisticated period, none but a devout mind would use" (*Bible Class Magazine* 5:299–300). Cf. Gen 4:1.

10.   "Of this we have ample evidence in the sacrifices brought by Cain and Abel (to the enlightened views and true faith of the latter of whom we have the testimony in Heb. xi. 4.), and in the early indications of piety in the world, both before Adam's removal hence, and immediately after. Even then we see a godly seed in the household of Seth, and in the person of Enoch, and it is only fair to attribute this to the pious instructions and devout example of our first parents after their removal from Eden" (*Bible Class Magazine* 5:300). Cf. Gen 5:4.

11.   "Our Saviour was the Lamb slain before the foundation of the world, in the purpose, and covenant, and thought of God. His sacrifice saved Adam, and Noah, and Moses, and David, and all the saints, before the name of Calvary had become illustrious" (*MTP* 33:573).

12.   December 25.

13.   "A manufacturer; *a low workman*" (Johnson's *Dictionary*, s.v. "mechanick").

14. Cf. Luke 2:41–52.   15. Cf. Isa 53:3.

16. Cf. Matt 14:1–12.   17. Cf. John 7:3–5.

18. Cf. John 5:18.   19. Cf. Matt 26:74–75.

20. Cf. Matt 27:50–54.

21. Cf. Matt 28:1–4; Mark 16:2–5; Luke 24:1–4; John 20:1.

22. "Though about to become the mother of Jesus, Mary did not think herself without sin. Her eyes still looked to him who should be her Saviour from guilt and condemnation" (*MTP* 44:383).

23. "Once there was free will in Paradise, and a terrible mess free will made there, for it all spoiled all Paradise and turned Adam out of the garden" (*NPSP* 1:234).

24. "Jesus Christ was not capable of sin; it was utterly impossible for Christ to have sinned, as for fire to drown or water to burn. I suppose both of these things might be possible under some peculiar circumstances; but it never could have been possible for Christ to have committed or to have endured the shadow of the commission of a sin. He did not know it. He knew no sin" (*NPSP* 3:276–77).

25. Cf. John 10:17–18.

26. "Certainly, sin did gain a great victory in the garden of Eden, and therein it abounded; but Paul shows that it was by this very principle of representation that "grace did much more abound," for it is through the death of One, even Jesus Christ our Lord, that all believers live" (*MTP* 58:253–254).

27. "When that solemn and decisive hour comes, your interview with God will have to be a personal one. Sponsors will be of no use to anyone upon a dying bed. It will be of no avail, then, to call upon Christian friends to take a share of your burden. They will not be able to give you of their oil, for they have not enough grace for themselves and you. If you live and die without accepting the aid of the one Mediator between God and man, all these questions will have to be settled between your Soul and God without anyone else coming between yourself and your Maker; and all this may happen at any moment" (*MTP* 50:440–441).

28. "I am not going to speak at length about the doctrine of the federal headship of the first Adam and of the second Adam, which is to my mind indisputably taught in this chapter [Rom. 5]. I have heard a great many objections to that truth which appears to me to be plainly revealed in scripture, namely, that we were all represented by Adam in the Garden of Eden, and that, when he sinned, he so sinned as to sin representatively, and we fell by virtue of his disobedience" (*MTP* 43:553). Cf. Rom 5:12–21.

29. "As the Apostle before proves the distinction of a natural and spiritual body, and gives instances of both in the two principal men in the world, the first and the last; and points out the difference between them, the one being animated, and having life given unto it, the other animating, and giving life to others; proceeds to observe the order of these, how that one was before the other" (John Gill, *An Exposition of the New Testament*, vol. 2 [London: printed for the author, 1747, The Spurgeon Library], 684).

30. Cf. Gen 3:6–7.   31. Cf. Matt 4:1–11.

32. Cf. Rom 8:34.   33. Cf. Rom 5:12–21

34. "We, who are now present, must not however throw blame on Adam; no man was ever yet damned for Adam's sin alone" (*NPSP* 3:265).

35. See "Infant Salvation" (*MTP* 7, Sermon 411).

36. Cf. 1 Tim 4:10.

37. See "The Lamb's Book of Life" (Sermon 204).

Prov. XV. 15. The merry hearted man. 207

"A merry Christmas" is the compliment of the
season — & if Solomon had said it — it would
have been all-right —.   Why we should feast
& rejoice at Christmas I know, but why we
should riot, take sinful license & go into sin
I cannot tell. Surely it is most out of character.

Yet I will say "a merry Christmas to you all."
I love true merriment — & will refuse none
of you your fill of it. — Let me look —

I. At merry folks whose feast soon ends.

1. The rioters of day — have lounged till noon
then ate some dainty fare & crammed them—
—selves with sumptuous viands — table
cleared comes wine & fruit — then cards —
then more wines — cards again — & wine
then comes a dance — & nearly drunk they
reel home —   The feast is Done.
Tomorrow they cannot get up to go to any
place of worship — lustful thoughts have
been brewed — bills to pay, Monday
comes as busy as ever & the fun is gone.

2. The spendthrift — who lives above his
means, too high for his wings to keep him
up, he speculates, he sobs, he falls Done

THE MERRYHEARTED MAN [1]

Proverbs 15:15

"All the days of the afflicted are evil: but he that is of a merry heart hath a continual feast."

"A merry Christmas" is the compliment of the season. And if Solomon had said it, it would have been all-right.

Why we should feast and rejoice at Christmas I know. But why we should riot, take sinful license, and go into sin, I cannot tell. Surely, it is most out of character.

Yet I will say "a merry Christmas to you all." I love true merriment and will refuse none of you your fill of it. Let me look:

I. AT MERRY FOLKS WHOSE FEAST SOON ENDS.

1. The rioters of day have lounged till noon. Then ate some dainty fare and crammed themselves with sumptuous viands. Table cleared, comes wine and fruit, then cards, then more wines. Cards again and wine, then comes a dance. And nearly drunk, they reel home. The feast is <u>Done.</u>

    Tomorrow, they cannot get up to go to any place of worship. Lustful thoughts have been brewed, bills to pay. Monday comes as busy as ever, and the fun is gone.

2. The spendthrift who lives above his means, too high for his wings to keep him up. He speculates,[2] he sobs, he falls. <u>Done</u>.

3. The man of lust — follows his passions, revels in delight, is entranced in sin, enamoured with lust — he is mad & rushes on but soon disease has him, melancholy marks him, pain & agony convey him away *He feast is* <u>**done**</u>

4. The lover of strong drink, a right jolly fellow is he, round & round goes the wassail bowl, merrily, merrily run the hours — higher, higher, the shout is raised blood grows warm & strife is there — a fight comes on — police — the goal. br tis still on & on — the belly swells, a barrel alive is he. the legs grows stout with gout, the hand of pain gives the man pay for drink. br money is gone & no credit —— then robbery or suicide — or the workhouse *He feast is* <u>**done**</u>

5. The innocent mirth man, leads a quiet life, his are the cooler & more shady vales. He loves quiet, business, money & self. He gets on, gains money — all is beautiful — it flies & he is done or worse he dies & leaves it all, the hearse, the coffin, the hall, all say. <u>*He Feast is done*</u>

3. The man of lust follows his passions, revels in delight, is entranced in sin, enamoured with lust. He is mad and rushes on, but soon disease has him, melancholy marks him, pain and agony convey him away. The feast is <u>done</u>.

4. The lover of strong drink, a right jolly fellow is he. Round and round goes the wassail bowl.[3] Merrily, merrily run the hours. Higher, higher, the shout is raised. Blood grows warm and strife is there. A fight comes on. Police. The gaol. But 'tis still on and on. The belly swells. A barrel alive is he. The leggs grows stout with gout, the hand of pain gives the man pay for drink. Or money is gone and no credit. Then robbery, or suicide, or the workhouse. The feast is <u>done</u>.

5. The innocent mirth man leads a quiet life. His are the cooler and more shady vales. He loves quiet, business, money, and self. He gets on, gains money. All is beautiful. It flies and he is done. Or worse, he dies and leaves it all. The hearse, the coffin, the hall, all say, <u>**The Feast is done**</u>.

II. Folks who cannot be merry.

1. Discontented people never can. especially
if that breeds envy, malice & covetousness.
The miser.

2. Dishonest people cannot — can they lay
their heads on a pillow if theft be there.

3. Men who have not a clear conscience
before both man & God —

4. The man who counts another his foe
& cannot now forgive.

5. The who has not a friend above to trust
in — who lives at an uncertainty,
without any real solid ground of trust.

6. The tattler can't — who carries lies abroad.
Give these all the appliances of mirth they
yet could not rise to substantial joy —

III. People that can be merry. —

1. The man whose life is insured in
Jesus Christs life office — whose life is hid.

2. The man who is out of debt to man
or God — & oweth nothing to divine justice

3. The man who can say all things
are mine — & work for my good.

4. The humble soul who knows he has
more than he deserves & lives thankfully
on his little, being therewith content

II. FOLKS WHO CANNOT BE MERRY.

1. Discontented people never can, especially if that breeds envy, malice and covetousness.[4] The Miser.

2. Dishonest people cannot. Can they lay their heads on a pillow if theft be there?

3. Men who have not a clear conscience before both man and God.

4. The man who counts another his foe and cannot now forgive.

5. The [man] who has not a friend above to trust in, who lives at an uncertainty without any real solid ground of trust.[5]

6. The tattler can't, who carries lies abroad. Give these all the appliances[6] of mirth. They yet could not rise to substantial joy.[7]

III. PEOPLE THAT CAN BE MERRY.

1. The man whose life is insured in Jesus Christ[']s life office, whose life is hid.[8]

2. The man who is out of debt to man or God, and oweth nothing to divine justice.[9]

3   The man who can say, all things are mine[10] and work for my good.[11]

4. The humble soul who knows he has more than he deserves and lives thankfully on his little, being therewith content.[12]

5. Men who can find wine in a promise
& hope one day to take the full fruition
of the things here promised. —
6. Any man may be merry who can
see his interest in Election, Redemption, Adoption, Glory &c.

<u>IV</u>. Odd times to be merry in.
1. Time of Loss of friends — the Christian can rejoice
2. Time of poverty, distress & famine he laughs
3. Time of sickness he enjoys much.
4. Time of storm & thunder he fears not.
5. Time of death he can sing aloud
  & rejoice in his departure. —

To be thus merry —
Your heart must be bruised, then broken,
then healed, then washed in blood, then
in water, & then bound to Jesus Christ.
  Be merry Child of God in the good
old style — Rejoice, Rejoice, Rejoice.

338
Waterbeach Dec 25/52

5. Men who can find wine in a promise and hope one day to take the full fruition of the things here promised.

6. Any man may be merry who can see his interest in Election,[13] Redemption,[14] Adoption,[15] Glory,[16] etc.

IV. ODD TIMES TO BE MERRY IN.

1. Time of loss of friends. The Christian can rejoice.[17]

2. Time of poverty, distress, and famine. He laughs.

3. Time of sickness. He enjoys much.[18]

4. Time of storm and thunder. He fears not.

5. Time of death. He can sing aloud and rejoice in his departure.[19]

To be thus merry:

Your heart must be bruised, then broken, then healed, then washed in blood, then in water, and then bound to Jesus Christ.

Be merry[,] Child of God, in the good old style. Rejoice. Rejoice. Rejoice.

338

Waterbeach Dec 25/52[20]

1. Charles never again preached from this passage. From his notes, it is clear he preached this sermon on Christmas Day of 1852.

2. "2. To lay out money with a view to more than usual success in trade; to incur risks in business in the hope of large remuneration" (Worcester's *Dictionary*, 1383, s.v. "speculate").

3. "1. A liquor made of apples, sugar, and ale, anciently much used by English good-fellows. 2. A drunken bout. 3. A merry song" (Johnson's *Dictionary*, s.v. "wassail").

4. Cf. Rom 1:29.

5. "There is no real contentment to a truly-awakened man until he is at peace with God, and it is a horrible thing for any man to be perfectly satisfied while he is under God's wrath, and in danger of eternal destruction, as he certainly is unless he has believed in the Lord Jesus Christ. I would like to put a few very sharp thorns into the pillow of any easy-going people here who are content out of Christ. I would even wound you that you may come to Christ for healing, and smite you that you may resort to the great Physician for the cure which he alone can work, for it is a dreadful thing that you should be at ease when you have such grave cause for disquietude. 'There is no peace, saith my God, to the wicked'" (*MTP* 47:377).

6. "The act of applying; the thing applied" (Johnson's *Dictionary*, s.v. "appliance").

7. "At the cross we find a substantial joy, a far-reaching satisfaction, 'the peace of God, which passeth all understanding.' Here, ye restless ones, is the cure of restlessness: here shall you say, 'O God, my heart is fixed, my heart is fixed. I will sing and give praise'" (*MTP* 28:86).

8. Cf. Col 3:3.

9. Cf. Ps 32:2; Rom 4:8.

10. Cf. 2 Pet 1:3.

11. Cf. Rom 8:28.

12. Cf. Phil 4:11.

13. Cf. Rom 9:11; 1 Thess 1:4; 2 Pet 1:10.

14. Cf. Eph 1:6–7. "That same light, also, reveals to man God's way of salvation — shows him the person of Christ, his work, its suitability, and its freeness, and lets him see how he may obtain an interest in redemption by the simple act of believing" (*MTP* 21:494).

15. Cf. Eph 1:5. "They come not there as servants; no servant has any right to the inheritance of his master; let him be never so faithful, yet is he not his master's heir. But because ye are sons—sons by God's adoption, sons by the Spirit's regeneration—because by supernatural energy ye have been born again—ye become inheritors of eternal life, and ye enter into the many mansions of our Father's house above" (*MTP* 7:81).

16. Cf. Rom 8:30. In a sermon titled "Justification and Glory," Charles speaks about how the Christian is glorified: "'Whom he justified, them he also glorified.' They follow close together you see. A little stream divides them, but the apostle says nothing about it, and you and I need not say much. It is a narrow stream called Death: there is no glory without passing through that, or through the great change when the Lord comes; but there is nothing said about it, and so we will not say anything. It is not worth thinking of, it is swallowed up in victory" (*MTP* 11:247).

17. "The man who believes in Jesus and is reconciled to God has nothing outside of him that he needs to fear. Is he poor? He rejoices that Christ makes poor men rich. Does he prosper? He rejoices that there is grace to sanctify his prosperity lest it become intoxicating to him. Does there lie before him a great trouble? He thanks God for his promise that as his day his strength shall be. Does he apprehend the loss of friends? He prays that the trial may be averted, for he is permitted so to pray, even as David begged for the life of his child; but, having so done, he feels sure that God will not take away an earthly friend unless it be with kind intent to gather up our trust and confidence more fully to himself" (*MTP* 24:77).

18. "The Minister in These Times," Charles reflected upon suffering and ministry, saying, "[T]he greatest earthly blessing that God can give to any of us is health, *with the exception of sickness.* Sickness has frequently been of more use to the saints of God than health has. If some men, that I know of, could only be favoured with a month of rheumatism, it would, by God's grace, mellow them marvelously. Assuredly, they need something better to preach than what they now give their people; and, possibly, they would learn it in the chamber of suffering. I would not wish for any man a long time of sickness and pain; but a twist now and then one might almost ask for him. A sick wife, a newly-made grave, poverty, slander, sinking of spirit, might teach lessons nowhere else to be learned so well. Trials drive us

to the realities of religion. You may feed on chaff until you have real work to do, or real grief to bear; but then you want the old corn of the land, and you must have it, or else you will faint and fail" (*ARM*, 384–85, italics in the original).

19. See Charles's inscription on the title page of this notebook, "I hope to die singing," in a drawing of a swan. "Like the swan, of whom the fable hath it, that it singeth never till [it] comes to its end, so many a child of God has begun to sing in his last hours; because he has done with the glooms of earth, he begins to sing here his swan song, intending to sing on for ever and ever" (*MTP* 18:105).

20. The marking "Waterbeach Dec 25/52" appears in pencil at the bottom of this page. Charles likely composed the sermon, preached it, and later marked the location and date. This appears to be the second sermon he preached on Christmas Day of 1852.

Ex. XXIII. 29. I will not drive them out 208. in one year.

'Tis well to measure time & mark the flow of our day — divisions of years, months &c are the tongue of time whereby we are warned of its flight & premonished of its end. —

Some men expect too little in a year & will be glad of this text to help their laziness, we must not think meanly of time. We must do a great deal, & grow a great deal in one year.

Some expect too much they are ready to give up because things do not come up to their rash surmises — these must be warned by that.

The driving out of the Canaanites & conquest of Canaan is a type of our getting to heaven, or the victory of our souls over Christ's enemies.

I. Note. The way enemies are to be routed.

God "drives them out". — —

1. The enemies in our heart will not come out by persuasion of man, nor by our unaided exertions, nor by our vows & promises made in our strength, nor by mere formal worship, nor by mere telling to go — no. God must drive them out. This implies — that they are firmly estab- lished, that they are loath to leave, that they strive to return, that much power

I WILL NOT DRIVE THEM OUT *in* ONE YEAR [1]

Exodus 23:29

"I will not drive them out from before thee in one year; lest the land become desolate, and the beast of the field multiply against thee."

'Tis well to measure time, and mark the flow of our days. Divisions of years, months, etc. are the tongue of time [2] whereby we are warned of its flight and premonished [3] of its end.

Some men expect too little in a year and will be glad of this text to help their laziness. We must not think meanly [4] of time. We must do a great deal and grow a great deal in one year.

Some expect too much. [T]hey are ready to give up because things do not come up to their rash surmises. [5] These must be warned by that.

The driving out of the Canaanites and conquest of Canaan is a type of our getting to heaven, or the victory of our souls over Christ's enemies. [6]

I. NOTE. THE WAY ENEMIES ARE TO BE ROUTED. GOD *"drives them out."*

   1. The enemies in our heart will not come out by persuasion of man, nor by our unaided exertions, nor by our vows and promises made in our strength, nor by mere formal worship, nor by mere telling to go. [7] No. God must drive them out. This implies that they are firmly established. That they are loath to leave. That they strive to return. That much power

is necessary to make them move at all.
Is it not so believer? Is it not truly so?
2. The enemies of God in the world must
be driven out too. What can we poor creatures
do? If they persecute & slander — Can we
make the gospel spread? can we make one
drunkard sober? can we renew one heart?
No Lord do thou arise!!! arise!!!
Sinners truly have to be driven, sometimes
driven away in anger — but Oh let us pray
that may be drawn by love, driven by divine
grace, constrained by omnipotence.
<u>II</u>. The caution. or what will not be done.
1. God will not free us from our cor-
-ruptions all at once, we are not to leap
into Canaan too speedily — the old man will
still live — If you get on slowly take
courage. If well bless your God. He lets
them remain to try your faith & glorify
his own divine power — if these were so
many vile beasts such as pride, self con-
-fidence, sloth &c would multiply too fast.
So God finds it for our benefit to leave
some still in the land — We must
look for wearisome wars & fightings.
2. The enemies of our holy religion are not

is necessary to make them move at all. Is it not so[,] believer? Is it not truly so?

2. The enemies of God in the world must be driven out, too. What can we poor creatures do? If they persecute and slander,[8] can we make the gospel spread? Can we make one drunkard sober? Can we renew one heart?

No, Lord, do thou. arise!!! arise!!!

Sinners truly have to be driven. Sometimes driven away in anger. But, oh, let us pray that [they] may be drawn by love, driven by divine grace, constrained by omnipotence.

II. THE CAUTION. OR WHAT WILL NOT BE DONE.

1. God will not free us from our corruptions all at once. We are not to leap into Canaan so speedily. The old man will still live.[9] If you get on slowly, take courage. If well, bless your God. He lets them remain to try your faith and glorify his own divine power.[10] If these were gone, many vile beasts such as pride, self confidence, sloth etc. would multiply too fast. So, God finds it for our benefit to leave some still in the land. We must look for wearisome wars and fightings.

2. The enemies of our holy religion are not

to be overcome in one day. Missions are not
to convert a world at once. Our village will
not be suddenly swept of sin – not in one year.
we have had some success – say not the gospel
has failed because it has not done all – it is
intended to work a gradual rejuveration.
Be not too sanguine – nor disappointed

<u>III</u>. The hidden promise. I will eventually
drive them out.
1. Our corruptions though their defeat is gradual
yet are to be overcome. they shall one day die
& be gone for ever – we pure, holy & without blemish
Doubter. on. on, victory comes surely though slowly
2. The cause shall prosper, its foes must
fall, men shall be saved, the gospel
shall cover the earth, prayer shall prevail.
Blessed jubilee. Come! Come. —

<u>IV</u>. The duty. –
1. Beleive what God says.
2. Persevere in thy labour.
3. Sinner thou art not driven to hell, not
all in one year, thou art spared. God
lead thee to repentance this year –

Help. my Lord. oh King.

340.

to be overcome in one day. Missions are not to convert a world at once. Our village will not be suddenly swept of sin. Not in one year.[11] We have had some success. Say not the gospel has failed because it has not done all. It is intended to work a gradual regeneration.[12] Be not too sanguine nor disappointed.

III. THE HIDDEN PROMISE. I WILL EVENTUALLY DRIVE THEM OUT.

1. Our corruptions, though their defeat is gradual, yet are to be overcome. They shall one day die and be gone for ever. We pure, holy and without blemish.[13] Doubter, on, on. Victory comes surely, though slowly.

2. The cause shall prosper. Its foes must fall. Men shall be saved. The gospel shall cover the earth. Prayer shall prevail.

    Blessed Jubilee. Come! Come.

IV. THE DUTY.

1. Believe what God says.

2. Persevere in thy labour.

3. Sinner, thou art not driven to hell. Not all in one year. Thou are spared.[14] God lead thee to repentance this year.[15]

    Help, my Lord, Oh King.

340.

1. Charles never again preached from this passage.

2. This phrase was common parlance for the manner in which one categorized time. See William Harrison, *The Tongue of Time: or, the Language of a Church Clock* (London: Cradock, 1842).

3. "To warn or admonish beforehand" (Johnson's *Dictionary*, s.v. "premonish").

4. "2. Without dignity; poorly. 3. Without greatness of mind; ungenerously. 4. Without respect." (Johnson's *Dictionary*, s.v. "meanly").

5. "Imagination not supported by knowledge" (Johnson's *Dictionary*, s.v. "surmise").

6. "Just as the corruptions of human nature remain with the people of God when converted, for the trial and exercise of their graces, and that they may have their dependance [*sic*] not on themselves, but on the grace of God to keep them in his ways, and to preserve them safe to eternal glory; and by compleating [*sic*] the work of grace, which is gradually done, they might be made meet for it" (John Gill, *An Exposition of the Old Testament*, vol. I [London: printed for the author, 1763, The Spurgeon Library], 423).

7. "If your contendings against sin be all on legal accounts, from legal principles and motives, what assurance canst you attain unto that sin shall not have dominion over you, which will be your ruin? Yea, know that this reserve will not long hold out. If your lust has driven you from stronger gospel forts, it will speedily prevail against this also. Do not suppose that such considerations will deliver you, when you hast voluntarily given up to your enemy those help and means of preservation which have a thousand times their strength. Rest assuredly in this, that unless you recover yourself with speed from this condition, the thing that you fear will come upon you. What gospel principles do not, legal motives cannot do" (John Owen, *The Works of John Owen, D.D.*, vol. 6 [London: Johnstone and Hunter, 1861, The Spurgeon Library], 47–48).

8. Cf. Matt 5:10–11.

9. "There are some persons who strongly object to the doctrine of progressive sanctification, and to our mentioning anything like growth in grace. My brethren are welcome to object if they like, but I am sure, if they read the Scriptures

(they will surely not object to Scriptural terms), they will find growth in grace very frequently mentioned; if that does not mean progressive sanctification, then I do not understand the term 'growth in grace' at all. It is quite certain that there are degrees in the development of grace" (*MTP* 46:531).

10. Cf. 2 Cor 12:7.

11. At the time of this sermon, Charles likely had been serving in Waterbeach for just over a year.

12. See Notebook 1, Sermon 54 for an account of the spiritual climate in Waterbeach (*LS* 1:339n25).

13. Cf. Eph 5:26–27.   14. Cf. Luke 13:6–9.

15. Cf. 2 Tim 2:25.

209 I Cor. XIII. 13. Faith, Hope & Charity.

This exquisite chapter is a panegyric on love. She is the fairest & the golden apple is hers.

Paul in the first 3 verses declares her to be better than gifts & then goes on – 4–7 to speak of her influence on the mind & heart – & concludes by once more setting her in competition with all gifts & graces.

May I be aided while I think & speak.

I Graces are preferable to Gifts or Acts.

There is the gift of Riches, wealth, influence. The Gifts of talent, education, eloquence, & There were once miraculous gifts of healing, prophecy, languages, understanding mysteries, mountain– –moving faith – But Graces are much to be preferred to these.

1. For Gifts are given to even the ungodly but graces are the jewels that come to the children.

2. For we may abuse gifts but not graces.

3. Graces are evidences of salvation, abused Gifts are causes of damnation.

4. Gifts may be lost but graces are entailed.

Again Graces are better than Acts.

There are acts of charity, dividing ones property into small portions to feed the poor.

FAITH, HOPE, *and* CHARITY[1]

1 Corinthians 13:13

"And now abideth faith, hope, charity, these three; but the greatest of these is charity."

This exquisite chapter is a panegyric[2] on love. She is the fairest, and the golden apple[3] is hers.

Paul, in the first 3 verses, declares her to be better than gifts, and then goes on, 4–7 to speak of her influence on the mind and heart, and concludes by once more setting her in competition with all gifts and graces.[4]

May I be aided while I think and speak.

I.   GRACES ARE PREFERABLE TO GIFTS OR ACTS.[5]

There is the gift of Riches, wealth, influence.[6]

The Gifts of talent, education, eloquence.

There were once miraculous gifts of healing,[7] prophecy, languages, understanding mysteries,[8] mountain-moving faith.[9] But graces are much to be preferred to these.

1.   For ~~these~~ Gifts are given to even the ungodly but graces are the jewels that come to the children.[10]

2.   For we may abuse gifts but not graces.[11]

3.   Graces are evidences of salvation.[12] Abused gifts are causes of damnation.

4.   Gifts may be lost but graces are entailed.

Again graces are better than Acts.[13] There are acts of charity, dividing one[']s property into small portions to feed the poor[,]

practising dreadful austerities, or being burned as
a martyr with a view of salvation by it.
Graces are better than the best works.
1. For the ungodly can do such works.
2. Even if good then grace is their parent.
3. Such works avail not to please God, or
ensure our salvation but graces prove our salvation

The Graces are.
Love. Faith & Hope. which I will mention anon,
then comes. The 4 quiet graces.
1 Humility. the sweet violet of the vale, the mark of a
gracious soul — this is worth more than gifts.
2. Godly Fear. another drooping flower. filial fear keeps
us from sin. makes us walk circumspectly.
3. Godly Sorrow or Repentance grows in a wet soil
but is more precious than all the brightest gifts
4 Patience — to endure persecution, trial, trouble
to wait our Maker's will

The 2 lively graces.
Zeal — burning — one grain of this is worth
a world of gold.
Joy. always rejoicing, a sweet grace
indeed & very honorable to Jesus.
All Graces are more precious than Gifts

preaching dread austeries,[14] or being burned as a martyrs [*sic*] with a view of salvation by it.

Graces are better than the best works.

1. For the ungodly can do such works.[15]

2. Even if good, then grace is their parent.

3. Such works avail not to please God[16] or ensure our salvation. But graces prove our salvation.[17]

The graces are:

Love, Faith, and Hope, which I will mention soon.

Then comes the 4 quiet graces:

1. Humility. The sweet violet of the vale, the mark of a gracious soul. This is worth more than gifts.

2. Godly Fear, another drooping flower. Filial fear keeps us from sin. Makes us walk circumspectly.

3. Godly Sorrow or Repentance grows in a wet soil but is more precious than all the brightest gifts.

4. Patience to endure persecution, trial, trouble. To wait our Maker's will.

The 2 lively graces:

Zeal. Burning one grain of this is worth a world of gold.

Joy. Always rejoicing. A sweet grace indeed, and very honorable to Jesus.

All Graces are more precious than Gifts.

II. Faith. Hope. & Love are the 3 brightest graces.
They are all 3 abiding, constant graces.
Faith is to be distinguished from the faith before
mentioned as working miracles. — the faith
here meant is saving faith of God's elect.
It is not a mere belief of certain doctrines.
A man may have faith even if he never has
confidence or full assurance — these are valuable
graces but they do not always abide as true faith

His is an exceedingly precious grace, since on it
rests our salvation or justification before God.
It shall not be taken from us, though weakened it
    cannot be slain — it abides for ever.

Hope. is the child of faith. faith believes & hope
expects what faith sees in the promise.
This is not presumption. — it is not fancy.
It "abides", so long as we are in the "now".
It cheers, & sweetens our weary pilgrimage.

Charity rather Love. — not giving of alms
for some do so & have not charity — not candour
to our opponent that is good but is not
intended here. — not natural love —
maternal, filial or connubial but another
Love — Love to Christ & all things for his sake.

II. FAITH, HOPE, AND LOVE ARE THE 3 BRIGHTEST GRACES.

They are all 3 abiding, constant graces.

Faith is to be distinguished from the faith before mentioned as working miracles. The faith here meant is saving faith of God's elect.[18]

> It is not a mere belief of certain doctrines. A man may have faith even if he never has confidence or full assurance.[19] These are valuable graces, but they do not always <u>abide</u> as true faith.
>
> This is an exceedingly precious grace since on it rests our salvation or justification before God. It shall not be taken from us. Though weakened, it cannot be slain. It abides for ever.[20]

Hope is the child of faith. Faith believes and hope expects what faith sees in the promise.[21] This is not presumption. It is not fancy. It "<u>abides</u>," so long as we are in the "<u>now</u>." It cheers and sweetens our weary pilgrimage.[22]

Charity, rather Love. Not giving of alms, for some do so and have not charity. Not candor to our opponents. That is good, but is not intended here. Not natural love, maternal, filial, or connubial.[23] But another Love. Love to Christ and all things for his sake.[24]

III. Love is the Queen of all. —

The other two are mightier because they are the most essential & useful of all the graces but this is the chief of the 3.

She surpasses even Faith.

not that she can justify, as the Catholics say, for in that matter faith is her superior. —

1. But she is the most Godlike grace. God cannot be said to have either faith or hope but God is love.

2. She is a giving grace. She looketh on others. She regardeth not herself — Love is universal. Faith & Hope — personal. the others are receiving graces — the giver is greater than the taker.

3. It is the most fruitful, the most patent evidence

4. Most Christians believe Love is superior because faith & hope will cease in heaven —

Some say not so. we must even in heaven have confidence in God — & hope for future continuance of glory — — but others say "what a man seeth that he cannot hope for, & faith will be lost in sight — Love is eternal.

1. Little-Faiths remember love is the best.

2. Get much of Love —

3. Sinner thou hast none.

Bless th. Love

348. 357.

III. LOVE IS THE QUEEN OF ALL.

The other two are mighties because they are the most essential and useful of all the graces, but this is the chief of the 3.

She surpasses even Faith.

Not that she can justify, as the Catholics say, for in that matter, faith is her superior.

1. But she is the most Godlike grace. God cannot be said to have either faith or hope, but God is love.[25]

2. She is a giving grace. She looketh on others. She regardeth not herself. Love is universal. Faith and Hope, personal. The others are receiving graces. The giver is greater than the taker.

3. It is the most fruitful, the most patent evidence.

4. Most Christians believe love is superior because faith and hope will cease in heaven.[26] Some say not so. We must, even in heaven, have confidence with in God and hope for future continuance of glory. But others say, "What a man seeth, that he cannot hope for, and faith will be lost in sight." Love is eternal.

   1. Little-Faith,[27] remember love is the best.

   2. Get much of love.

   3. Sinner, thou hast none.

Bless, Oh <u>Love</u>.

348. 357.

1. Charles never again preached on this passage, but he does preach twice from
1 Cor 13. See "Now, and Then" (*MTP* 17, Sermon 1002) and "Love's Labours"
(*MTP* 27, Sermon 1617).

2. "Panegyrical; laudatory, containing praise; bestowing praise" (Johnson's
Dictionary s.v. "panegyrick," "elogy," and "encomiastick").

3. Spurgeon is referencing the Greek myth "The Judgment of Paris." In the story,
the mortal Paris of Troy is called upon by Zeus to judge who is the fairest of
three goddesses: Hera, Athena, or Aphrodite. The one judged most beautiful
by Paris received a golden apple as a reward. Samuel Boyse, *The Pantheon: or, The
Fabulous History of the Heathen Gods, Goddesses, Heroes, etc.* (London: n.p., 1777, the
Spurgeon Library), 94–95.

4. Cf. 1 Cor 13:1–13.

5. "True grace is much more excellent than any spiritual gifts whatever. And faith,
hope, and love, are the three principal graces, of which charity is the chief, being
the end to which the other two are but means" (Matthew Henry, *An Exposition of
the New Testament* [London: Thomas C. Jack, n.d., The Spurgeon Library], 8:116).

6. "All that men have they must trace to the Great Fountain, the giver of all good.
Hast thou talents? They were given thee by the God of talents. Hast thou time?
Hast thou wealth, influence, power? Hast thou powers of tongue? Hast thou
powers of thought? Art thou poet, statesman, or philosopher? Whatever be thy
position and whatever be thy gifts, remember that they are not thine, but they
are lent thee from on high. No man hath anything of his own, except his sins"
(*NPSP* 4:81).

7. "How far the gifts of healing may still remain in the Church, I should not like
to be forced to say; — either to say that they remain, lest any should be led into
fanaticism; or to say that they are utterly gone, lest I should be denying some
things which, at any rate, look like facts. God does, I doubt not, still hear the
believing prayers of his servants concerning the sick; at least, in certain cases, and
still should it be, as I judge, an ordinance to be observed, 'Is any sick among you?
let, him call for the elders of the church; and let them pray over him, anointing
him with oil in the name of the Lord: and the prayer of faith shall save the sick,
and the Lord shall raise him up'" (*MTP* 46:458–59).

8.   Cf. Mark 4:11; 1 Cor 2:7; Col 1:26; 1 Tim 3:16; Rom 16:25; Eph 1:9, 3:3.

9.   Cf. Matt 17:20.

10.   "Gifts and graces, charismata and charis, greatly differ. Both indeed were freely given of God. But where grace is given it is for the salvation of those who have it. Gifts are bestowed for the advantage and salvation of others. And there may be great gifts where there is not a dram of grace, but persons possessed of them are utterly out of the divine favour. They are great instances of divine benignity to men, but do not by themselves prove those who have them to be the objects of divine complacency" (Henry, *An Exposition of the New Testament*, 8:101).

11.   "[N]ot that the special grace of the Spirit is given to every individual man in the world, nor to every member of a visible church, for some are sensual, not having the Spirit; but as the same graces of the Spirit are given to every regenerate man, for all receive the same spirit of faith, so the gifts of the Spirit, more or less, either ordinary or extraordinary, are given to all such persons" (John Gill, *An Exposition of the New Testament*, vol. 2 [London: printed for the author, 1747, The Spurgeon Library], 641, The Spurgeon Library).

12.   "A soul sanctified by saving grace, is the only proper soil for gifts to flourish in. . . . When the actings of grace and gifts are inseparable, as when in prayer the Spirit is a spirit of grace and supplication, the grace and gift of it working together, when utterance in other duties is always accompanied with faith and love, then is God glorified, and our own salvation promoted" (John Owen, *Works of John Owen* [London and Edinburgh: Johnstone and Hunter, 1852, The Spurgeon Library], 4:438).

13.   "Paul assures us that the two principles of grace and merit can no more mix together than fire and water; that if man is to be saved by the mercy of God, it must be by the mercy of God and not by works; but if man is to be saved by works, it must be by works entirely and not by mercy mixed therewith, for mercy and work will not go together. Jesus saves, but He does all the work or none. He is Author and Finisher, and works must not rob Him of His due. Sinner, you must either receive salvation freely from the hand of Divine Bounty, or else you must earn it by your own unassisted merits, which last is utterly impossible. Oh that you would yield to the first!" (*MTP* 12:426–27).

14. "Severity, cruelty" (Johnson's *Dictionary,* s.v. "austerity").

15. "The most important thing to remember about religion in Victorian England is that there was an awful lot of it. The nineteenth century was marked by a revival of religious activity unmatched since the days of the Puritans. This religious revival shaped that code of moral behavior, or rather that infusion of all behavior with moralism, which we still call, rightly or wrongly, 'Victorianism.' Above all, religion occupied a place in the public consciousness, a centrality in the intellectual life of the age, which it had not had a century before and did not retain in the twentieth century" (Josef L Althotz, "The Warfare of Conscience with Theology" in *Religion in Victorian Britain,* vol. 4, *Interpretations,* ed. Gerald Parsons [Oxford Road, Manchester: Manchester University Press, 1988], 150).

16. Cf. Heb 11:6; Rom 3:20.

17. Cf. 1 John 3:10: "Yea, in the very graces themselves of faith and uprightness of heart, there is such a seal and stamp, impressing the image of God upon the soul, as, without any reflex act or actual contemplation of those graces themselves, have an influence into the establishment of the souls of men in whom they are unto a quiet, comfortable, assured repose of themselves upon the love and faithfulness of God" (Owen, *Works of John Owen,* 11:83).

18. "[This] faith is to be understood, not of a faith of miracles, for that does not abide; nor of an historical one, or mere assent to truth; persons may have this faith, and believe but for a while; but of that faith, which is peculiar to God's elect; is a fruit and effect of electing grace, and for that reason abides" (Gill, *An Exposition of the New Testament,* 2:654).

19. "It is a great mistake to fancy that to endorse sound doctrine is the same thing as possessing saving faith, for while saving faith accepts the truth of God, it mainly concerns itself with the person and work of the Lord Jesus Christ, and its essence lies in reliance upon Jesus himself. I am not saved because I believe the Scriptures, or because I believe the doctrines of grace, but I am saved if I believe Christ; or, in other words, trust in him" (*MTP* 18:62).

20. "Learn from this that a measure of doubt is consistent with saving faith; that weak faith is true faith, and a trembling faith will save the soul. If thou

believest, even though thou be compelled to say, 'Help thou mine unbelief,' yet that faith makes thee whole, and thou art justified before God" (*MTP* 18:67).

21. Cf. Heb 11:1.

22. See "Hopeful" in John Bunyan, *The Pilgrim's Progress* (London: J. Haddon, 1847, The Spurgeon Library), 116.

23. "Matrimonial; nuptial; pertaining to marriage" (Johnson's *Dictionary*, s.v. "connubial").

24. "What persons very often mean by 'charity,' in their ordinary conversation, is a disposition to hope and think best of others, and to put a good construction of their words and behavior; and sometimes the word is used for a disposition to give to the poor. But these things are only certain particular branches, or fruits of that great virtue of charity which is so much insisted on throughout the New Testament. The word properly signifies *love* . . . so that by charity in the New Testament, is meant the very same things as Christian love; and though it be more frequently used for love to men, yet it be sometimes used to signify not only love to men, but love to God" (Jonathan Edwards, *Charity and its Fruits; or, Christian Love as Manifested in the Heart and Life. Edited from the Original Manuscripts, with an Introduction, by Tyron Edwards* [New York: Robert Carter and Brothers, 1852], 1–2).

25. Cf. 1 John 4:8. "When faith and hope are at an end, true charity will burn for ever with the brightest flame. Note, Those border most upon the heavenly state and perfection whose hearts are fullest of this divine principle, and burn with the most fervent charity. It is the surest offspring of God, and bears his fairest impression. For God is love" (Henry, *An Exposition of the New Testament*, 8:102).

26. "[I]n heaven faith will be swallowed up in vision, and hope in fruition. There is no room to believe and hope, when we see and enjoy. . . . When faith and hope are at an end, true charity will burn for ever with the brightest flame" (Henry, 8:102).

27. See the story of "Little-Faith" in *Pilgrim's Progress* (Bunyan, *The Pilgrim's Progress*, 150–56).

210. Deut. XXII. 11. Linsey-woolsey forbidden.

This command is no longer binding upon us — only such commands as enjoin moral duties can be said to be binding upon us. & not even these in exact form. for instance that command of the Sabbath-day to be on the seventh — is now superseded by a day on which a more glorious ~~work~~ work is commemorated — — — What a mercy that we are free from the rigours of the ceremonial dispensation & that we are more at liberty in things indifferent. Outward dress is now no longer the badge of an Israelite — yet we are bound to be neat, modest & becoming in dress.

Wherefore was this command given. — Some (as Josephus) think it was because the priests alone might wear such garments & they were not to trespass on the office of the priest — — as Uzziah, Korah —

But surely God designed more than this — we are not to find spiritual meaning where there is none as some do — but in the types of the law we are warranted to do it.

I. We are not to seek salvation by grace & by works.

LINSEY-WOOLSEY FORBIDDEN [1]

Deuteronomy 22:11

"Thou shalt not wear a garment of divers sorts, as of woolen and linen together."

This command is no longer binding upon us. Only such commands as enjoin moral duties can be said to be binding upon us. And not even these in exact form. For instance, that command of the Sabbath-day to be on the seventh [2] is not superseded by a day on which a more glorious work is commemorated.

What a mercy that we are free from the rigours of the ceremonial dispensation [3] so that we are more at liberty in things indifferent. Outward dress is now no longer the badge of an Israelite. [4] Yet we are bound to be neat, modest, and becoming in dress. [5]

Wherefore was this command given. Some (as Josephus) [6] think it was because the priests alone might wear such garments, and they were not to trespass on the office of the priest, as Uzziah, Korah. [7] But surely, God designed more than this. We are not to find spiritual meaning where there is none, as some do. But in the types of the law we are warranted to do it.

I. WE ARE NOT TO SEEK SALVATION BY GRACE AND BY WORKS. [8]

The apostle Paul will not have it so.
The Pharisee said it was all works & acted consist-
- ently. some pray like a publican & yet at least
are true Pharisees & their very prayer is hyppocrisy.
The Tractarians say it is all by ceremonies.
Others say that God for Christs sake accepts
our imperfect obedience if it be sincere.
& some say our sanctification must justify
us before God. But away with mixtures.
My Grace are ye saved — through the
Sole merit of Jesus Christ. Look now
Ye sons of God & see if any flax be with the
wool & if so pull it out

II. We are not to ascribe the new-birth
to God & man conjointly.
This is by some divided between God & the
clergyman & water — by others God & the
minister & by others God & the sinner. —
But the new birth is entirely by divine power
for man dead if made alive does not help
in the matter.
man does not understand it — see. Nicodemus
man does not love & desire it but rather
hates the light — so then it is by the
Holy Spirit altogether unassisted.

The apostle Paul will not have it so. The Pharisee said it was all works and acted consistently.[9] Some pray like a publican,[10] and yet at least are true Pharisees and their very prayer is hypocrisy.

The Tractarians say it is all by ceremonies.[11] Others say that God, for Christ's sake, accepts our imperfect obedience if it be sincere.[12] And some say our sanctification must justify us before God.[13] But away with mixtures.

By grace are ye saved through the sole merit of Jesus Christ.[14] Look now, ye sons of God, and see if any flax be with the wool. And if so[,] pull it out.

II. WE ARE NOT TO ASCRIBE THE NEW-BIRTH TO GOD AND MAN CONJOINTLY.

This is, by some, divided between God and a clergyman's water.[15] By others, God and the minister[,] and by others[,] God and the sinner.

But the new birth is entirely by divine power, for man [is] dead. If made alive, [man] does not help in the matter. Man does not understand it. See Nicodemus.[16] Man does not love and desire it but rather hates the light.[17] So then, it is by the Holy Spirit altogether unassisted.[18]

after regeneration the man assisted & prompted
by the divine agency of the Spirit does perform
good works but yet these come of sin —
   Election is all of God. Adoption is all his.
Final Perseverance is his — He is Alpha & Omega.
__III__. We are not to join sin & religion.
   This is often attempted — the same man
who drinks & swears will yet boast of being
a child of God — Bad men of all denominations do this. He Antinomian does it
because he says he is free from the law —
He Puseyite does it because he is saved
in baptism — the Catholic can be pardoned
by the priest — He Arminian can be
renewed just when he pleases — He mere
Calvinist makes his perseverance a plea
for sin — but such will be wrong at last
Be one thing or the other. Linsey-woolsey
will not do in heaven. Members, professors
see that ye walk circumspectly for the
days are evil — purge out the old leaven
   be not conformed to the world but transformed
__IV__ We are not to have two
aims in view.

After regeneration, the man, assisted and prompted by the divine agency of the Spirit, does perform good works[,] but yet these come of him.

Election is all of God. Adoption is all his. Final Perseverance is his.[19] He is Alpha and Omega.[20]

III. WE ARE NOT TO JOIN SIN AND RELIGION.

This is often attempted. The same man who drinks and swears will yet boast of being a child of God. Bad men of all denominations do this. The Antinomian does it because he says he is free from the law.[21] The Puseyite does it because he is saved in baptism. The Catholic can be pardoned by the priest. The Arminian can be renewed just when he pleases. The mere Calvinist makes his perseverance a plea for sin. But such will be wrong at last.

Be one thing or the other. Linsey-woolsey[22] will not do in heaven. Members, professors, see that ye walk circumspectly, for the days are evil.[23] Purge out the old leaven.[24] Be not conformed to the world but transformed.[25]

IV. WE ARE NOT TO HAVE TWO AIMS IN VIEW.

This will touch those who are the most moral.
Religion is attended to because it is respectable
& helps business — but we ought to have a
single eye to God's glory.   Business, the
world are followed so hotly & religion too
cooly. —   Surely this is God & Baal — but
God must be our aim, his service our delight.
When we are too anxious, or too elevated
by our affairs — there is much danger.
Hands too full, make a heart too dull. —
    May God make us wholly his ~~~~~~~~~~~~

V. Rather make this III —
    We must not have a creed partly
founded on Scripture & part on man. —
    It must be wholly what the Bible says & not
at all what John Calvin, John Wesley, John Gill,
or any mortal man says.   Not the Bible
& the Prayer-book, nor the Hymn Book.
No arguments must be allowed from tradition
for infant sprinkling or believer's immersion either.
No pope, no canons, no synods, decrees, Nicene creed
or Athanasian creeds. —   If experience so called
opposes Scripture throw it away.   We must not
aim so much at consistency with ourselves
    as with the word of God. —
                            Bless me my Father —

349.

This will touch those who are the most moral. Religion is attended to because it is respectable and helps business.[26] But we ought to have a single eye to God's glory. Business, the world, are followed so hotly and religion too cooly. Surely this is God and Baal. But no. God must be our aim. His service, our delight. When we are too anxious or too elevated by our affairs, there is much danger. Hands too full make a heart too dull.

May God make us wholly his . . . .

V. RATHER MAKE THIS III. WE MUST NOT HAVE A CREED PARTLY FOUNDED ON SCRIPTURE AND PART ON MAN.

It must be wholly what the Bible says and not at all what John Calvin, John Wesley, John Gill, or any mortal man says.[27]

Not the Bible and the Prayer-book,[28] nor the Hymn Book.[29]

No arguments must be allowed from tradition for infant sprinkling or believer's immersion either. No pope, no canons, no synods, decrees, Nicene creed or Athanasian creeds.[30] If experience, so called, opposes Scripture, throw it away. We must not aim so much at consistency with ourselves as with the Word of God.

<u>Bless me[,] my Father.</u>

349.

1. "Made of linen and wool mixed. Vile; mean; of different and unsuitable parts" (Johnson's *Dictionary*, s.v. "linseywoolsey"). Charles never again preached on this passage, but he mentions the content of it in "God, the Father of a Family" (Notebook 2, Sermon 129).

2. Cf. Exod 20:8–11.   3. Cf. Rom 6:14.

4. Cf. Lev 19:19; Deut 22:5.   5. Cf. 1 Pet 3:1–6.

6. "There were peculiar garments appointed for the priests, and for all the rest, which they call Cahanaeae [priestly] garments, as also for the high priests, which they call Cahanaeae Rabbae, and denote the high priests' garments" (Flavius Josephus, *The Works of Flavius Josephus*, trans. William Whiston [London: printed for William Allason, 1818, The Spurgeon Library], 1:137).

7. Cf. Num 16:1–3, 31–35; 2 Chr 26:18–19.

8. "[The law's] object is this—to make you accept salvation as the free gift of God—to make you stand and own that you are a sinner, and accept a free, full, perfect forgiveness, according to the infinite grace of the eternal Father. The law is meant to keep you always holding on to salvation by grace. For my part, I cannot bear that preaching which is partly law and partly grace. I have had enough of the law. If you had known five years of its rigor—five years discipline of the pedagogue—you would never want to see even his back any more. When a man once knows what law-work is in his soul, he knows the difference between that and the gospel, and he will not have linsey-woolsey: he wants to have the pure white linen all of one material, and that material free grace" (*MTP* 20:559).

9. Cf. Matt 15:1–9.   10. Cf. Luke 18:9–14.

11. "Tractarians" is another term for Puseyites. For other early sermons in which Charles spoke against Puseyism, see "Salvation in God Only" (Notebook 1, Sermon 24); "The Fight and the Weapons" (Notebook 1, Sermon 37a); "Justification By Imputed Righteousness" (Notebook 2, Sermon 117); "Come Ye Out from Among Them" (Notebook 2, Sermon 119); and "More for Us Than against Us" (Notebook 3, Sermon 1:80).

12. See where Charles addressed antinomianism: "Pleasure in the Stones of Zion" (Notebook 1, Sermon 53); "Making Shipwreck of Faith" (Notebook 3, Sermon 161); and "Following Jesus with a Cross on Our Back (Notebook 3, Sermon 187).

13. Charles would address Wesleyan perfectionism often in later writings. See *Autobiography* 1:262–64 and *TD* 6:21.

14. Cf. Eph 2:8.

15. Charles revised this sentence in light pencil after its initial composition, adding "the" after "a" and "sprinkled by a" after "water," circling "clergyman's," and indicating that "clergyman's" comes after "water" with an arrow. The revised sentence, then, reads this way: "This is by some divided between God & sprinkled by the clergyman's water." See "Baptismal Regeneration" (*MTP* 10, Sermon 573).

16. Cf. John 3:4, 9.   17. Cf. John 3:19.

18. "[T]ake effectual calling. By what power is a man called? There are some who say that it is by the energy of his own will, or at least that while God gives him grace, it depends upon him to make use of it: some do not make use of the grace and perish, others make use of the grace and are saved; saved by their own consenting to allow grace to be effectual. We, on the other hand, say no, a man is not saved against his will, but he is made willing by the operation of the Holy Ghost. A mighty grace which he does not wish to resist enters into the man, disarms him, makes a new creature of him, and he is saved. We believe that the calling which saves the soul is a calling which owes nothing at all to man, but which comes from God, the creature being then passive, while God, like the potter, moulds the man like a lump of clay. Clearly the calling, we think must be through God; for so it coincides with this principle 'of him, and through him, and to him are all things'" (*MTP* 10:308–9).

19. See "Final Perseverance" (Notebook 1, Sermon 8); "Final Perseverance Certain" (Notebook 2, Sermon 82); and "Making Shipwreck of Faith" (Notebook 3, Sermon 161).

20. Cf. Rev 1:7, 11; 21:6, 22:13.

21. "In my first pastorate, I had often to battle with Antinomians—that is, people who held that, because they believed themselves to be elect, they might live as they liked. I hope that heresy has to a great extent died out, but it was sadly prevalent in my early ministerial days. I knew one man, who stood on the table of a public-house, and held a glass of gin in his hand, declaring all the while that he

was one of the chosen people of God. They kicked him out of the public-house, and when I heard of it, I felt that it served him right. Even those ungodly men said that they did not want any such 'elect' people there. There is no one who can live in sin—drinking, swearing, lying, and so on—who can truly declare that he is one of the Lord's chosen people . . . From my very soul, I detest everything that in the least savours of the Antinomianism which leads people to prate about being secure in Christ while they are living in sin" (*Autobiography* 1:258).

22. Cf. Deut 22:11.   23. Cf. Eph 5:15–17.

24. Cf. 1 Cor 5:7.   25. Cf. Rom 12:2.

26. "I do not doubt that many people have put religion as a show-card into their business, and have tried to make money by it. Like Mr. By-ends, they thought that if, by being religious, they could get a good wife, — if, by being religious they could be introduced into respectable society, — if, by being religious they would bring some excellent religious customers to their shop, and if, indeed, by being religious they could get themselves to be esteemed, it would be a very proper thing. Now, this is making religion into irreligion" (*MTP* 22:230).

27. "The Holy Ghost revealed much of precious truth and holy precept by the apostles, and to his teaching we would give earnest heed; but when men cite the authority of fathers, and councils, and bishops, we give place for subjection, no, not for an hour. They may quote Irenaeus or Cyprian, Augustine or Chrysostom; they may remind us of the dogmas of Luther or Calvin; they may find authority in Simeon, or Wesley, or Gill—we will listen to the opinions of these great men with the respect which they deserve as men, but having so done, we deny that we have anything to do with these men as authorities in the Church of God, for there nothing has any authority, but 'Thus saith the Lord of hosts.' Yea, if you shall bring us the concurrent consent of all tradition—if you shall quote precedents venerable with fifteen, sixteen, or seventeen centuries of antiquity, we burn the whole as so much worthless lumber, unless you put your finger upon the passage of Holy Writ which warrants the matter to be of God" (*MTP* 10:535).

28. "We will follow Ben-hadad, *and hear the king at his prayers.* He has come before the king of Israel, and he has a petition to offer. What will it be? Bring the big book; turn to the collect for Quinquagesima Sunday—will that not suit him? Will not

our beautiful liturgy serve his turn? No, no; living souls must have living words, and their own words too, for I cannot adopt another man's petition, they must be my own children, sprung from my own loins. The dead soul may parrot out a printed prayer, but the living soul pants to be rid of such tag-rags—such bondage. The living spirit can no more be content with a mere form of prayer, than the blazing, flaming comet could be chained, belted, and held fast in prison. It must have words of its own" (*MTP* 9:585).

29. "I leave this point [discussing the various works of the Holy Spirit], only endeavouring to urge each one to enquire, 'What do I know of all this?' I am afraid many of you know nothing at all about it. You are a good sort of people; you were sprinkled when you were infants, and have been regularly to church or chapel all your lives; you do not owe anything, and live as you should live in many respects, and you think that outward morality and outward religion are everything. You use your hymn book and prayer books, and behave yourselves like respectable people; but if you have not the Spirit you are lost. The external without the inward is good for nothing. It is all good for nothing. A waggon-load [*sic*] of profession is not worth an ounce of grace" (*MTP* 13:321).

30. "The text does not say, 'These are written that ye might believe the Nicene creed,' for, good as that creed is, it was not then composed, and is not the chief object of faith. It does not say, 'These are written that ye might believe the Athanasian creed;' a very good creed, but rather savage, and also not then devised. No, no: 'These are written that ye might believe that Jesus is the Christ, the Son of God, and that believing ye might have life through his name [John 20:31].' That is to say, the faith which brings life to the soul is faith in the person, offices, nature, and work of Jesus; and though you may be in the dark about a thousand things, and may make mistakes about ten thousand more, yet if you believe in the Messiah, the Son of God, you have eternal life" (*MTP* 27:659–60).

211.   Col. I. 12.   Meet for the Inheritance.

The Verse before this one is a true martyr's verse
it is the carrying out of the verse "When men
persecute you, rejoice & be exceeding glad &c. —
He leaps from suffering to rejoicing yea from the
bitter he extracteth sweet. —   He speaks of 3 things.

I. Of a heaven provided.

II. Of a meetness given.

III. Of a conduct expected   "giving thanks".

I. Of a heaven provided. this he describes
    in 3 different particulars.

1. It is an "inheritance"   — —
It is so called in allusion to Canaan which
was by covenant made with Abram, the inheritance
of all his sons.   There was a portion a lot
for every tribe & every family.

It is so called that we may see that it is all
of grace, not of free will, merit, or purchase.

To show us that Adoption is the only title a
man can shew for a possession there.

2, It is the "inheritance of the saints."
Not of what Catholics call saints — not of
the eminently good alone — not of perfect being
but of scriptural saints who are to

MEET *for the* INHERITANCE [1]
Colossians 1:12

*"Giving thanks unto the Father, which hath made us meet to be
partakers of the inheritance of the saints in light[.]"*

The Verse before this one is a true martyr's verse.[2] It is the carrying out of the verse,
"When men persecute you, rejoice and be exceeding glad, etc."

He leaps from suffering to rejoicing. Yea, from the bitter he extracteth sweet. He
speaks of 3 things:

I.   OF A HEAVEN PROVIDED.

II. OF A MEEKNESS GIVEN.

III. OF A CONDUCT EXPECTED. *"giving thanks."*

I.   OF A HEAVEN PROVIDED.

This he describes in 3 different particulars:

   1. It is an "<u>inheritance</u>."

      It is so called in allusion to Canaan,[3] which was, by covenant made with
      Abram,[4] the inheritance of all his sons. There was a portion, a lot, for
      every tribe and every family.[5]

      It is so called that we may see that it is all of grace. Not of free will,
      merit, or purchase.

      To show us that Adoption is the only title a man can show for to a
      possession there.

   2. It is the "<u>inheritance of the saints</u>."

      Not of what Catholics call saints. Not of the eminently good alone. Not
      of perfect beings. But of scriptural saints who are so

called from the two meanings the word has.

It means selected, chosen, thus the sacraficial bulls were selected & so are God's people they are elect

It means also holy — for the act of selection made the beast holy — & God makes his elect "holy" — he puts on them the holiness of Jesus & works in them the graces of the Holy Spirit — every child of God is a saint,

None but these can enjoy the inheritance.

3. It is the "inheritance of the saints in light"

The saints bodies are doubtless all glorious so as to be as if they were made of "light" — Jesus transfigured shone — their bodies like his may be ethereal, far lighter & more spiritual than ours.

But it describes also their knowledge; here we are dark, they are light, suns without spots.

It describes their glorious habitation where all is resplendent because God is there, he who dwells in light inaccessible.

& it implies their beatific happiness, when neither doubt, distress, fear, nor trial shall annoy.

II. He speaks of a meetness given.

He gives thanks that he is meet & ascribes it all to supreme power "made us meet," not caused us to be born meet, not helped us to make ourselves meet. — but "made" us meet.

Paul would not wish by this to say

called from the two meanings the word has.

It means selected, chosen. Thus, the sacrificial bulls[6] were selected and so are God's people. They are elect.

It means also holy, for the act of selection made the beast holy. And God makes his elect "holy." He puts on them the holiness of Jesus and works in them the graces of the Holy Spirit. Every child of God is a saint.

None but these can enjoy the inheritance.

3. It is the "<u>inheritance of the saints in light</u>."

The saints['] bodies are doubtless all glorious so as to be as if they were made of "light." Jesus transfigured shone.[7] Their bodies, like his, may be ethereal, far lighter and more spiritual than ours.[8]

But it describes also their knowledge. Here, we are dark. They are light. Suns without spots. It describes their glorious habitation where all is resplendent because God is there. He who dwells in light inaccessible.[9]

And it implies their beatific happiness when neither doubt, distress, fear, nor trial shall annoy.

II. HE SPEAKS OF A MEETNESS GIVEN.

He gives thanks that he is meet and ascribes it all to supreme power. "Made us meet." Not caused us to be born meet. Not helped us to make ourselves meet. But "made" us meet.

Paul would not wish by this to say

that he thought himself "perfect", or fully prepared to enter heaven. — he meant that he had the embryo of that perfection, & he had the earnest & pledge of it. Note, He is not here speaking of meetness wrought by the Holy Ghost as by the Father. The whole divine Trinity have hand in it. The Son has cried it "is finished" his part is done. The Spirit has but commenced his though with a certainty of completion — but the meetness worked by the Father for us is perfect it consists in

Election — without this we could not be "meet for the inheritance is for saints. "select one"

Justification — without this we could not be saints —

Adoption. which entitles us to an inheritance

This is the meetness the Father works & in this sense our meetness is perfect the moment we believe. A christian a day old is fit to enter heaven at once so far as the meetness conferred by the Father is concerned.

that he thought himself "perfect"[10] or fully prepared to enter heaven. He meant that he had the embryo of that perfection, and he had the earnest and pledge of it.

Note. He is not here speaking of meetness wrought by the Holy Spirit as by the Father. The whole divine Trinity have hand in it. The Son has cried[,] it "is finished." His part is done. The Spirit has but commenced his thought with a certainty of completion. But the meetness worked by the Father for us is perfect. It consists in:

Election. Without this, we could not be "meet," [f]or the inheritance is for saints. "Select one."

Justification. Without this, we could not be saints.

Adoption, which entitles us to an inheritance.

This is the meetness the Father works. And in this sense, our meetness is perfect the moment we believe. A Christian a day old is fit to enter heaven at once, so far as the meetness conferred by the Father is concerned.

These things make us fit not to be lookers on in
heaven but partakers. not crumb-pickers, not
beggars but partakers of a rich inheritance.

<u>III</u>. The conduct expected.

Grumbling - no - no - let that be Satan's own.
Silence - far from it - down - down with our harps.
Giving "<u>mere</u>" thanks, mere words, not to
no thanks are worth having, but those that
bring the whole man with them.

not Have <u>given</u>, & have done - but giving
still on & on as long as we live anywhere,
Thanks in prisons or palaces, health or sickness,
joy or sorrow, life or death. ever, ever.

In God's house, in your closet, in your
life - give thanks, be a walking hymn book
Be like a well tuned harp at all times
Come you must see to the screws & strings
but with your worm - eaten psalm, bring
the lyre, & an instrument of ten strings

Help me th. Helper.
I <u>trust in thee</u>.

352

These things make us fit, not to be lookers on in heaven, but partakers. Not crumb-pickers, not beggars, but partakers of a rich inheritance.

III. THE CONDUCT EXPECTED.

Grumbling. No, no. Let that be Satan's own.[11]

Silence. Far from it. Down, down with our harps.[12]

Giving "<u>mere</u>" thanks, mere words. Not so. No <u>thanks</u> are worth having but those that bring the whole man with them.

Not <u>Have given</u> and have done, but giving still on and on as long as we live anywhere. Thanks in prisons or palaces, health or sickness, joy or sorrow, life or death.[13] "Ever, ever."

In God's house, in your closet, in your life, give thanks. Be a walking hymn book. Be like a well tuned harp at all times. Come, you must see to the screws and strings. But with your worm-eaten psalm, bring the lyre, and an instrument of ten strings.[14]

Help me, Oh Helper.

<u>I trust in thee.</u>

352

1.   Charles never again preached on this passage.

2.   Colossians 1:11: "Strengthened with all might, according to his glorious power, unto all patience and longsuffering with joyfulness[.]"

3.   Cf. Gen 17:8.   4.   Cf. Gen 17:2–4.

5.   Cf. Josh 14:1–5.

6.   "And what are we to do? To present our bodies to God, not our souls alone, to make real, practical work of it. Let this flesh and blood in which your body dwells be presented unto God, not to be killed and to be a dead sacrifice, but to live and still to be a sacrifice, a living sacrifice unto God, holy and acceptable to him. This is reasonable. God help us to carry it out" (*MTP* 62:298–99).

7.   Cf. Matt 17:1–8.

8.   "[Paul] declares the nature of the new body and teaches that its fashion shall be the same as that of our ascended Lord" ("The Resurrection Body" [Notebook 3, Sermon 185]).

9.   Cf. 1 Tim 6:16.   10.   Cf. Phil 3:12.

11.   Cf. Phil 2:14.   12.   Cf. Ps 137:1–3.

13.   Cf. Phil 4:11–12.   14.   Cf. Pss 33:2; 92:3; 144:9.

212.   John VI. 37. Nowise cast out.

Upon reading this verse one feels inclined to break out with the angelic song — "behold I bring you glad tidings of great joy &c"

Here are two sets of doctrine, the high & the low conjoined, surely it will suit all from the Hyper down to the Primitive.

I. The Eternal "shall" — positive.

II. The Eternal "will" — negative.

I. The Positive. Eternal "shall".
These words may be regarded as

1. A prophecy of our Lord, the prophet of his people.
2. As a solemn oath of God the Son.
3. As a triumphant boast of Jesus the Conqueror
4. As a challenge to death & hell.

In these words he speaks like one

1. Who knows the number of his people "all".
2. Who regards past & present as one "giveth"
3. Who knows his rights are good &
4 Who is convinced of his own power to keep

But this is of no comfort to us

NOWISE CAST OUT[1]
John 6:37

*"All that the Father giveth me shall come to me; and him
that cometh to me I shall no wise cast out."*

Upon reading this verse, one feels inclined to break out with the angelic song. "Behold, I bring you glad tidings of great joy, etc."[2]

Here are two sets of doctrine, the high and the low conjoined. Surely, it will suit all from the Hyper[3] down to the Primitive.[4]

I. THE ETERNAL *"Shall"*—POSITIVE.

II. THE ETERNAL *"Will"*—NEGATIVE.

I. THE POSITIVE, ETERNAL *"Shall."*

These words may be regarded as:

    1. A prophecy of our Lord, the prophet of his people.[5]

    2. As a solemn oath of God the Son.

    3. As a triumphant boast of Jesus the Conqueror.[6]

    4. As a challenge to death and hell.

In these words he speaks like one:

    1. Who knows the number of his people. "All."[7]

    2. Who regards past and present as one. "Giveth."

    3. Who knows his rights are good,[8] and

    4. Who is convinced of his own power to perform it.[9]

But this is no comfort to us

unless we can see

1. That he has given us the Holy Spirit.
2. That we have given ourselves to him

if we have then glory in the words & sing them

All that the Father giveth me shall come
to me. — —

<u>II</u>. The Negative. Eternal "will".

Notice here the speaker ... the Father has never
spoken thus in his absolute character — it were
an insult to go to him, when he has made
his Son the only medium of access.

Notice the character ___ not the few that cometh
not the King or rich that cometh — not the
good man that cometh — not the young or old
but "him that cometh" <u>whosoever</u>, it be,

Notice the no-wise — it is strong in the
original — it is — not — not — or never, never.
I will not cast them out when they come.

1. Not because of their great sins.
2. Not because of their long delays
3. Not because of their trying other saviours.
4. Not because of the hardness of their hearts,
5. Not because of their little faith.

unless we can see:

1. That he has given us the Holy Spirit.

2. That we have given ourselves to him.

If we have then glory in the words and sing them:

["]All that the Father giveth me shall come to me.["]

II. THE NEGATIVE, ETERNAL *"Will"*.

Notice here the speaker . . . The Father has never spoken thus in his absolute character. It were an insult to go to him when he has made his Son the only medium of access.[10]

Notice the character . . . Not the Jew that cometh. Not the king or rich that cometh. Not the good man that cometh. Not the young or old but "him that cometh." <u>Whosoever</u>[11] it be.

Notice the no-wise. It is strong in the original.[12] It is "not not," or "never never."

I will not cast them out when they come.

1. Not because of their great sins.

2. Not because of their long delays.

3. Not because of their trying other saviours.

4. Not because of the hardness of their hearts.

5. Not because of their little faith.

6. not because of their poor & dull prayers.
7. not because every-one else passes them by.
He will not cast them out when they are
    once in — in for ever —
1. not for their unbelief.
2. not for their old corruptions.
3. not for their backslidings.
Read, write, print, shout.
    I will in nowise cast out.

well what is to come —
    Men do not know what it is they fancy it is
to reform, to be immensely good &c &c.
but no it is — to trust — to believe.
    Believe & thou shalt be saved.
Great one, I thank thee for the text,
    Help thou me —

353. 356. 366. 379.

6. Not because of their poor and dull prayers.

7. Not because every-one else passes them by.

He will not cast them out when they are once in – in for ever –

1. Not for their unbelief.[13]

2. Not for their old corruptions.

3. Not for their backsliding.

Read. Write. Print. Shout.

I will in nowise cast out.

Well, what is to come?

Men do not know what it is they fancy. It is to reform, to be immensely good, etc. etc.[14]

But no. It is to trust, to believe.

Believe, and thou shalt be saved.[15]

Great one, I thank thee for the text.

Help thou me.

353. 356. 366. 379.

1. Charles preached on this passage six more times during his later ministry: "The Certainty and Freeness of Divine Grace" (*MTP* 10, Sermon 599–600); "High Doctrine and Broad Doctrine" (*MTP* 30, Sermon 1762); "All Comes to Christ Welcomed" (*MTP* 40, Sermon 2349); "The Big Gates Wide Open" (*MTP* 51, Sermon 2954); "No. 3000; Or, Come and Welcome" (*MTP* 52, Sermon 3000); and "The Last Message for the Year" (*MTP* 56, Sermon 3230). In addition, this sermon outline appears in *Autobiography* 1:225.

2. Cf. Luke 2:10–11.

3. "I do not think I differ from any of my Hyper-Calvinistic brethren in what I do believe, but I differ from them in what they do not believe. I do not hold any less than they do, but I hold a little more, and, I think, a little more of the truth revealed in the Scriptures. . . . That God predestines, and yet that man is responsible, are two facts that few can see clearly. They are believed to be inconsistent and contradictory; but they are not. The fault is in our weak judgment. Two truths cannot be contradictory to each other. If, then, I find taught in one part of the Bible that everything is fore-ordained, that is trite; and if I find, in another Scripture, that man is responsible for all his actions, that is true; and it is only my folly that leads me to imagine that these two truths can ever contradict each other. I do not believe they can ever be welded into one upon any earthly anvil, but they certainly shall be one in eternity. They are two lines that are so nearly parallel, that the human mind which pursues them farthest will never discover that they converge; but they do converge, and they will meet somewhere in eternity, close to the throne of God, whence all truth doth spring" (*Autobiography* 1:176).

4. "Propriety very greatly objects to the praise which is rendered by Primitive Methodists at times; their shouts and hallelujahs are thought by some delicate minds to be very shocking. I would not, however, join in the censure, lest I should be numbered among the Pharisees who said, 'Master, rebuke thy disciples.' I wish more people were as earnest and even as vehement as the Methodists used to be" (*MTP* 12:125).

5. Cf. Deut 18:15–19; Acts 7:37.

6. Cf. 2 Cor 2:14; Col 2:15.

7. Cf. 2 Tim 2:19; Rev 13:8.

8. Cf. John 13:3; 16:28; 17:25–26.

9. Cf. Heb 12:2.   10. Cf. 1 Tim 2:5; Heb 8:6; 9:15; 12:24.

11. Cf. John 3:15–16; 3:36.

12. "OY, an adv. . . . *not, no.* . . . With μη following the negation is made more intense, Ου μη, *In no wise, by no means*" (John Parkhurst, *A Greek and English Lexicon to the New Testament* [London: printed for William Baynes and Son, 1822, The Spurgeon Library], 400, italics in the original).

13. "When we see any of our friends falling into sin and unbelief, we must seek to deal wisely with them,—always kindly,—never harshly. Let us reserve all our severity for ourselves, as I have already urged upon you. Still, I am sure that it is quite possible for us to be doing our fellow-Christians serious harm by excusing their unbelief, and by pitying them for it, instead of pointing out to them, tenderly, yet faithfully, the great sin they are committing by this doubting" (*MTP* 50:314).

14. "The true Christian is not only to be seen in the singing of hymns and the offerings of prayers, but he is to be distinguished by the honesty and integrity, the courage and the faithfulness, of his ordinary character. In the streets and in the marketplaces, or wherever else the providence of God may call him, he witnesses the good confession. It is easy to secularize religion in a wrong sense" (*MTP* 22:229–30).

15. "What a multitude of religions there is in this poor wicked world of ours! Men have taken it into their heads to invent various systems of religion and if you look round the world, you will see scores of different sects; but it is a great fact that, while there is a multitude of false religions, there is but one that is true. While there are many falsehoods, there can be but one truth; real religion is, therefore, one. There is but one gospel--the gospel of our Lord Jesus Christ. What a wonderful thing it is that Jesus Christ, the Son of God, should be born of humble parents, and live as a poor man in this world, for the purpose of our salvation! He lived a life of suffering and trial, and at length, through the malignity of his enemies, was crucified on Calvary as an outcast of society" (*MTP* 61:73).

Job XIV . 1. 2. Shortness of Life.

No doubt we look forward with a hope of living
long, certainly the young have more reason to hope
for long life than the older ones have.

I. Job's first sentence blasts our hopes & say.
we are of few days — Some ve many babies die.
Bigger ones die. Young men die, & even old men
say it is but a span — Then ought we
not to prepare to die, not think of living here

II. again we look forward for happiness and
pleasure. but Job says they are full of trouble.
Wicked men have many trouble, good
men have some but grace comforts & cheers
them & then heaven is their home at last

III. Our youth promises much but Job says
it is like the frail flower. the flower of the
field, tender, soon mowed down, or it withers
it is gone, all gone.

IV. Our whole life he compares to a passing
shadow which is not, it only seems to be
& at last even the seeming is gone.

354.

213

CHILDREN'S SERMON. NUMBER 2.[1]

SHORTNESS *of* LIFE

Job 14:1–2

"Man that is born of a woman is of few days, and full of trouble. He cometh forth like a flower, and is cut down: he fleeth also as a shadow, and continueth not."

No doubt we look forward with a hope of living long. Certainly the young have more reason to hope for long life than the older ones have.

I.   Job's first sentence blasts our hopes and say[s] we are of few days. Some, yea many, babies die. Bigger ones die. Young men die. And even old men say it is but a span. Then ought we not to prepare to die, not think of living here?[2]

II.   Again we look forward for happiness and pleasure, but Job says they are full of trouble. Wicked men have many trouble[s]. Good men have some, but grace comforts and cheers them and then heaven is their home at last.

III. Our youth promises much, but Job says it is like the frail flower. The flower of the field, tender, soon mowed down, or it withers. It is gone, all gone.[3]

IV. Our whole life he compares to a passing shadow, which is not[;] it only seems to be. And at last, even the seeming is gone.

354.

1. Charles never again preached on this passage. This is the second sermon in this volume that Charles has written specifically for children. See "Sermon to Children" (Sermon 191).

2. "I cannot tell how much I owe to the solemn words of my good mother. It was the custom, on Sunday evenings, while we were yet little children, for her to stay at home with us, and then we sat round the table, and read verse by verse, and she explained the Scripture to us. After that was done, then came the time of pleading; there was a little piece of Alleine's *Alarm*, or of Baxter's *Call to the Unconverted*, and this was read with pointed observations made to each of us as we sat round the table; and the question was asked, how long it would be before we would think about our state, how long before we would seek the Lord" (*Autobiography* 1:68, italics in the original).

3. Ps 103:15–16; Isa 40:8; Jas 1:10.

214   II Cor XIII. 5. Examine yourselves.

The Corinthians demanded proof of Paul's apostleship
& were very nice in their examination of him.
after vindicating his own character he bids them
turn their attention within & make an examination
of their own souls.   This advice is equally
suitable now & to show my belief in it.

I. We shall explain the exhortation.

"Examine yourselves" — this we may interpret according
to our various occupations — — the schoolmaster
examines his pupils to see if they improve & catechise yourself
— the purchaser of horses, cattle, goods, furniture
will examine them — the engineer, or guard
will examine the carriages & train — the money-
-taker examines his money — the wife examines
her husbands linen, her household &c — — here
we are exhorted to examine ourselves.

"Prove your own-selves" — the buyer of oxen will
plough a furrow to prove them — the axe is
tried to see if it will cut — the metal is essayed
this is more trying work even than examination.

"Know ye not your own selves" If not ye have
neglected your most proper study — —

This passage implies that we ought to know
our own state — Paul knew his — doubts

EXAMINE YOURSELVES [1]
2 Corinthians 13:5

"Examine yourselves, whether ye be in the faith; prove your own selves. Know ye
not your own selves, how that Jesus Christ is in you, except ye be reprobates?"

The Corinthians demanded proof of Paul's apostleship and were very nice in their examination of him. After vindicating his own character, he bids them turn their attention within and make an examination of their own souls.

This advice is equally suitable now, and to show my belief in it [. . .]

I. WE SHALL EXPLAIN THE EXHORTATION.

"Examine yourselves." This we may interpret according to our various occupations. The schoolmaster examines his pupils to see if they improve. So, catechize yourselves. The purchaser of horses, cattle, goods, furniture will examine them.[2] The engineer, or guard, will examine the carraiges [*sic*] and train. The money-taker examines his money. The wife examines her husband[']s linen, her household, etc. Here we are exhorted to examine ourselves.

"Prove your own-selves." The buyer of oxen will plough a furrow to prove them. The axe is tried to see if it will cut. The metal is essayed.[3] This is more trying work even than examination.

"Know ye not your own selves." If not, ye have neglected your most proper study.[4] This passage implies that we ought to know our own state. Paul knew his. Doubts

oughts not to be extolled as grand evidences —
they are not very valuable ✠ signs. —
"Reprobates" has no connection with the doctrine
of reprobation — whether that be true or no. For
many of the elect are yet without Christ in
their hearts — — it is in opposition to genuine
means false, notional, hypocrites. If Christ
be in us we are true, if not false.
Christ in us as our hope, joy, end, master &c &c.

<u>II</u>. We shall show its reasonableness.

1. It is too important a matter to take on guess. —
we may take a penny without examination but not gold.
A £5 note we might not look at so much but we would
look very sharp at £1000 note — so this is Heaven & Salvation

2. Remember this is thy last chance, thy only shilling,
their will be no other place for rectifying mistakes.
       Examine your — selves before as you leave this box
of time as mistakes cannot afterwards be recognized.
This is a life & death matter! 'Tis kill or cure — therefore examine

3. The Deceitfulness of thy heart will incline thee to be
a partial judge — therefore examine well.

4. The Devil will cheat thee if he can — he does
not like thee to examine thyself — he says thou
art right when thou art wrong —

5. Multitudes have been ruined by taking it on
trust instead of testing & proving matters.
They have reaped a bitter disappointment through
their carelessness. —

ought not to be extolled as grand evidences. They are not very valuable designs.

"Reprobates." Has no connection with the doctrine of reprobation, whether that be true or no[t]. For any of the elect are yet without Christ in their hearts. It is in opposition to genuine means. False, notional, hypocrites.

If Christ be in us, we are true. If not false. Christ in us as our hope, joy, end, master[,] etc., etc.

II. WE SHALL SHOW ITS REASONABLENESS.

1. It is too important a matter to take on guess. We may take a penny without examination, but not gold. A £5 note we might not look at so much, but we would look very sharp at [a] £1000 note. So this is Heaven and Salvation.

2. Remember, this is thy last chance, thy only shilling. Their [*sic*] will be no other place for rectifying mistakes. Examine your-*selves* before as you leave this box of time, as mistakes cannot afterwards be recognized. This is a life and death matter! 'Tis kill or cure. Therefore, examine.

3. The Deceitfulness of thy heart will incline thee to be a partial judge. Therefore, examine well.

4. The Devil will cheat thee if he can. He does not like thee to examine thyself. He says thou art right when thou art wrong.[5]

5. Multitudes have been ruined by taking it on trust instead of testing and proving matters. They have reaped a bitter disappointment through their carelessness.

6. Examine yourselves for if wrong now is the time
to right thyself — if doubting this may clear thine
eyes — if it distress thee, It is better to be right
& fear than to be wrong & presume.

7. Examine thyself I say — for God will examine
thee & sift thee. He will not take thee at hear-say.

__III__. We would direct you how to do it, —

1 Look for Experimental Evidences —
Search & see if thou hast been convinced of sin.
Hast thou been born again — has a mighty-change come
o'er thee or art thou the same as ever thou
wert — can'st thou remember answers to prayer.
Emptyings of self & fillings with Jesus.
Dost thou ever enjoy his divine presence & smile?
Hast thou been upheld & comforted in trouble?

2. Look for External Practical Evidence
Dost thou frequent the house of prayer & love to do so?
Dost thou mingle with the saints & share their
persecutions? — Dost thou forgive thine enemies?
Dost thou live honestly, soberly, & righteously?
Dost thou long to live better than thou dost.

3. Look for Secret Practical Evidence.
Dost thou enter into thy closet & pray in secret?
Dost thou enjoy the Holy word of Truth.
What are thy thoughts? what thy secret
deeds — dost thou love the saints or no.

6. Examine yourselves, for if wrong, now is the time to right thyself. If doubting, this may clear thine eyes. If it distress[es] thee, it is better to be right and fear than to be wrong and presume.

7. Examine thyself, I say, for God will examine thee and sift thee.[6] He will not take thee at hear-say.

III. WE WOULD DIRECT YOU HOW TO DO IT.

1. Look for Experimental Evidences.[7]

   Search and see if thou hast been convinced of sin. Hast thou been born again[?] Has a mighty change come o'er thee, or art thou the same as ever thou wert? Can'st thou remember answers to prayer[?] Emptyings of self and fillings with Jesus[?] Dost thou ever enjoy his divine presence and smile? Hast thou been upheld and comforted in trouble?

2. Look for External, Practical Evidence.

   Dost thou frequent the house of prayer and love to do so? Dost thou mingle with the saints and share their persecutions? Dost thou forgive thine enemies? Dost thou live honestly, soberly, and righteously? Does thou long to live better than thou dost[?][8]

3. Look for Secret, Practical Evidence.

   Dost thou enter into thy closet and pray in secret? Dost thou enjoy the Holy Word of Truth? What are thy thoughts? What thy secret deeds? Dost thou love the saints, or no?

4. Above all try thyself by the ~~touch~~ touchstone
Is Jesus Christ in you?—

Dost thou venture wholly on him? Dost thou
esteem him exceedingly precious? Is he thy
advocate, confidante, lover, friend.
Oh if he is — then Heaven is thine.

Oh Father For Jesus Christ's sake send down
thy Spirit in more than usual abundance —
amen —
359. 363. 364. 406.

Dan, IV. 14.   Hew down the tree.   215

Though originally to be taken in connection with the rest
of the context, I here sever it from its connection in order
that I may make it the theme of a pointed & telling
sermon — for this I invoke thine aid O ever glorious Spirit.

In the fulfilment of this dream, these words were
spoken by the watcher at the moment when Nebuchad-
-nezzar boasted of Babylon which he had built — Oh my
friends I bid ye take heed lest your pride should
rise & destruction follow.   Sinner I would first

I. Inform thee who cries "Hew down the tree".
1. The Law & Justice of God are clamourous for
thy destruction, — thou hast no pardon — no justification
thou art the bondslave of law & he longeth for thee.
2. Death whose belly is greedy, wants to mow thee
down with his sharp sickle, he has touched
thy roots more than once & longs to cut thee down

4. Above all[,] try thyself by the ~~touch~~ touchstone[.][9]

Is Jesus Christ in you?

Dost thou venture wholly on him? Dost thou esteem him exceedingly precious? Is he thy advocate,[10] confidante, lover,[11] friend[?][12]

Ah[,] if he is then Heaven is thine.

Oh, Father. For Jesus Christ[']s sake, send down thy Spirit in more than usual abundance.   Amen.

359. 363. 364. 406.

HEW DOWN *the* TREE [1]
Daniel 4:14

"He cried aloud, and said thus, 'Hew down the tree, and cut off his branches; shake off his leaves, and scatter his fruit: let the beasts get away from under it, and the fowls from his branches."

Though originally <u>to</u> be taken in connection with the rest of the context, I here sever it from its connection in order that I may make it the theme of a pointed and telling sermon.[2] For this, I invoke thine aid, O ever glorious Spirit.

In the fulfillment of this dream, these words were spoken by the watcher at the moment when Nebuchadnezzar boasted of Babylon, which he had built.[3] Oh my friends, I bid ye take heed lest your pride should rise and destruction follow.[4] Sinner[,] I would first:

I.   INFORM THEE WHO CRIES, *"Hew down the tree."*

1. The Law and Justice of God are clamourous for thy destruction.[5] Thou hast no pardon, no justification.[6] Thou art the bondslave of law,[7] and he longeth for thee.

2. Death, whose belly is greedy, wants to mow thee down with his sharp sickle. He has touched thy roots more than once[8] and longs to cut thee down.

3, Satan – thy greatest foe next to thyself – doth wait anxiously for thee – that he may glut his eyes on thy eternal damnation.

4. Hell – & its inhabitants – think it long till thou comest, thy dead companions think thy time is too long & in bonds cry vengeance on thee.

5. But – God – holdeth the thread & by & by he will hear thine accusers & decree thy fall.

Surely thou dost wonder why thou art spared so long – I will try & tell thee

II. Tell why thou art not hewn down.

1. Because God maketh thee a monument of longsuffering – he gave the old world time & respite

2. Jesus hath begged a reprieve for thee. He whom thou despisest has saved thy life more than once — to him thou owest much.

3. You are spared that digging & dunging may be tried a little longer, if perhaps thou mayest repent & believe the Gospel.

4. Your pious friends, your parents, brethren – the church & minister have prayed for mercy. Thou art spared for their sakes.

III. I assure thee however thou wilt come down.

1. Hath not sickness prophesied this to thee, surely in thy life thou hast been near the borders of the grave

3. Satan, thy greatest foe next to thyself, doth wait anxiously for thee[9] that he may glut his eyes on thy eternal damnation.

4. Hell and its inhabitants think it long till thou comest. Thy dead companions think thy time is too long and, in bonds, cry vengeance on thee.[10]

5. But God holdeth the thread, and by and by, he will hear thine accusers and decree thy fall.[11] Surely thou dost wonder why thou art spared so long. I will try and tell thee.

II. TELL WHY THOU ART NOT HEWN DOWN.

1. Because God maketh thee a monument of longsuffering. He gave the old world time and respite.[12]

2. Jesus hath begged a reprieve for thee.[13] He whom thou despises has saved thy life more than once. To him thou owest much.

3. You are spared that digging and dunging may be tried a little longer[14] if perhaps thou mayest repent and believe the Gospel.

4. Your pious friends, your parents, brethren, the church, and ministers have prayed for mercy. Thou art spared for their sakes.[15]

III. I ASSURE THEE, HOWEVER, THOU WILT COME DOWN.

1. Hath not sickness prophesied this to thee? Surely in thy life thou hast been near the borders of the grave.

2. Have ye not seen others die & are ye immortal
young & old are borne to their long home — & will
you persuade your silly self that you must die.
3. Some of you in your persons give signs of
decay — gray hairs &c — many have their deaths
disease for many a year before they die & may
not you have something deadly in your breast.
But anyhow thou wilt acknowledge thou must die

<u>II</u>. I will give thee reasons why thou
          deservest to be hewn down at once.
1. Thou hast no fruit — thou never hast had
any — save a few figs & apples of Sodom. which
are worse than none. Thou art old enough
to bear — thou art in a good situation,
2. Thou takest up the room of a better than
thyself — another might use thy money better
he would not drink it away — Another's house
would have prayer in it. Another's time would
be improved — but thou art useless,
3. Thou cumberest the ground & keepest others
from fruitfulness — the saints are hindered
by thee & many are enticed by thy company
to sin — It were good for society that thou wouldest go —
4. The pruning knife of affliction hath
been at work upon thee but alas in vain —
thou hast revolted more, though thou didst
promise to mend thy ways.

2. Have ye not seen others die, and are ye immortal? Young and old are borne to their long home, and will you persuade your silly self that you must die?

3. Some of you in your persons give signs of decay. Gray hairs etc. Many have their death[']s disease for many a year before they die. And may not you have something deadly in your breast?

But anyhow, thou wilt acknowledge thou must die.

IV. I WILL GIVE THEE REASONS WHY THOU DESERVEST TO BE HEWN DOWN AT ONCE.

1. Thou hast no fruit.[16] Thou never hast had any, save a few figs and apples of Sodom,[17] which are worse than none. Thou art old enough to bear.[18] Thou art in a good situation.

2. Thou takest up the room of a better than thyself.[19] Another might use thy money better. He would not drink it away. Another's house would have prayer in it. Another's time would be improved. But thou art useless.

3. Thou cumberest the ground and keepest others from fruitfulness. The saints are hindered by thee and many are enticed by thy company to sin. It were good for society that thou wouldest go.

4. The pruning knife of affliction hath been at work upon thee, but alas, in vain.[20] Thou hast revolted more, though thou didst promise to mend thy ways.

5. Digging & Dunging have failed on thee.
Thou hast had waggon loads of sermons.
Years of digging — privileges, opportunities
but all in vain — why spare thee then.

V. I would solemnly address —

1. You that are getting old — why you are
falling now — the axe has cut almost through.

2. You that have been hearers of long
standing — perhaps — God has given you
up — since nothing affects you.

3. Perhaps the last year is come, ye
are marked for the axe. —

4. Backsliders how the axe doth long
to be at you — for ye are the worst of cumber-
—grounds — —

Lord help me to dig & manure a little
by telling them of the way to escape
from hell & fly to heaven.

360. 564

Cottenham young man brought out 360

5. Digging and Dunging have failed on thee.[21] Thou hast had wagon loads of sermons. Years of digging, privileges, opportunities. But all in vain. Why spare thee then?

V. I WOULD SOLEMNLY ADDRESS:

1. You that are getting old. Why you are falling now[.] The axe has cut almost through.[22]

2. You that have been hearers of long standing, perhaps God has given you up since nothing affects you.[23]

3. Perhaps the last year is come. Ye are marked for the axe.

4. Backsliders, how the axe doth long to be at you, for ye are the worst of cumber[24]—grounds[.]

Lord, help me to dig and manure[25] a little by telling them of the way to escape from hell and fly to heaven.

360. 564.

Cottenham. Young man brought out. 360[26]

1. Charles preached on this text on two other occasions: "Self-Examination" and "The Proof of Our Ministry" (*MTP* 30, Sermon 1788). "Self-Examination" was likely based on this sermon.

2. "HOW TO BUY A HORSE. In order to make a thorough examination, it becomes necessary to consider the height and condition of the horse, not only in the stable, but also when led out of the stall, and outside the stable; in a state of repose, and in motion." This article goes on to detail further ways to examine and determine a horse worthy of purchase. ("How to Buy a Horse," *Southern Reporter and Cork Daily Commercial Courier*, July 27, 1863, capitalization in the original).

3. "3. To try the value and purity of metals" (Johnson's *Dictionary*, s.v. "to essay").

4. "Muse, I pray you, unregenerate man, *upon your present state*. 'Dead in trespasses and sins,' as you now are, the wrath of God abideth on you. Heirs of wrath even as others, afar off, without God, without hope, and without Christ in the world, I pray you bethink you of the hole of the pit where you now are, and out of which you have never yet been digged. Perhaps I have thought more about your soul than you have ever thought about it in your life; I pray you now let your own thoughtfulness begin to exercise itself; examine yourself; see what your state is" (*MTP* 10:362, italics in the original).

5. "When the devil says to me, 'You are no saint,' I say to him, 'Nor are you, either.' 'Ah!' says he, 'You are a deceiver,' and I reply, 'And so are you.' 'Ah!" says he, 'but you are mistaken, your experience has been a delusion, you are no child of God.' 'What am I, then? Tell me, if you know so much about me.' 'You are a Sinner,' says he. 'All right, Satan! I thank you for that word, for Jesus Christ came into the world to save sinners.' So I begin again; and if you begin again like that, you will very often find that this is a short cut to comfort. If it comes to a question between the devil and you whether you are a saint or not, you will have a hard battle to fight, let me tell you" (*MTP* 39:633–34).

6. Jer 17:10; Acts 15:8; Rom 8:27.

7. "We have direct experimental evidence of God's ever-watchful care over his Church. He does not deal with his people only through instruments, but he

himself takes the Church in his own hands. This is his own declaration, 'I the Lord do keep it; I will water it every moment: lest any hurt it, I will keep it night and day.' Thus doth he speak of his vineyard" (*MTP* 54:169).

8. "How many, who frequent the house of prayer, worship God carelessly? They sing, but with no more heart than if they were singing in their own houses some common ditty. The prayer is offered, and often that is the dullest part of the service, and their eyes are gazing about here and there; or if the eyes of the head be shut, the eyes of their heart are open enough, looking not, however, to God, but to vanity. And when the sermon is delivered they care but little for its precious message, or if they lend some attention, yet what a weariness it is! You see in some congregations nodding heads, and eyes that are given to slumber. They think there is nothing particular in hearing the gospel; they listen to the entreaty of God's ambassador as to a thrice told tale, but that is all" (*MTP* 8:135).

9. "1. Stone by which metals are examined. 2. Any test or criterion" (Johnson's *Dictionary*, s.v. "touchstone").

10. Cf. 1 John 2:1–2.   11. Cf. Eph 5:25.

12. Cf. John 15:12–17.

1. Charles never again preached on this passage.

2. "A great deal of real good may be done by occasionally taking forgotten, quaint, remarkable, out-of-the-way texts; and I feel persuaded that if we appeal to a jury of practical, successful preachers, who are not theorizers but men actually in the field, we shall have a majority in our favour" (*Lectures*, vol. 1:102–3).

3. Cf. Dan 4:29–31.   4. Cf. Prov 16:18.

5. Cf. Ps 37:38; Prov 11:21; Isa 13:11; 26:21; Rom 2:12.

6. Cf. Gal 2:16.   7. Cf. John 8:34; Rom 6:20; Gal 4:7.

8. Cf. Matt 3:10.   9. Cf. 1 Pet 5:8.

10. "There is no sleep in hell. Oh, what a blessing sleep would be if it could enter the habitation of the damned! Alas! If any of you should lift up your eyes there, what a sight you will behold! Here, if you drop off to sleep, and wake up in the Tabernacle, you see the faces of attentive listeners hearing words of mercy; there, when first you lift up your eyes, you will gaze into visages more marred with pain than any you have ever seen before; and if you ask them the cause of their awful grief, and why agony, as with a red-hot ploughshare, has made such deep furrows in their cheeks, they will tell you that you need not ask them, for you will soon learn the reason yourself" (*MTP* 53:633).

11. "O sinner! consider the fearful danger you are in: it is a great furnace of wrath, a wide and bottomless pit, full of the fire of wrath, that you are held over in the hand of that God, whose wrath is provoked and incensed as much against you, as against many of the damned in hell. *You hang by a slender thread, with the flames of divine wrath flashing about it, and ready every moment to singe it, and burn it asunder;* and you have no interest in any Mediator, and nothing to lay hold of to save yourself, nothing to keep off the flames of wrath, nothing of your own, nothing that you ever have done, nothing that you can do, to induce God to spare you one moment" (Jonathan Edwards, *The Works of Jonathan Edwards, A.M.*, ed. Edward Hickman [London: Ball, Arnold, and Co., 1840, The Spurgeon Library], 10, emphasis added).

12. Cf. Gen 6:3.

13. See "Jesus Interceding for Transgressors" (*MTP* 23, Sermon 1385).

14. Cf. Luke 13:6–9.   15. Cf. Matt 5:44–45.

16. Cf. Matt 7:16.   17. Cf. Deut 32:32; 1 Cor 6:9–11; Gal 5:21; Rev 21:8.

18. See "Infant Salvation" (*MTP* 7, Sermon 411).

19. Cf. Rom 11:11–24.

20. "At any rate, so far as personal sorrows are concerned, it would be a very sharp and trying experience to me to think that I have an affliction which God never sent me, that the bitter cup was never filled by his hand, that my briars were never measured out by him, nor sent to me by his arrangement of their weight and quality. Oh, that were bitterness indeed! But, on the contrary, the prophet here [Mic 7:9] sees the hand of God in all his trials, and I pray that you and I may do the same. May we see that our heavenly Father fills the cup with loving tenderness, and holds it out, and says, 'Drink, my child; bitter as it is, it is a love-potion which is meant to do thee permanent good.' The discerning of the hand of God is a sweet lesson in the school of experience" (*MTP* 57:99-100).

21. Cf. Luke 13:6–9.   22. Cf. Matt 3:10.

23. Cf. Rev 3:15–16.

24. "Vexation; burdensomeness; embarrassment; obstruction; hindrance; disturbance; distress" (Johnson's *Dictionary*, s.v. "cumber").

25. Cf. Luke 13:6–9.

26. Charles may be indicating here that a young man was converted when Charles preached at Cottenham on his 360th preaching occasion, likely in early 1853.

Eccles. III. 1. Time for every purpose. 216

This sermon is intended for my young compeers
in age. May Solomon's words lead us to make
Solomon's choice. — In looking on to the
future it is as well — to lay out our work. —
As the man who has so much to do will look
at the work & the time. — —

I. As God has given us time for every —
— thing he has given time for religion.

1 Men find time — for all necessary actions.
such as eating — who will starve because he has
not time to eat:
   dressing — we do not go without coats or gowns.
   sleeping — we never say I have no time — except it
be in most extreme emergency.
   business — man toils at all day long —
"recreation" too comes in for its share of time.
   sympathy; in joy or sorrow we have time for.
   for seeking cure or relief of pain we find time. —
times to talk, plant, pull up, build, dance, love, &
   why sure then there is time for religion.

2. Take all ages at which men die — they
have time enough — the babe needs none but
is safe — the accountable child has much
time to think — the young man is often
a Christian & middle aged men are in our
ranks. Old men have no pretence here.

TIME *for* EVERY PURPOSE [1]
Ecclesiastes 3:1

"To every thing there is a season, and a time to every purpose under the heaven[.]"

This sermon is intended for my young compeers in age.[2] May Solomon's words lead us to make Solomon's choice.[3] In looking on to the future, it is as well to lay out our work.[4] As the man who has so much to do will look at the work and the time.

I. AS GOD HAS GIVEN US TIME FOR EVERYTHING HE HAS GIVEN TIME FOR RELIGION.

1. Men find time for all necessary actions:

   Such as eating.[5] Who will starve because he has not time to eat?

   Dressing. We do not go without coats or gowns.[6]

   Sleeping. We never say, I have no time, except it be in most extreme emergency.

   Business. Man toils at [it] all day long.[7]

   "Recreation," too, comes in for its share of time.

   Sympathy. In joy or sorrow, we have time for.

   For seeking cure or relief of pain, we find time.

   Times to talk, plant, pull up, build, dance, love. And why, sure then, there is time for religion.[8]

2. Take all ages at which men die.[9] They have time enough. The babe needs none, but is safe. The accountable child has much time to think. The young man is often a Christian, and middle aged men are in our ranks. Old men have no pretence here.[10]

3. Men of all ranks & occupations have found time. artizans, clerks, politicians.

4. Besides religion will not put us off from other pursuits — If a man can work & sing a song — he can work & pray — If he can swear & drive his horse — he could sing praises & see to the team too ~

II Why cannot men find time for religion.

The only answer is because they do not love it. One finds time to hunt & another wonders but he need not it is because one loves it. So all men find time, if their hearts are set on it — where there is a will there's a way.

III. Where is the time gone to you cannot find. Perhaps part of it is spent in gossip. perhaps you spend some of it in the tavern perhaps you are lazy — perhaps you spend it in day-dreams — But anyhow you have had it & are accountable.

IV What time seems naturally meant for religious purposes.

There are hours & seasons — which are they. 1. The Sabbath which can never be too sacredly regarded — it is to our

3. Men of all ranks and occupations have found time: artizans [*sic*], clerks, politicians.

4. Besides, religion will not put us off from other pursuits. If a man can work and sing a song, he can work and pray. If he can swear and drive his horse, he could sing praises and see to the team, too.[11]

II. WHY CANNOT MEN FIND TIME FOR RELIGION[?]

The only answer is because they do not love it. One finds time to hunt, and another wonders. But he need not. It is because one loves it. So all men find time if their hearts are set on it. Where there is a will there's a way.

III. WHERE IS THE TIME GONE TO YOU CANNOT FIND[?]

Perhaps part of it is spent in gossip. Perhaps you spend some of it in the tavern. Perhaps you are lazy. Perhaps you spend it in day-dreams. But anyhow, you have had it and are accountable.

IV. WHAT TIME SEEMS NATURALLY MEANT FOR RELIGIOUS PURPOSES[?]

There are hours and seasons, which are they:

1. The Sabbath, which can never be too sacredly regarded.[12] It is to our

advantage to rest on the Sabbath, it oils the
wheels of business.

2. Early morning, as soon as we wake —
seems naturally the hour of praise & prayer.
Ere thou goest to the world have a word or
two with God.

3. Eventide, with its shades calls for a
vesper song & prayer. —

4. Youth seems as the morning of life
so fitted for holy resolve, serious deliberation,
virgin consecration, unprejudiced judgment
may it be ours to employ our young
hours in sacred labour & divine employ
& shall our gray head if spared wear
crowns of glory.

Help me. Help thKing —

361

Eph. I. 8. The prudence of God   217

This is about the only place in the Scriptures, where
prudence is ascribed to God. It is a very
useful attribute of a wise man & we shall
see that is is also an attribute of God.

When a man is involved in difficulties
& yet steers clear of all we say he is prudent.
When a man insures his life or in other ways
provides for future necessities we say he is

advantage to rest on the Sabbath[;] it oils the wheels of business.

2. Early morning, as soon as we wake. Seems naturally the hour of praise and prayer.[13] Ere thou goest to the world, have a word or two with God.

3. Eventide, with its shades, calls for a vesper song and prayer.

4. Youth seems as the morning of life. So filled for holy resolve, serious deliberation, virgin consecration, unprejudiced judgment.

    May it be ours to employ our young hours in sacred labour and divine employ.

    So shall our gray head[s] if spared wear crowns of glory.[14]

Help me. Help, Oh King.

361

THE PRUDENCE *of* GOD [1]
Ephesians 1:8

"Wherein he hath abounded toward us in all wisdom and prudence[.]"

This is about the only place in the Scriptures where prudence is ascribed to God. It is a very useful attribute of a wise man, and we shall see that it is also an attribute of God.[2]

When a man is involved in difficulties and yet steers clear of all, we say he is prudent.[3] When a man insures his life or in other ways provides for future necessities[,] we say he is prudent. When a man refuses to undertake what is beyond his power he is prudent. But God is never in difficulties, has no future to provide for, nothing is beyond him — so that in none of these can he exercise prudence.

I. Let us look in Scripture for instances of prudence.

1. His provision for his people during the great famine. It was the most fit way to do it. If he had given them extra crops they might have sold them — or if prophecy had warned them of the famine the nations would have robbed them of the precious store. Joseph is not killed but sold — not sold to Ethiops but Egyptians — by them not to any save Potiphar — a prison forms an appropriate portal to a palace & thus it is done.

2. The Israelites were a people used to a Bedouin life but Egypt taught them the arts, & sciences of settled life. At the same time as a mass they were mere slaves incapable of being formed into a nation. Forty years of the wilderness schooled them — they might have gone in a few days but here was prudence.

3. When Canaan was to be conquered, it was not done in a day or two — nor in a year — the wild beasts would have been too numerous — the air tainted with corpses.

prudent. When a man refuses to undertake what is beyond his power, he is prudent.[4] But God is never in difficulties, has no future to provide for, nothing is beyond him, so that in none of these can he exercise prudence.

I. LET US LOOK IN SCRIPTURE FOR INSTANCES OF PRUDENCE.

1. His provision for his people during the great famine.[5] It was the most fit way to do it. If he had given them extra crops, they might have sold them. Or if prophecy had warned them of the famine, the nations would have robbed them of the precious store. Joseph is not killed, but sold. Not sold to Ethiops, but Egyptians.[6] By them, not to any save Potiphar.[7] A prison forms an appropriate portal to a palace,[8] and thus it is done.

2. The Israelites were a people used to a Bedouin life, but Egypt taught them the arts and sciences of settled life. At the same time, as a mass they were mere slaves, incapable of being formed into a nation. Forty years of the wilderness schooled them.[9] They might have gone in a few days, but here was prudence.

3. When Canaan was to be conquered, it was not done in a day or two.[10] Nor in a year. The wild beasts would have been too numerous.[11] The air tainted with corpses.

4... But let us be content with these in the Old & let us look in the New Testament.

He laid the whole world under the Roman yoke & by making it one empire he opened doors for the gospel in every country.

5. He sent his gospel by poor fishermen that the excellency of his power might be seen. Peter was by his fall made more fit to be an earthen vessel — receiving no honour to himself. Paul too, born out of due time; the chief of sinners was the very person to be the chief in-strument of enlightening the nations.

6. For a short time the ear of the masses was gained by miracles — now these cease & rightly lest the world should say we practised juggling tricks & magic.

7. The Scriptures themselves are monuments of the prudence of God. For the Hebrew & Greek becoming dead have remained un-altered & so truth has been sealed up. English, French &c would have so much altered in the time as to be unintelligible. The Kings printers prevent any other than the authorized version from being printed, thus preventing bad translations.

Herein is prudence. —

4. But let us be content with these in the Old, and let us look in the New Testament. He laid the whole world under the Roman yoke, and by making it one empire he opened doors for the gospel in every country.

5. He sent his gospel by poor fishermen that the excellency of his power might be seen.[12] Peter was, by his fall, made more fit to be an <u>earthen</u> vessel,[13] receiving no honour to himself. Paul, too, born out of due time,[14] the chief of sinners,[15] was the very person to be the chief instrument of enlightening the nations.[16]

6. For a short time, the ear of the masses was gained by miracles.[17] Now these cease, and rightly, lest the world should say we practiced juggling tricks and magic.[18]

7. The Scriptures themselves are monuments of the prudence of God. For the Hebrew and Greek, becoming dead have remained unaltered. And so truth has been sealed up.[19] English, French, etc. would have so much altered in the time as to be unintelligible. The King[']s printers prevent any other than the authorized version from being printed, thus preventing bad translations.

Herein is prudence.

<u>II</u>   Let us look in the economy of grace.
1. In Election — as to persons choosing the base things of this earth — as to reasons not for our works or merits foreseen & all this to the praise of grace —   here is prudence
2. In Redemption — saving us not in an unjust way   but satisfying justice — finding a ransom, providing a complete righteousness — not allowing us to subscribe a farthing.
3. In our temporal estate — making us subject to trouble & sickness, shewing us thus our dependance, weaning us from earth, making us long more for heaven —
4. In our Spiritual estate — was not our conversion just in time — our hourly dependance on his grace is prudent — the temptations of Satan — the length of our pilgrimage — {our coldness & our trouble {so far as from constitution} is all prudent — if it were otherwise many dangers would attend us.

Christian trust his care — admire his love — imitate his prudence —

Help. My Lord. I crave. —

367.

II. LET US LOOK IN THE ECONOMY OF GRACE.

1. In Election. As to persons choosing the base things of this earth,[20] as to reasons not for our works, or merits foreseen. And all this to the praise of grace.[21] Here is prudence.

2. In Redemption. Saving us not in an unjust way, but satisfying justice,[22] finding a ransom,[23] providing a complete righteousness,[24] not allowing us to subscribe a farthing.[25]

3. In our temporal estate. Making us subject to trouble and sickness, shewing us thus our dependence, weaning us from earth, making us long more for heaven.[26]

4. In our spiritual estate. Was not our conversion just in time? Our hourly dependence on his grace is prudent. The temptations of Satan,[27] the length of our pilgrimage,[28] {our coldness, so far as from constitution},[29] our trouble, is all prudent. If it were otherwise, many dangers would attend us.

Christian, trust his care, admire his love, imitate his prudence.

Help, My Lord, I crave.

367.

1. Charles never preached again on this passage.

2. Charles was eighteen when he preached this sermon.

3. Cf. 1 Kgs 3:9.

4. Cf. Prov 12:24; 16:3; Eccl 9:10; Col 3:17; 2 Thess 3:10–12.

5. Cf. Prov 26:15.   6. Cf. Matt 6:31–33.

7. For a description of the challenging working conditions in Victorian England, see Sally Mitchell, *Daily Life in Victorian England* (Westport, CT: Greenwood Press, 1996], 41–42.

8. Cf. Eccl 3:1–8.

9. The average Victorian in 1850 could only expect to live about forty years (Patricia Jalland, *Death in the Victorian Family* [New York: Oxford University, 1996], 143).

10. "Who is too old to trust Christ? Who is too old to seek and find the Saviour? . . . I do thank God that, even in this building, I could point out a great many who I know were baptized after their hair had grown grey. . . . However old you are, friend, come along. If Methuselah were here, I would preach to him the same gospel that I would teach to one of these dear girls; for, however old a sinner is, there is nothing in the gospel about limiting it to persons of a certain age" (*MTP* 42:297).

11. Cf. Eph 5:19; 1 Thess 5:17.

12. "[The Sabbath] is, first, a *perfect* rest. They are wholly at rest in heaven. Here rest is but partial. . . . Here, on Sabbath days a vast multitude of you sit in God's house, but many of you are obliged to stand, and rest but little except in your mind; and even when the mind is at rest the body is wearied with the toil of standing. You have a weary mile, perhaps, many miles, to go to your homes on the Sabbath day. And let the Sabbatarian say what he will, you may work on the Sabbath day, if you work for God; and this Sabbath day's work of going to the house of God is work for God, and God accepts it. For yourselves you may not labor, God commands you to rest, but if you have to toil these three, these four, these five, these six miles,

as many of you have done, I will not and I must not blame you. 'The priests in the sanctuary profane the Sabbath, and are blameless.' It is toil and labor, it is true, but it is for a good cause—for your Master" (*NPSP* 3:214).

13. "We cannot praise God too soon. Our very first breath [upon waking] is a gift from God, and it should be spent to the Creator's praise. The early morning hour should be dedicated to praise: do not the birds set us the example?" (*MTP* 32:293).

14. Cf. Prov 16:31.

1. Charles never again preached on this passage.

2. "Wisdom is a perfection in God, and is in him in its utmost perfection; it is consummate and infinite wisdom he is possessed of. No one that believes the being of a God, can admit the least doubt of it. An unwise Being cannot be God" (John Gill, *Gill's Complete Body of Practical and Doctrinal Divinity: Being a System of Evangelical Truths, Deduced from the Sacred Scriptures. Abridged by William Staughton, D.D.* [Philadelphia: printed for Delaplaine and Hellings, by B. Graves, 1810, The Spurgeon Library], 1: 120).

3. Cf. Prov 22:3; 27:12.

4. "A man must be prudent in such a world as this. He will soon cut his feet if he do[es] not pick his steps. He will soon tear his garments with thorns and briars if he do[es] not choose his way. This is a land full of enemies; we must be wise, or the arrow will suddenly find out a vulnerable place in our armor. We must be cautious, for we are not travelling in noon-day on the king's highway, but rather at night-fall, and we may, therefore, be attacked by robbers, and may lose our precious treasures. He who is in a wilderness, and in a wilderness infested with robber bands, must handle matters wisely if he would find good" (*MTP* 7:354).

5. Cf. Gen 45:16–28.   6. Cf. Gen 37:25–28.

7. Cf. Gen 37:36; 39:1.

8. Cf. Gen 39:20. "Like a cork, which you may push down, but it is sure to come up again, so was Joseph: he must swim, he could not drown, the Lord was with him. The Lord's presence made him a king and a priest wherever he went, and men tacitly owned his influence. In the little kingdom of the prison Joseph reigned, for 'God was with him.' He will rise higher than that, however, when opportunity arises for a display of *prophetic power*" (*MTP* 27:417, italics in the original).

9. Cf. Num 32:13.   10. Cf. Deut 7:22. See also Sermon 208.

11. Cf. Exod 23:29.   12. Cf. 2 Cor 4:7.

13. Cf. Luke 22:54–62.   14. Cf. 1 Cor 15:8.

15. Cf. 1 Tim 1:15.   16. Cf. Eph 3:1–7.

17. Cf. Acts 2:1–4:4.

18. "The age of miracles passed off, it was well it should. Miracles are but the cradle in which the man-child, the Church, must be rocked. When the Church becomes strong enough to stand alone, she leaves her swaddling bands behind her; but the name of Jesus hath not less power to-day because no risen dead, no opened eyes follow our train. At this hour, dead *souls* hear the voice of God and live. At this moment, spiritual eyesight is restored; hearts that were stone are turned to flesh, and tongues that were ready enough at cursing begin to sing" (*MTP* 9:707–8, italics in the original).

19. "[Spurgeon] urged the brethren to be diligent students, to read all books that would help them to understand the Scriptures; but, above all, to study the Word itself, in the original languages if possible, and to saturate themselves with what he termed Bibline, the very essence of *The Book*" (*Autobiography* 1:267, italics in the original).

20. Cf. 1 Cor 1:27–28.   21. Cf. Eph 1:6.

22. Cf. Rom 3:27.   23. Cf. 1 Tim 2:6.

24. "True justification by faith is the surface soil, but then imputed righteousness is the granite rock which lies underneath it; and if you dig down through the great truth of a sinner's being justified by faith in Christ, you must, as I believe, inevitably come to the doctrine of the imputed righteousness of Christ as the basis and foundation on which that simple doctrine rests" (*MTP* 7:381). Cf. Rom 3:21–22.

25. "1. The fourth of a penny; the smallest English coin. 2. Copper money. 3. It is used sometimes in a sense hyperbolical: as, it is not worth a *farthing*; or proverbial" (Johnson's *Dictionary*, s.v. "farthing," italics in the original). "When Christ redeemed his people, he did it thoroughly, he did not leave a single doit unpaid, nor yet one farthing for them to settle afterwards. God demanded of Christ the payment for the sins of all his people; Christ stood forward, and to the utmost

farthing paid whate'er his people owed. The sacrifice of Calvary was not a part payment; it was not a partial exoneration, it was a complete and perfect payment, and it obtained a complete and perfect remittal of all the debts of all believers that have lived, do live, or shall live, to the very end of time" (*NPSP* 3:154).

26. "Wait a little longer. Ah, beloved! How despicable our troubles and trials will seem when we look back upon them! Looking at them here in the prospect, they seem immense; but when we get to heaven, they will seem to us just nothing at all. . . . Let us go on, therefore; and if the night be ever so dark, remember there is not a night that shall not have a morning; and that morning is to come by-and-by" (*MTP* 44:104).

27. Cf. 1 Pet 5:8.   28. Cf. 1 Pet 2:11–12.

29. "*Coldness of heart towards God* is another cause of the loss of enjoyment of his favour. When the heart grows spiritually cold, the whole being soon gets out of order. If the heart be warm and vigorous, the pulsations throughout the entire frame will be kept strong and healthy; but when the heart is cold, the blood will be chilled in the veins, and all the powers will be benumbed and paralyzed" (*MTP* 57:138–39, italics in the original).

Mark. XV. 33. 34. (Death Scenes of Christ Jesus. 218

The more closely we examine Scripture the more we see in it — So it is with that portion which tells of the love of dying Jesus. A hasty reader sees little but let us bend devoutly over the words.

I. What means the darkness.

Is it night? No. It is mid-day — noon — twelve Is the Sun eclipsed? No for 'tis full moon when eclipses never come — besides did an eclipse ever last so long as three hours? What then is doing? Yonder cross gives an answer Jesus the man, the God, is expiring —

1. This darkness was a sort of revelation of the inner darkness & horror Jesus was just enduring.

2. It was an increase of his pains, sent by his Father — for our sins.

3. It was a sign of nature's sympathy with him.

4. It the funeral of the Jewish nation or rather the black seal of their death-warrant

5. It was the fulfilment of prophecy — Amos. 8. 9. Note now the conduct of Jesus —

1. Just before the darkness he spoke to the dying thief — learn hence to work while it is day.

2. In the whole 3 hours he said nothing he was dumb — he complained not, but endured the cross, despising the shame.

DEATH SCENES *of* CHRIST JESUS [1]

Mark 15:33–34

"And when the sixth hour was come, there was darkness over the whole land until the ninth hour. And at the ninth hour Jesus cried with a loud voice, saying, Eloi, Eloi, lama sabachthani? which is, being interpreted, My God, my God, why hast thou forsaken me?"

The more closely we examine Scripture, the more we see in it. So it is with that portion which tells of the love of dying Jesus. A hasty reader sees little, but let us bend devoutly over the words.

I. WHAT MEANS THE DARKNESS[?]

Is it night? No. It is mid-day. Noon. Twelve. Is the sun eclipsed? No, for 'tis full moon when eclipses never come. Besides, did an eclipse ever last so long as three hours? What then is [it] doing? Yonder cross gives an answer.

Jesus the man, the God, is expiring.

1. This darkness was a sort of revelation of the inner darkness and horror Jesus was just enduring.

2. It was an increase of his pains sent by his Father for our sins.

3. It was a sign of nature's sympathy with him.[2]

4. It [was] the funeral of the Jewish nation, or rather the black seal of their death-warrant.[3]

5. It was the fulfillment of prophecy. Amos.8.9.[4]

Note now the conduct of Jesus:

1. Just before the darkness he spoke to the dying thief.[5] Learn hence to work while it is day.[6]

2. In the whole 3 hours he said nothing. He was [mute]. He complained not,[7] but endured the cross, despising the shame.[8]

<u>II</u>. Why speaks he at the ninth hour?
About 3 o'clock, in the afternoon. —
1. To show us that we are not always to keep silence but may tell our Lord our griefs. —
2. That was the time of the evening offering when the daily lamb was to be slaughtered. Jesus thus identified himself with the evening oblation.

<u>III</u>. Why cries he so loud? —
1. That unbelievers might look on him as the Messiah — might think on Psalm <u>XXII</u> & be led to see the striking fitness of those words to his case.
2. To show his earnestness — he felt com—pelled to cry for he panted after the light of God's countenance.
3. To show that he was strong as ever, his voice yet most powerful & thus to manifest his power to keep his life or not.

<u>IV</u> Why such a cry? —
1. Here note that it is scriptural — he used a quotation let us do so too —
2. Mark his confidence in God. <u>My God</u> <u>My God</u> — this showed his strong faith.

II. WHY SPEAKS HE AT THE <u>NINTH</u> HOUR?[9]

About 3 o'clock in the afternoon.[10]

1. To show us that we are not always to keep silence, but may tell our Lord our griefs.

2. That was the time of the evening offering when the daily lamb was to be slaughtered. Jesus thus identified himself with the evening oblation.

III. WHY CRIES HE SO LOUD?[11]

1. That unbelievers might look on him as the Messiah. Might think on Psalm XXII[12] and be led to see the striking fitness of those words to his case.

2. To show his earnestness. He felt compelled to cry, for he panted after the light of God's countenance.[13]

3. To show that he was strong as ever. His voice yet most powerful, and thus to manifest his power to keep his life or not.[14]

IV. WHY SUCH A CRY?

1. Here note that it is Scriptural. He used a quotation. Let us do so, too.

2. Mark his confidence in God. "<u>My God[,] My God</u>."[15] This showed his strong faith,

his unmoved love & affiance. As man God
was God over Jesus — he became a servant.

3. Mark his enquiry — why forsaken me?
Well might he ask it — he was much loved,
had no sin, was about his father's business.
He did not suppose his Father was for ever
gone — it was a temporary absence he mourned
— never had he been thus deserted before.
Now was the climax of suffering — Satan
was most fierce, pain greatest, friends fewest.

His spotless purity — his frequent fellowship with
God, his intense love to him all made this
desertion a thousand-fold more painful.
Saints suffer this but never when in such a
plight — & never do they pant so after quick
deliverance as Jesus did. —

This was necessary as part of our purchase
money, & that he might be like his brethren

1. Brother, love Jesus more.
2. Why so easy amid hidings of his face.
3. Sinner what will hell be to thee
    where God's face doth frown fearfully.

368

his unmoved love and affiance.[16] As man, God was God over Jesus. He became a servant.[17]

3. Mark his enquiry. "Why forsaken me?" Well might he ask it. He was much loved, had no sin,[18] was about his father's business.[19]

He did not suppose his Father was for ever gone. It was a temporary absence he mourned. Never had he been thus deserted before. Now was the climax of suffering. Satan was most fierce, pain greatest, friends fewest.[20]

His spotless purity,[21] his frequent fellowship with God,[22] his intense love [for] him, all made this desertion a thousand-fold more painful.

Saints suffer this, but never when in such a plight, and never do they pant so after quick deliverance as Jesus did.

This was necessary as part of our purchase money,[23] and that he might be like his brethren.[24]

1. Brother, love Jesus more.

2. Why so easy amid hidings of his face[?]

3. Sinner, what will hell be to thee where God's face doth frown fearfully[?]

368.

1. Charles never again preached on this passage.

2. Cf. Rom 8:22. See also "Creation's Groans and the Saints' Sighs" (*MTP* 14, Sermon 788).

3. Cf. Rom 11:13–15.

4. Amos 8:9: "And it shall come to pass in that day, saith the Lord God, that I will cause the sun to go down at noon, and I will darken the earth in the clear day."

5. Cf. Luke 23:32–43.   6. Cf. John 9:4.

7. Cf. Isa 53:7.   8. Cf. Heb 12:2.

9. Cf. Matt 27:46.

10. John Gill, *An Exposition of the New Testament* 1:325.

11. Cf. Matt 27:50; Mark 15:37; Luke 23:46.

12. Cf. Psalm 22. See also "The Church and Its Boast" (*Notebook 1*, Sermon 75).

13. Cf. Ps 40:8; 42:1.   14. Cf. John 10:17–18.

15. Cf. Psalm 22; Matt 27:47; Mark 15:34.

16. "2. Trust in general; confidence; secure reliance. 3. Trust in the divine promises and protection. To this sense it is now almost confined" (Johnson's *Dictionary*, s.v. "affiance").

17. "[Jesus] claims to be Master and Lord to those who ask salvation at his hands; and is not the claim a just one? Whom should we serve but the Lord who became a servant for our sakes? It must be so, or salvation is impossible; those who serve sin are not saved, nor can they be except by being brought to serve the Christ of God" (*MTP* 22:363). Cf. Rom 15:8; Phil 2:7.

18. Cf. 2 Cor 5:21.   19. Cf. Luke 2:49.

20. Cf. Mark 14:50.   21. Cf. 1 Pet 1:19.

22. Cf. Luke 5:16.   23. Cf. Rom 6:23; 1 Cor 6:20.

24. Cf. Heb 2:9–18.

219.   Matt. III. 12.   The Church is to be purged.

God never will destroy the righteous with the wicked
nor suffer the bad to share the felicity of the holy.

I. The place to be purged. "his floor". —
the Jewish nation — though highly favoured. — though outwardly
good was to be tried — God will not let any pass.
     The visible Church is as the floor where lie the
chaff & the wheat mingled — we sift — but still the
chaff will get in — the hypocrite — formalist — deceiver.
     The floor shall have the fan first.

II. The instrument of severance "his fan" —
     He has small fans such as — — a faithful ministry —
heresy — persecution — temptation &c — but
     Judgment will be his great winnowing fan.

III. The destination of the wheat "the garner"
     none of it — not even the shrivelled grain will
perish but all shall be lodged in the garner
          What a garner!

IV. The end of the chaff "unquenchable fire".
"fire" — the torments of conscience, remorse, despair.
     never to be extinguished by our tears, time
the mercy of God — nor aught in the universe
     "unquenchable" — is the hell of hell.

378.

THE CHURCH IS *to* BE PURGED[1]

Matthew 3:12

"Whose fan[2] is in his hand, and he will thoroughly purge his floor, and gather his wheat into the garner; but he will burn up the chaff with unquenchable fire."

God never will destroy the righteous with the wicked, nor suffer the bad to share the felicity of the holy.[3]

I. THE PLACE TO BE PURGED. *"his floor."*

The Jewish nation, though highly favoured, though outwardly good[,] was to be tried.[4] God will not let any pass.

The visible Church is as the floor where lie the chaff and the wheat mingled. We sift,[5] but still the chaff will get in: the hypocrite, formalist, deceiver.

The floor shall have the fan first.

II. THE INSTRUMENT OF SEVERANCE. *"his fan."*

Heresy—persecution—temptation etc.—but judgment will be his great winnowing fan.[6]

III. THE DESTINATION OF THE WHEAT. *"the garner."*

None of it, not even the shriveled grain, will perish. But all shall be lodged in the garner.

What a garner!

IV. THE END OF THE CHAFF. *"unquenchable fire."*

"Fire." The torments of conscience, remorse, despair. Never to be extinguished by our tears, time, the mercy of God, nor ought[7] in the universe.

"Unquenchable" is the hell of hell.

378.

1. Charles never again preached on this passage.

2. "3. The instrument by which the chaff is blown away when corn is winnowed" (Johnson's *Dictionary*, s.v. "fan").

3. Cf. Gen 18:23–25.

4. "By the *fan*, here is meant, either the Gospel which Christ was just ready to publish; by which he would effectually call his chosen people among the *Jews*, and so distinguish and separate them from others, as well as purify and cleanse them; or rather the awful judgment of God, which Christ was ready to execute, and in a short time would execute on the unbelieving and impenitent *Jews*" (John Gill, *An Exposition of the New Testament* 1:23, italics in the original).

5. Charles was "prepared to maintain this position against the attacks of the Strict Communionist and the Open Membership man, both of whose principles he believed to be unscriptural. He would rather give up his pastorate than admit any man to the Church who was not obedient to his Lord's command; and such a course would certainly promote the downfall of any Church that practised it" (*MTP* 7:260). "A month after the Tabernacle was opened[,] 77 persons were received for baptism and church membership, the following month another 72 were thus received, and when another month had passed[,] a further 121 were added. If we bear in mind the evidence of true conversion that Spurgeon required—in contrast with the methods often used today—these figures become all the more noteworthy" (Arnold Dallimore, *Spurgeon: A Biography* [Chicago: Moody Press], 99–100).

6. Cf. Matt 25:1–13, 31–46; Luke 13:25–28.

7. "Any thing; not nothing" (Johnson's *Dictionary*, s.v. "ought").

Col. IV. 2. —   Continue in prayer.   220.

Many are the exhortations to prayer because much needed.

I. The apostle supposes that all Christians pray.

This is the commencement, means, sign, help, & close of our life

never do we get too wise, too strong, or too old to need it.

1. Faith, an essential part of a Xⁿ cannot develop itself without it.

2. Penitence cannot make its confession without it.

3. Weakness & sense of need do naturally produce it

II. Many things hinder us or seek to do so.

1 Our heart — our nature is averse to it.

2 Wordly cares & troubles do distract us.

3. Satan tempts us to cease our cries.

4. Delays in our answers — make us ready to despair

III. Means for maintaining devotion.

1. Reading of the Scriptures — especially Psalms.

2. Attendance on every means of grace

3. Much prayer when we feel aright.

The exercises of a Christian are Siamese twins they will

be healthy or sick together —

IV. Motives —

1. Consider thy vile heart.

2. Consider thine other enemies & difficulties

3. Consider the end —

4. Consider the happiness enjoyed in the exercise

5. Consider the sins good men commit through

neglect of this —

372. 374. 380. 381,

CONTINUE *in* PRAYER[1]

Colossians 4:2

"Continue in prayer, and watch in the same with thanksgiving[.]"

Many are the exhortations to prayer because [it is] much needed.[2]

I. THE APOSTLE SUPPOSES THAT ALL CHRISTIANS PRAY.

This is the commencement, means, sign, help, and close of our life.[3] Never do we get too wise, too strong, or too old to need it.[4]

1. Faith, an essential part of a X^n [,][5] cannot develop itself without it.[6]

2. Penitence cannot make its confessions without it.[7]

3. Weakness and sense of need do naturally produce it.[8]

II. MANY THINGS HINDER US, OR SEEK TO DO SO.

1. Our heart. Our nature is averse to it.

2. Worldly cares and troubles do distract us.

3. Satan tempts us to cease our cries.

4. Delays in our answers make us ready to despair.

III. MEANS FOR MAINTAINING DEVOTION.

1. Reading of the Scriptures, especially Psalms.[9]

2. Attendance on every means of grace.[10]

3. Much prayer when we feel aright.

The exercises of a Christian are Siamese[11] twins. They will be healthy or sick together.

IV. MOTIVES.

1. Consider thy vile heart.[12]

2. Consider thine older enemies and difficulties.

3. Consider the end.

4. Consider the happiness enjoyed in the exercise.

5. Consider the sins good men commit through neglect of this.

372. 374. 380. 381.

1. Charles preached on this text one other time in his later sermon "A Sermon for the Week of Prayer" (*MTP* 7, Sermon 354).

2. Cf. Acts 10:2; Rom 12:12; 1 Thess 5:17; 2 Tim 1:3.

3. "It might have been more in order that the aged minister should himself address the people; but nevertheless, as it is his own choice, so it must be; and I shall draw my consolation from the third verse, where it is declared, that though God be the God of the close of our life, yet he is also the God of its beginning" (*MTP* 2:217).

4. Augustus H. Strong, after visiting with Charles, concluded "that the secret of Mr. Spurgeon's success was his piety and his faith. Above all things he seemed to be a man of prayer" (Augustus H. Strong, *Autobiography of Augustus Hopkins Strong*, ed. Crerar Douglas [Valley Forge, PA: Judson Press, 1981], 300). "Oh! May God help me, if you cease to pray for me! Let me know the day, and I must cease to preach. Let me know when you intend to cease your prayers, and I will cry, 'O my God, give me this day my tomb, and let me slumber in the dust" (*NPSP* 3:255–56).

5. Abbreviation of "Christian."

6. "The movements of God's servants may be controlled by prayer. You cannot tell how much of blessing will come to your own souls, through the ministry, if you are in the habit of praying about it. The man who comes up to God's house, having prayed for God to bless the preacher, is not likely to go away unprofited" (*MTP* 40:204).

7. "Trembling penitent, let a living Saviour cheer thee. Exercise faith in him who only hath immortality. He lives to hear thy prayer; cry to him, he lives to present that prayer before his Father's face. Put yourself in his hands; he lives to gather together those whom he bought with his blood, to make those the people of his flock who were once the people of his purchase. Sinner, dost thou believe this as a matter of fact? If so, rest thy soul on it, and make it thine as a matter of confidence, and then thou art saved" (*MTP* 9:197).

8. "Prayer is now as much a necessity of our spiritual life as breath is of our natural life" (*MTP* 34:15).

9. See Charles's *The Treasury of David*.

10. "There are many means of grace, and let us speak as highly of them as ever we can; we would be far from depreciating them; they are of the highest value; blessed are the people who have them; happy is the nation which is blessed with the means of grace. But my brethren, no man was ever saved by the means of grace apart from the Holy Spirit" (*NPSP* 4:107). See Charles's comments on "means of grace" in "God's Grace Given to Us" (Notebook 1, Sermon 14).

11. Conjoined.

12. Cf. Jer 17:9.

221.   Zeph. III. 9.   The pure language.

The "then" refers to the time of preaching the gospel
immediately after the destruction of "the oppressing city"
   This prophecy then concerns the language, worship,
and service which the sons of God shall render.
   I. Their language. "then will I turn to the people
                              a pure (or choice) language.
   The Jews had once the pure language but Egypt & the
nations among whom they dwelt previously much polluted it.
Then again the nations of Canaan led them astray — the Syrian,
Edomites, Philistines, Babylonians & Persians — corrupted
their conversation more & more — yet — shall the pure
language be restored.   Man by nature spoke
this celestial tongue, but fallen he has lost it —
The language every babe speaks is one of sin, anger, pride &c
— we imitate others too & so get further from the pure.
But yet grace divine — — can restore the pure language.
   1. How can this language be known?
   Look at its letters & you shall see Jesus Alpha & Omega.
Its first grammar is prayer — its syntax the
Bible — its poetry is holy praise.
   It is the language of an importunate beggar —
a ransomed slave — an adopted child —
   Its highest branch is the language of triumph
Its hardest words are words of constant trust.
   It is a language not spoken by natural man

THE PURE LANGUAGE [1]
Zephaniah 3:9

"For then I will turn to the people a pure language, that they may all call upon the name of the LORD, to serve him with one consent."

The "then" refers to the time of preaching the gospel immediately after the destruction of "the oppressing city."[2]

This prophecy, then, concerns the language, worship, and service which the sons of God shall render.[3]

I. THEROJECT **THEIR LANGUAGE.** *"then will I turn to the people a pure (or choice) language.*["]

The Jews had once the pure language, but Egypt and the nations among whom they dwelt previously much polluted it. Then again, the nations of Canaan led them astray.[4] The Syrians,[5] Edomites,[6] Philistines,[7] Babylonians and Persians[8] corrupted their conversation more and more. Yet shall the pure language be restored.

Man, by nature, spoke this celestial tongue, but fallen, he has lost it. The language every babe speaks is one of sin, anger, pride, etc. We imitate others too, and so get further from the pure.

But yet grace divine can restore the pure language.

1. How can this language be known?

Look at its letters and you shall see Jesus, Alpha and Omega.[9] Its first grammar is prayer. Its syntax, the Bible. Its poetry is holy praise. It is the language of an importunate beggar, a ransomed slave, an adopted child.[10] Its highest branch is the language of triumph.[11] Its hardest words are words of constant trust. It is a language not spoken by natural man.[12]

2. <u>Wherein does the purity of this language consist?</u>
1. It has been purged of all boasting words. — to man or God —
2. It has not one slavish word — nor one repining word.
3. No hypocritical word can be found in it.
4. No lustful, evil, lascivious sentence can it form.
5. No angry, hot, or passionate word. —
6. No lukewarm, denying, fearful, coward word —
   It is a pure language — God teach me it.
It is called a "choice language" — it is God's choice.
Oh may it be mine. — Amen

<u>3 Where is this language spoken?</u>
Not in distant lands, lordly palaces, or learned colleges.
But it may be read in the word of God. It is heard
in some of its purity from the Gospel Minister.
It is spoken in broken accents by every son of God
but Heaven is the place where its sweet, melodious,
charming, enrapturing sound is heard in perfection.
   May God turn to his people more & more this
         pure language — choice tongue.

<u>II. Their worship.</u> "that they may all call upon
         the name of the Lord"

1. This refers to the worship carried on in
the public sanctuary. All true sons of God will
go up thither to adore Jesus & call on his name.
God alone shall be the object of their adoration.
"All" shall "call on his name" no stay-at-homes.
   No careless hearers — but all calling on God
alone — each for himself.

2. <u>Wherein does the purity of this language consist?</u>

   1. It has been purged of all boasting words. To man or God.[13]

   2. It has not one slavish word, nor one repining[14] word.

   3. No hypocritical word can be found in it.[15]

   4. No lustful, evil, lascivious sentence can it form.[16]

   5. No angry, hot, or passionate word.[17]

   6. No lukewarm,[18] denying[19], fearful, coward word.

It is a pure language. God teach me it.

It is called a "choice language." It is God's choice. Oh may it be mine. <u>Amen</u>

3. <u>Where is this language spoken?</u>

   Not in distant lands, lordly palaces, or learned colleges.[20] But it may be read in the word of God. It is heard in some of its purity from the Gospel Minister.[21] It is spoken in broken accents by every son of God, but Heaven is the place where its sweet, melodious, charming, enrapturing sound is heard in perfection.

   May God turn to his people more and more [with] this pure language, choice tongue.

II. THEIR WORSHIP. *"<u>that they may all call upon the name of the Lord</u>."*

   1. This refers to the worship carried on in the public sanctuary. All true sons of God will go up thither to adore Jesus and call on his name. God alone shall be the object of their adoration.

   "<u>All</u>" shall "call on his name." No stay-at-homes. No careless hearers. But all calling on God alone, each for himself.

2. This refers to the secret devotions of Christians.
Secret prayer is _the_ test of a Christian.
At all times, in all trials, for all our needs to the
throne, we fly — "all" — each for himself.
3. This refers to an open avowal of conversion.
an open profession is often styled "calling on d' name"
this all the faithful will do — or ought to do —
<u>III</u>. Their service. to serve him with one consent

Mark. / each one must serve in various ways — for
God giveth different gifts & offices but all must serve.

Mark 2. they must serve unitedly "with one consent"
"with one shoulder" — as the margin reads it.
This excludes desire of preeminence — one ox
must not go before the other lest the plough overturn
this excludes all quarrelling & disagreement
& recommends love & unity —

Mark 3. they should serve willingly "consent"
not by constraint — not pressmen but
volunteers.. gifts not taxes — no need
of driving but glad to serve —

Lord be with thine unworthy one.
For my Redeemer's sake.

375.

2. This refers to the secret devotions of Christians. Secret prayer is the test of a Christian. At all times, in all trials, for all our needs, to the throne we fly. "All." Each for himself.

3. This refers to an open avowal[22] of conversion. An open profession is often styled "calling on his name."[23] This, all the faithful will do, or ought to do.

III. THEIR SERVICE. *["]to serve him with one consent.["]*

Mark 1. Each one must serve in various ways, for God giveth different gifts and offices. But all must serve.[24]

Mark 2. They must serve unitedly "with one consent." "With one shoulder," as the margin reads it.[25] This excludes desire of preeminence. One ox must not go before the other, lest the plough overturn. This excludes all quarrelling and disagreement and recommends love and unity.

Mark 3. They should serve willingly. "Consent," not by constraint. Not press men, but volunteers. Gifts, not taxes. No need of driving,[26] but glad to serve.

Lord be with thine unworthy one,

For my Redeemer's sake.

375.

1. Charles never again preached on this passage.

2. Cf. Zeph 3:1. "That is, at or about the time of the destruction of *Jerusalem* by the *Romans*; when the *Jews*, both in their own land, and in the *Gentile* world, would have the gospel first preached to them, but would reject it; upon which the apostles and first ministers of the word would turn to the *Gentiles*, as the Lord commanded them; when he would turn or change his speech and language towards them, and their speech and language towards him would be turned and changed also: for the words may be taken either way" (John Gill, *An Exposition of the Books of the Prophets of the Old Testament, Both Larger and Lesser* [London: printed for the author and sold by G. Keith at the Bible and Crown in Grace-church-street; and by J. Robinson at Dock-head, Southwark, 1758], 2:628, italics in the original).

3. "[The Gospel] is a *pure* speech or language; a pure doctrine, fetched out of the sacred scriptures; free from the dross of error; unmixed, consistent, and all of a piece; and which has a tendency to promote purity of heart, life and conversation: or, is a *choice speech*, as some render it" (Gill, 2:628, italics in the original).

4. Cf. Exod 34:14–16; Num 25:1.

5. Cf. 2 Kgs 18:11.

6. Cf. Amos 1:11.

7. Cf. Zeph 2:5.

8. Gill lists "*Philistines, Moabites, Ethiopians,* and *Assyrians*" as the nations that were utterly cut off by God. He also mentions that Jerusalem was corrupted "not as before the *Babylonish* captivity, but after their return from it, under the second temple" (Gill, *An Exposition of the Books of the Prophets of the Old Testament,* 2:625, 627, italics in the original).

9. Cf. Rev 1:8, 11; 21:6; 22:13.

10. Cf. Luke 18:1–8; Rom 8:15; Eph 1:5; 1 Tim 2:6.

11. Cf. 2 Cor 2:14.

12. Cf. 1 Cor 2:13–15; Col 1:9.

13. Cf. Rom 3:27.

14. "1. To fret; to vex himself; to be discontented: with *at* or *against*. 2. To envy" (Johnson's *Dictionary*, s.v. "to repine," italics in the original).

15. "Beware of seeking respect by a hypocritical godliness. Honour gained by a heartless profession is, in God's sight, the greatest disgrace. The actor may strut in his mimic royalty, but he must take off his crown and robes when the play is over; and what will he then be?" (*MTP* 35:306). Cf. Matt 6:2, 5, 16; 7:5.

16. Cf. Gal 5:16; Eph 4:22. 17. Cf. Eph 4:26.

18. Cf. Rev 3:16.   19. Cf. Matt 10:33.

20. Charles was fascinated with exotic lands and languages. This is evidenced by the multitude of adventure and travel books he had in his personal collection. One is titled *Rough Notes Taken During Some Rapid Journeys Across the Pampas and Among the Andes* ([London: John Murray, 1846], The Spurgeon Library), which details Sir Francis Head's travels across South America. Another has the title *A Voyage up the River Amazon, Including a Residence at Para.* In the preface to this book, the author writes, "In these stirring times . . . all Anglo-Saxondom is on the qui-vive for novelty, and the discovery of a new watering-place is hailed with more enthusiasm than the discovery of a new planet" (William H. Edwards, *A Voyage up the River Amazon, Including a Residence at Para* [London: John Murray, Albemarle Street, 1847, 2, The Spurgeon Library]). As a final example, Charles had a book titled *Recent Polar Voyages. A Record of Adventure and Discovery* (London: T. Nelson and Sons, 1876, The Spurgeon Library), which gives account of daring expeditions to the North Pole. The book includes picture captions such as "a bear at anchor" (page 425). This one shows a polar bear chained to an anchor. "Charging an iceberg" is on page 369; it shows a ship in tumultuous waters crashing through an iceberg. The book also has a foldout color map of the North Pole.

21. "For the herald of the gospel to be spiritually out of order in his own proper person is, both to himself and to his work, a most serious calamity; and yet, my brethren, how easily is such an evil produced, and with what watchfulness must it be guarded against! Traveling one day by express from Perth to Edinburgh, on a sudden we came to a dead stop, because a very small screw in one of the engines — every railway locomotive consisting virtually of two engines — had been broken, and when we started again we were obliged to crawl along with one piston-rod at work instead of two. Only a small screw was gone[;] if that had been right[,] the train would have rushed along its iron road, but the absence

of that insignificant piece of iron disarranged the whole. A train is said to have been stopped on one of the United States' railways by flies in the grease-boxes of the carriage wheels. The analogy is perfect; a man in all other respects fitted to be useful, may by some small defect be exceedingly hindered, or even rendered utterly useless. Such a result is all the more grievous, because it is associated with the gospel, which in the highest sense is adapted to effect the grandest results. It is a terrible thing when the healing balm loses its efficacy through the blunderer who administers it. You all know the injurious effects frequently produced upon water through flowing along leaden pipes; even so the gospel itself, in flowing through men who are spiritually unhealthy, may be debased until it grows injurious to their hearers" (*Lectures* 1:2–3).

22. "Justificatory declaration; open declaration" (Johnson's *Dictionary*, s.v. "avowal").

23. Cf. Rom 10:13.   24. Cf. 1 Pet 4:10–11.

25. *The Holy Bible, According to the Authorized Version; with Notes, Explanatory and Practical; Taken Principally from the Most Eminent Writers of the United Church of England and Ireland: Together with Appropriate Introductions Tables, Indexes, Maps, and Plans: Prepared and Arranged by the Rev. George D'Oyly, B.D. and the Rev. Richard Mant, D.D., Domestick Chaplains to His Grace the Lord Archbishop of Canterbury, under the Direction of the Society for Promoting Christian Knowledge. Vol. I, Part II.* [Oxford: printed for the Society at the Clarendon Press by Bensley, Cooke, NS Collingwood and sold by F. C. and J. Rivington, St. Paul's Church-Yard; and by all other booksellers in the United Kingdom, 1817, "Zephaniah 3:9," The Spurgeon Library]).

26. "2. To force along by impetuous pressure.... 6. To force or urge in any direction.... 9. To convey animals; to make animals march along under guidance" (Johnson's *Dictionary*, s.v. "to drive").

Zeph. I. 4. 5. 6. Zephaniah's warnings —
Zephaniah's prophecy opens with a chapter full of
solemn things, in solemn language.

✗. He denounces woes against four classes.

I. Open & acknowledged sinners. The Remnant of Baal
the Chemarims (or black ones – black with Molech fires) the priests
& worshippers of the stars.   All open sinners of
whatever kind – though they may say "my sin
is not like such an one's – all must be cut off.
All drunkards, swearers, adulterers, Sabbath-breakers
in fact the devil's professing people, his church.

Permit me, oh Father, to remind such of thy love
through the atonement of thy beloved son. Help me
to argue the matter – & strive with them –
Divine Spirit speak thou & they shall hear.
But if ye hear not, neither regard – then my God
biddeth me declare his wrath. Zeph. I. 14 – 17.
Joel. II. 10 – 14.   Prov. I. 24 to end.

II. Hypocritical professors. persons serving God & Mammon
"they swear by the Lord & swear by Molech"
this class sit securely – they are on their lees, their
fancy has given laudanum to their conscience
Sabbath day is to atone for the other days – a
few prayers are – to make amends for many
sins – they are chameleons –
These are even worse than the first class.

ZEPHANIAH'S WARNINGS [1]
Zephaniah 1:4–6

"I will also stretch out mine hand upon Judah, and upon all the inhabitants of Jerusalem; and I will cut off the remnant of Baal from this place, and the name of the Chemarims with the priests; and them that worship the hosts of heaven upon the house tops; and them that worship and that swear by the LORD, *and that swear by Malcham; And them that are turned back from the* LORD; *and those that have not sought the* LORD, *nor enquired for him."*

Zephaniah's prophecy opens with a chapter full of solemn things, in solemn language.

Ɨ.   He denounces woes against four classes:

I.   OPEN AND ACKNOWLEDGED SINNERS.

The Remnant of Baal,[2] the Chemarims (or black ones,[3] black with Molech fires), the priests and worshippers of the stars.[4] All open sinners of whatever kind. Though they may say, "My sin is not like such an one's,["][5] all must be cut off. All drunkards, swearers, adulterers, sabbath-breakers[,] in fact, the devil's professing people, his church.

Permit me, Oh Father, to remind such of thy love through the atonement of thy beloved son. Help me to argue the matter and strive with them.

Divine Spirit[,] speak thou and they shall hear. But if ye hear not, neither regard. Then my God biddeth me declare his wrath. Zeph. I. 14-17.[6] Joel II. 10–14.[7] Prov. I. 24 to end.[8]

II.   HYPOCRITICAL PROFESSORS, PERSONS SERVING GOD AND MAMMON.[9] *"They swear by the Lord and swear by Molech."*

This class sit[s] securely. They are on their lees.[10] Their fancy has given laudanum[11] to their conscience[s].

Sabbath day is to atone for the other days. A few prayers are to make amends for many sins. They are chameleons.

These are even worse than the first class.

Come ye Both-ites listen — no man can serve two masters — can ye marry two wives — live at once in two houses — enlist in two armies.

Ye are hypocrites, liars to God & yourselves. Ye have reason enough to repent & turn to God. Some take the Sacrament at Church & slew in the public house. — Some in different villages act different — Some make gain of religion — Some really like both & halt between two opinions.

III. Backsliders. "turned back from the Lord".
Of this character there are to be found more than a few — & this class are in a sad state. for their sin in itself is immense — the mischief it does is great — the likelyhood of return is very little — the man Knows & has sinned against it — has felt & yet subdued his feelings he is almost hopeless.

But Backslider 'ere I read thy doom let me admonish thee — & invite thee — to the arms of mercy — yet unclosed.

If thou wilt go on however — nothing can save thee the cry comes against thee whatever thou art. Howl. Howl.

IV. Neglecters of God — who never seek his name — some think that if they make no profession sin is nothing but — they are wrong.

Come, ye Both-ites, listen. No man can serve two masters.[12] Can ye marry two wives[?][13] Live at once in two houses[?] Enlist in two armies[?]

Ye are hypocrites, liars to God and yourselves. Ye have reason enough to repent and turn to God.

Some take the sacrament at Church and then in the public house.[14] Some in different villages act different.[15] Some make gain of religion. Some really like both and halt between two opinions.[16]

III. BACKSLIDERS. *"turned back from the Lord."*

Of this character there are to be found more than a few. And [those in] this class are in a sad state, for their sin in itself is immense. The mischief it does is great. The likelyhood [*sic*] of return is very little. The man knows, and has sinned against it. Has felt, and yet subdued his feelings.[17] He is almost hopeless.

But Backslider, 'ere I read thy doom, let me admonish thee and invite thee to the arms of mercy yet unclosed.

If thou wilt go on, however, nothing can save thee. The cry comes against thee, whatever thou art. Howl. Howl.

IV. NEGLECTERS OF GOD WHO NEVER SEEK HIS NAME.

Some think that if they make no profession, sin is nothing. But they are wrong.

If the night prowler must be punished – shall the man who goes to robbery by day escape. –

It is a sin not to be a Christian, not to believe whatever your rank, or character a woe hangs over you if you are not a follower of Jesus.

Cursed are you so long as you are under the curse – by your deeds ye cannot be justified.

Your position under a master will not excuse you. v. 9 – Your trade will not help to make a plea – Maktésh must fall – Hope not to escape. the candle shall find you out – Boast not infidelity – wait a moment & wrath shall be revealed – but I pray God avert it.

The woes I proclaim shall not be mere words – they are decrees & shall be executed – turn thine eye on Nineveh or the proud cities of the Nile, or Edom in the rock. or Babel – Look down into the pit that burneth & see if thou wilt not see enough to convince thee of thine error in supposing they shall be unexecuted

Turn or die. Repent or Perish. Believe or be damned –

Lord help me to preach faithfully. through thy dear Son.

If the night prowler must be punished, shall the man who goes to robbery by day escape[?][18]

It is a sin not to be a Christian, not to believe.[19] Whatever your rank or character, a woe hangs over you if you are not a follower of Jesus.

Cursed are you so long as you are under the curse.[20] By your deeds, ye cannot be justified.[21]

Your position under a master will not excuse you.[22] v.9. Your trade will not help [you] to make a plea.[23] Maktesh[24] must fall. Hope not to escape. The candle shall find you out. Boast not infidelity.[25] Wait a moment and wrath shall be revealed. But I pray God avert[s] it.

The woes I proclaim shall not be mere words. They are decrees and shall be executed. Turn thine eye on Nineveh,[26] or the proud cities of the Nile,[27] or Edom in the rock,[28] or Babel.[29] Look down into the pit that burneth[,] and see if thou wilt not see enough to convince thee of thine error in supposing they shall be unexecuted.

Turn or die. Repent or Perish.

Believe or be damned.

Lord, help me to preach faithfully,

<u>through thy dear Son.</u>

376.

1. Charles never again preached from this passage.

2. Cf. 1 Kgs 18:20–40.

3. "[They were] so called, either from the black garments they wore, as some think; or from the colour of their faces, smutted with the smoke of the incense they frequently offered; or of the fires in which they sacrificed, or made the children to pass thro' to *Molech*" (John Gill, *An Exposition of the Books of the Prophets of the Old Testament*, 2:614, italics in the original).

4. "Some take them [the Chemarims] to be a sort of servants or ministers to the priests of *Baal*, who waited on them at the time of service; and so are distinguished from them in this clause, taking the word *priests* in it to design the priests of *Baal*" (Gill, 2:614 italics in the original).

5. Cf. Luke 18:10–14.

6. Zephaniah 1:14–17: "The great day of the LORD is near, it is near, and hasteth greatly, even the voice of the day of the LORD: the mighty man shall cry there bitterly. That day is a day of wrath, a day of trouble and distress, a day of wasteness and desolation, a day of darkness and gloominess, a day of clouds and thick darkness, A day of the trumpet and alarm against the fenced cities, and against the high towers. And I will bring distress upon men, that they shall walk like blind men, because they have sinned against the LORD: and their blood shall be poured out as dust, and their flesh as the dung."

7. Joel 2:10–14: "The earth shall quake before them; the heavens shall tremble; the sun and the moon shall be dark, and the stars shall withdraw their shining: and the LORD shall utter his voice before his army: for his camp is very great: for he is strong that executeth his word: for the day of the LORD is great and very terrible; and who can abide it? Therefore also now, saith the Lord, turn ye even to me with all your heart, and with fasting, and with weeping, and with mourning: And rend your heart, and not your garments, and turn unto the LORD your God; for he is gracious and merciful, slow to anger, and of great kindness, and repenteth him of the evil. Who knoweth if he will return and repent, and leave a blessing behind him, even a meat-offering and a drink-offering unto the LORD your God?"

8. Proverbs 1:24–33: "Because I have called, and ye refused; I have stretched out my hand, and no man regarded; but ye have set at nought all my counsel, and

would none of my reproof: I also will laugh at your calamity; I will mock when your fear cometh; when your fear cometh as desolation, and your destruction cometh as a whirlwind; when distress and anguish cometh upon you. Then shall they call upon me, but I will not answer; they shall seek me early, but they shall not find me: for that they hated knowledge, and did not choose the fear of the Lord: They would none of my counsel: they despised all my reproof. Therefore shall they eat of the fruit of their own way, and be filled with their own devices. For the turning away of the simple shall slay them, and the prosperity of fools shall destroy them. But whoso hearkeneth unto me shall dwell safely, and shall be quiet from fear of evil."

9. Cf. Matt 6:24.

10. "Dregs; sediment; it has seldom a singular" (Johnson's *Dictionary*, s.v. "lees").

11. "A soporific [sleep-inducing] tincture" (Johnson's *Dictionary*, s.v. "laudanum").

12. Cf. Matt 6:24.   13. Cf. Gen 2:24; Matt 19:6; 1 Tim 3:2.

14. "Perhaps someone asks, 'How do we feed on Jesus Christ?' and there are some who say that we feed upon Christ in what is called 'the sacrament.' I do not like that word 'sacrament' as applied to the ordinance of the Lord's supper; at all events, there is no mention in Scripture of such a thing as a 'sacrament.' It is an old heathenish word, applying to the oath which a soldier swore to be faithful to his commander. I like neither swearing nor sacraments, and I do not like either one of them any more than the other, for both of them are contrary to the Word of God. Out of that word 'sacrament' a great mass of mischief has grown up; it is a bed of rottenness out of which all sorts of evil fungi have sprung. Let us keep clear of that once and for all" (*MTP* 46:604).

15. "There was another man, of that [hypocritical] sort, who at one time frequently walked out with me into the villages where I was going to preach. I was glad of his company till I found out certain facts as to his manner of life, and then I shook him off, and I believe he hooked himself on to somebody else, for he must needs be gadding abroad every evening of the week. He had many children, and they grew up to be wicked men and women; and the reason was, that the father, while he was constantly busy at this meeting and that, never tried to bring his

own boys and girls to the Saviour. He said to me, one day, 'I never laid my hand upon my children;' so I answered, 'Then I think it is very likely that God will lay His hand upon you.' 'Oh!' he said, 'I have not even spoken sharply to them.' 'Then,' I replied, 'it is highly probable that God will speak very sharply to you; for it is not His will that parents should leave their children unrestrained in their sin'" (*Autobiography* 1:259).

16. Cf. 1 Kgs 18:21.

17. "In cases of backsliding, where there is a sound heart towards God, the backslider is soon brought back, but where the heart is rotten, the backslider goes from bad to worse. I was struck with a story of two men who were accustomed to give exhortations at meetings, who had fallen out with each other, and one of their brethren, who grieved to think two servants of God should be at difference with each other, went to reconcile them. He called upon the first, and said, 'John, I am very sorry to find you and James have quarrelled [*sic*]. It seems a great pity, and it brings much dishonour on the church of God.' 'Ah,' said John, 'I am very grieved, too, and what grieves me most is, that I am the sole cause of it. It was only because I spoke so bitterly, that James took offense.' 'Ah, ah,' said the good man, 'we will soon settle this difficulty, then,' and away he went to James. 'James, I am very sorry that you and John cannot agree.' 'Yes,' he said, 'it is a sad thing we don't, we ought to do so, for we are brethren; but what troubles me most is, that it is all my fault. If I had not taken notice of a little word John said, there would have been an end of it.' The matter, as you may guess, was soon rectified. You see there was at bottom a true friendship between them, so that the little difficulty was soon got over, and so where there is a true union between God and the soul, the backsliding will soon be recovered" (*MTP* 16:131).

18. Cf. Prov 11:21.

19. "To have been almost persuaded, and yet not to be a Christian, *will lead to endless regrets*; for will not this thought bubble up in the seething soul amidst its torments for ever: 'I was almost persuaded to repent: why did I go on in my sin? I was almost persuaded to put my trust in Jesus, wherefore did I cling still to my self-righteousness and vain ceremonies? I was almost persuaded to forsake my evil companions, and to become a servant of God, but I am now cast away for ever, where no more persuasions can melt my heart'" (*MTP* 15:287–88, italics in the original).

20. Cf. Gal 3:10.   21. Cf. Gal 2:16.

22. Cf. Rom 6:16.

23. "You know more about your trade than I do. No doubt there are trades which pander to the vices of men, and become all the more profitable in proportion to the growth of drunkenness and impurity. These must be given up. Moreover, there are traders who live by puffery, and lying, and cheating; and I do not recommend you to profess to be a Christian if that is your line of things. It is better to give up all profession of religion when you go in for unrighteous gain" (*MTP* 36:20).

24. Cf. Zeph 1:11.   25. Cf. Phil 3:18–19.

26. Cf. Nahum 2.   27. Cf. Exod 7:21.

28. Cf. Gen 11:9.

29. Cf. 2 Chr 25:12; 2 Kgs 14:7.

223. Rom. XII. 2. Nonconformity.

It is strange but yet true — that God's people have ever been inclined to lose their nationality & become as the world —

In Noah's time, — — the Israelites sighing for Egypt — sinning in the matter of Peor — marrying Canaanites — going to Egypt for horses — shaping altars like foreign nations — &c.&c. So now we ever need to hear the cry "be not conformed." —

The congregation before me & myself need this as much, perhaps more, than the Romans.

In Explaining the Text.

I. The apostle enjoins nonconformity to the world.
II. He tells us the only means of maintaing it.
III. He tells us the uses of this Nonconformity.

I. He enjoins nonconformity to the world —
"Be not conformed to this world"

The Quakers for this reason wear a dress which is peculiar — but we see no command for this — though neatness in dress is commended. They also by the use of the pronoun "thou"

NONCONFORMITY[1]
Romans 12:2

"And be not conformed to this world: but be ye transformed by the renewing of your mind, that ye may prove what is that good, and acceptable, and perfect will of God."

It is strange but yet true that God's people have ever been inclined to lose their nationality and become as the world.

In Noah's time,[2] the Israelites sighing for Egypt,[3] sinning in the matter of Peor,[4] marrying Canaanites,[5] going to Egypt for horses,[6] shaping altars like foreign nations,[7] etc. etc. So now we ever need to hear the cry, "be not conformed."[8]

The congregation before me, and myself, need this as much, perhaps more, than the Romans.[9]

In Explaining the Text.

I.   THE APOSTLE ENJOINS NONCONFORMITY TO THE WORLD.

II. HE TELLS US THE ONLY MEANS OF MAINTING IT.

III. HE TELLS US THE USES OF THIS NONCONFORMITY.

I.   HE ENJOINS NONCONFORMITY TO THE WORLD.
"Be not conformed to this world."

The Quakers, for this reason, wear a dress which is peculiar.[10] But we see no command for this, though neatness in dress is commended. They also [prefer] the use of the pronoun "thou"

"thee" — by giving numerical names to days & months
do in a sort render their language peculiar.
   Though this be over-straining — yet we ought to
maintain a pure language — banishing all
profane, filthy words, songs, taking God's name in vain
      We ourselves are called nonconformists, since
we (on good grounds) object to the State religion —
we must stand by our Bible never giving way —
not following the religion of a multitude.
      In common trade — an irreligious man will
do many things which a Christian should
studiously avoid — Shop-nonconformity is
meant, market, house, street & business nonconⁿ
      In our company & pursuits, our aims
& objects — our looks & actions let us be separate.

II. He tells us the means of maintaining it.
   "Be ye transformed by the renewing of your minds"
By this is meant not the first, beginning
of the great work, but the after progress —
Progressive Sanctification — Growth in
grace alone can keep us from going into sin.
We need pray constantly for the Holy Ghost to
come & enliven us, & renew us day by day.
   The "mind" must be renewed every day, the
colour though indelible needs fresh varnish.

[and also] "<u>thee</u>." By giving numerical names to days and months [they] do, in a sort, render their language peculiar.[11]

Though this be over-straining, yet we ought to maintain a pure language, banishing all profane, filthy words, songs, taking God's name in vain.

We ourselves are called nonconformists since we (on good grounds) object to the state religion. We must stand by our Bible, never giving way, not following the religion of a multitude.[12]

In common trade, an irreligious man will do many things a Christian should studiously avoid. Shop nonconformity is meant. Market, house, street and business noncon[ty.13]

In our company and pursuits, our aims and objects, our looks and actions, let us be separate.

II. HE TELLS US THE MEANS OF MAINTAINING IT.
"<u>Be ye transformed by the renewing of your minds</u>.["]

By this is ~~imp~~ meant not the first, beginning of the great work, but the after progress.

Progressive Sanctification.[14] Growth in grace alone can keep us from going into sin. We need [to] pray constantly for the Holy Ghost to come and enliven us and renew us day by day.[15]

The "mind" must be renewed every day. The colour though indelible needs fresh varnish.

Backsliding will bring us to the world but growth in grace will separate us more.

Increase in prayer, diligence, holiness, meditation &c.

III. The uses of this nonconformity.
"that ye may prove what is that good & acceptable & perfect will of God"

This I think means

1. That ye may approve the sincerity of your religion to others — they seeing your good works. Worldly Christianity is ever suspected by the world. Christ is wounded in his friend's house.

2. That ye may to your own comfort, prove & enjoy your religion — None know half the bliss of religion but true nonconformists. Conformity to the world causes doubts, trouble distress & a thousand sorrows — therefore "Be not conformed to this world"

In Enforcing the Exhortation.

I shall use the doctrines of Grace. & turn Calvinistic doctrines as motives to Calvinists. for Christian nonconformity to this world.

1. Election. You & I believe that God hath from all eternity chosen a number whom

Backsliding will bring us to the world, but growth in grace will separate us more.

Increase in prayer, diligence, holiness, meditation etc.

III. THE USES OF THIS NONCONFORMITY.

"*that ye may prove what is that good and acceptable and perfect 'will of God.'*"

This I think means:

1. That ye may approve[16] the sincerity of your religion to others. They, seeing your good works.[17] Worldly Christianity is ever suspected by the world. Christ is wounded in his friend's house.

2. That ye may, to your own comfort, prove and enjoy your religion. None know half the bliss of religion but true nonconformists.

Conformity to the world causes doubts, trouble, distress, and a thousand sorrows, therefore "Be not conformed to this world."

In Enforcing the Exhortation.

I shall use the doctrines of Grace and turn Calvinistic doctrines as motives to Calvinists for Christian nonconformity to this world.

1. Election. You and I believe that God hath from all eternity chosen a number whom

no man can number, who shall be holy,
& enjoy felicity — Believing this, & considering
yourselves as elect— how holy ought ye to be.
Otherwise how is God's purpose in election to be
accomplished in you. Ye are select & chosen.
2. Universal & Utter Depravity is another of
your peculiar tenets & mine too — We believe
our hearts to be utterly vile & rotten.
Surely then we ought not to carry such
a heart into evil company— it were like
laying a bomb-shell on your hearth.
With such lusts, passions, wills & hearts we
ought to walk exceedingly circumspect.
3. Effectual Calling again calls us to holiness.
We think that we are not come to the
feast of our own will but by the sweet
drawing & compulsion of the Holy Ghost.
Well, if so, show that your religion
excells the free-willers religion. Ah! Ah!
Bigotry would be good if you Bigots did this.
It is to be feared that old Gill-ism is not so
productive of heat & life as — the religion
which has a spice of Wesley in it —
But yet, it ought to be. If true it will
be. Therefore Calvinistic Christians be holy — —

no man can number, who shall be holy and enjoy felicity.[18] Believing this, and considering yourselves as elect, how holy ought ye to be.[19] Otherwise, how is God's purpose in election to be accomplished in you[?][20] Ye are select and chosen.

2. Universal and Utter Depravity is another of your peculiar tenets, and mine too. We believe our hearts to be utterly vile and rotten.

    Surely then, we ought not to carry such a heart into evil company. It were like laying a bomb-shell on your hearth. With such lusts, passions, wills, and hearts we ought to walk exceedingly circumspect.[21]

3. Effectual Calling again calls us to holiness. We think that we are not come to the feast of our own will, but by the sweet drawing and compulsion of the Holy Ghost.[22]

    Well, if so, show that your religion excells [*sic*] the free-willers religion.[23] Ah! Ah! Bigotry would be good if you Bigots did this. It is to be feared that old Gill-ism[24] is not so productive of heat and life as the religion which has a spice of Wesley in it.[25]

    But yet, it ought to be. If true, it will be. Therefore, Calvinistic Christians be holy.

4. Particular Redemption is held by you
of Cottenham. You believe Christ died
for none but believers ~ I myself cannot
help seeing a degree of speciality in the
intention of that act ___ but be it as
it may - I say - believing this you ought
to be more holy than those you call the
unredeemed - if Jesus blood be yours you
owe him much more than others, be
then concerned to serve him more.
5. Final Perseverance - a doctrine
which is my darling theme - my well
beloved note of sweetest harmony - you too
believe it in all its amplitude -
Come friends & brethren - if heaven is
as surely ours as if we were there
let us be holy, undefiled, for this is
the right behaviour for an heir of glory.
Ye are everlasting Christians, lay not
aside your helmet or sword but hold on to
the end. My Father help thy Babe
for thy son's sake.

382

4. Particular Redemption is held by you of Cottenham. You believe Christ died for none but believers. I myself cannot help seeing a degree of speciality in the intention of that act. But be it as it may. I say, believing this, you ought to be more holy than those you call the unredeemed. If Jesus['s] blood be yours, you owe him much more than others. Be then concerned to serve him more.

5. Final Perseverance, a doctrine which is my darling theme, my well beloved note of sweetest harmony. You too believe it in all its amplitude.

Come, friends and brethren, if heaven is as surely ours as if we were there, let us be holy, undefiled,[26] for this is the right behaviour for an heir of glory.[27]

Ye are everlasting, Christians. Lay not aside your helmet or sword,[28] but hold on to the end.

My Father, help thy Babe

<u>for thy son's sake.</u>

382

1. Charles never again preached from this passage.

2. Cf. Gen 6:5–8. This could also refer to Noah's failure in Gen 9:20–22.

3. Cf. Exod 16:2–3.   4. Cf. Num 25:1–3.

5. Cf. Ezra 9:1–2.   6. Cf. Isa 30:1–2, 15.

7. Cf. 2 Kgs 23:8; Jer 19:4–6.

8. Cf. Rom 12:2.

9. As he states later, Charles is preaching at Cottenham, where he had preached on two other occasions. See "The Corner Stone" (Notebook 2, Sermon 128) and "Hew Down the Tree" (Sermon 215). Thus, he likely had some degree of familiarity with this congregation.

10. "From the first they had a fondness for drab, or otherwise dingy-coloured garments, for splendour of apparel they thought, did not become men who clothed themselves simply to cover their nakedness, and protect themselves from the cold, and not to pamper a sinful pride" (John Cunningham, *The Quakers from Their Origin Till the Present Time: An International History* [Edinburgh: John Menzies 1868, The Spurgeon Library], 103). See also Sermon 119 in *LS* 2:390n9.

11. "The old pagan Saxons, in their idolatry, brought in the names of the days after their gods; and these called Christians have retained them to this day . . . and yet you say the Scripture is your rule, and yet disobey both the command of God, and the holy Scriptures of Truth, and are often angry with, and deride the People of God, whom you in scorn call *Quakers*, because they do not call the Months and Days after the Heathens' Gods and Goddesses, but do call them according as the Holy Men of God in the Scripture of Truth have first called them, and cannot call them after the Idolatrous Heathens' Gods and Goddesses, nor mention their Gods' and Goddesses' Names, as you do, without the Breach of the Command of God, as in *Exod. 23. 13.* and the Scriptures of Truth" (George Fox, *Gospel Truth Demonstrated, in a Collection of Doctrinal Books, Given Forth by That Faithful Minister of Jesus Christ, George Fox: Containing Principles Essential to Christianity and Salvation, Held Among the People Called Quakers* [Philadelphia: Marcus T. C. Gould; New York: Isaac T. Hopper, 1831], 348–49, italics in the original).

12. "As Protestant Dissenters[,] we see the truths we preach assailed by an army of Anglican Papists whom we are compelled to support that they may oppose our most cherished designs. Popery is this day installed and endowed among us, and we are compelled to acknowledge its myrmidons as the clergy of our own national church. That which our fathers died to overthrow we are compelled to support. We cannot help being indignant; we should be less than men if our blood did not boil within us at such injustice. If men want Popery, or any other form of error, let them pay for it themselves, and call it their own; but to foist their superstition on us as part of the nation is an oppression against which we appeal to the Judge of all the earth" (*MTP* 19:51).

13. Charles appears to use this abbreviation for nonconformity due to space restrictions.

14. "[G]oing on gradually till it comes to perfection" (John Gill, *A Body of Doctrinal Divinity* [London: 1769], 2:882). "I do not admire the term 'progressive sanctification,' for it is unwarranted by Scripture; but it is certain that the Christian does grow in grace, and though his conflict may be as severe in the last day of his life as in the first moment of conversion, yet he does advance in grace, and all his imperfections and his conflicts within cannot prove that he has made no progress" (*MTP* 10:570).

15. "So he had him about to the back side of the Wall, where he saw a Man with a Vessel of Oyl in his hand, of the which he did also continually cast (but secretly,) into the fire. Then said *Christian, What means this?* The *Interpreter* answered, This is *Christ,* who continually with the Oyl of his Grace, maintains the work already begun in the heart; By the means of which, notwithstanding what the Devil can do, the souls of his People prove gracious still. And in that thou sawest, that the Man stood behind the Wall to maintain the fire; this is to teach thee, that it is hard for the tempted to see how the work of Grace is maintained in the soul" (Bunyan, *The Pilgrim's Progress* [London: J. Haddon, 1847, The Spurgeon Library], 31–32, italics in the original).

16. "3. To prove; to shew; to justify" (Johnson's *Dictionary,* s.v. "to approve").

17. Cf. Matt 5:16.

18. "Happiness; prosperity; blissfulness; blessedness" (Johnson's *Dictionary*, s.v. "felicity").

19. Cf. 1 Pet 1:16.   20. Cf. Rom 9:6–21; Eph 1:4; 1 Thess 1:4.

21. Cf. Eph 5:15.

22. "What did [Christ] foresee about my faith? Did He foresee that I should get that faith myself, and that I should believe on Him of myself? No; Christ could not foresee that, because no Christian man will ever say that faith came of itself without the gift and without the working of the Holy Spirit. I have met with a great many believers, and talked with them about this matter; but I never knew one who could put his hand on his heart, and say, 'I believed in Jesus without the assistance of the Holy Spirit'" (*Autobiography* 1:171).

23. "It has often been said that the doctrines we believe have a tendency to lead us to sin. I have heard it asserted most positively, that those high doctrines which we love, and which we find in the Scriptures, are licentious ones. I do not know who will have the hardihood to make that assertion, when they consider that the holiest of men have been believers in them. I ask the man who dares to say that Calvinism is a licentious religion, what he thinks of the character of Augustine, or Calvin, or Whitefield" (*Autobiography* 1:177).

24. "Gill is Coryphaeus of Hyper-Calvinism, but if his followers never went beyond their master, they would not go very far astray" (C. H. Spurgeon, *Commenting and Commentaries: Two Lectures Addressed to the Students of The Pastors' College, Metropolitan Tabernacle, Together with a Catalogue of Biblical Commentaries and Expositions* [London: Passmore and Alabaster, 1890, The Spurgeon Library], 9).

25. As Charles notes in his *Autobiography*, in these years he encountered problems with antinomianism (*Autobiography* 1:256–60).

26. Cf. Ps 119:1; 1 Pet 1:4.   27. Cf. Rom 8:17.

28. Cf. Isa 59:17; Eph 6:17; 1 Thess 5:8.

Job. _XXXIII_ .   I have found a ransom. 224

The greatest work of the ministry is to preach Christ
crucified to poor sinners, ⋔ to show them
their own state & their only refuge —

I. Why did man need redemption.

1. Because the whole race are now by nature the
   property & slaves of law — by Adam's fall.
2. They are infinitely in debt on their own
   several & personal account —
3. Their master is too strong to allow of escape
   they are well watched & guarded.
4. Their master has no mercy & will not
   let them run off — he will not diminish a dust.
5. The master will not die or grow old
   not one title shall pass away
6. They may not live peacefully in their
   bondage — for the pit must soon have
   them. nothing but their damnation will do.

II. Where can we find a ransom.
   Man is in dreadful circumstance what
shall be done —
   1. Can he pay it himself? — no it is too
much — give him time! — no eternity
cannot do it — let her help one! no the whole
race are alike in debt & if not none
   can redeem his brother —

I HAVE FOUND *a* RANSOM
Job 33[1]

The greatest work of the ministry is to preach Christ crucified[2] to poor sinners, & to show them their own state and their only refuge.[3]

I. WHY DID MAN NEED REDEMPTION?

1. Because the whole race are now by nature the property and slaves of law by Adam's fall.[4]

2. They are infinitely in debt on their own several[5] and personal accounts.

3. Their master is too strong to allow of escape. They are well watched and guarded.

4. Their master has no mercy and will not let them run off. He will not diminish a dust.[6]

5. The master will not die or grow old. Not one tit[t]le[7] shall pass away.

6. They may not live peacefully in their bondage—for the pit must soon have them.[8] Nothing but their damnation will do.

II. WHERE CAN WE FIND A RANSOM[?]

Man is in dreadful circumstance. What shall be done[?]

1. Can he pay it himself? No[,] it is too much. <u>Give him time</u>! No[,] eternity cannot do it. <u>Let her help one</u>! No[,] the whole race are alike in debt. And if not, none can redeem his brother.

They are slaves. They cannot run away. Hell is their doom.

2. Can angels do it? Michael, Gabriel, the cherubim & seraphim? — — No man must pay it to meet the decree. — — Besides creatures cannot merit — they cannot but do their duty — certainly. no more.

In far off worlds none are to be found the search made even by Gods eyes is vain

but

Eureka. Eureka —

I have found a ransom

where? where?

3 In the person of my son, Jesus, the firstborn of every creature, the God becomes man — Emanuel suffers bleeds dies — wish you to see the ransom Go to Gethsemane, Gabbatha & Golgotha.

Surely Jesus at the resurrection. ascension & each day of his glory doth utter these glorious words.

III. When ransomed what then?

1. we are slaves no longer.

2. The pit is not our doom.

3. Everlasting glory is our portion.

2. Can angels do it? Michael, Gabriel, the cherubim and seraphim? No, man must pay it, so runs the decree. Besides, creatures cannot merit. They cannot but do their duty. Certainly[9] no more.

   In far off worlds, none are to be found. The search made even by God[']s eyes is vain but

Eurēka[!] Eurēka[!]

I have found a ransom[!]

Where? Where?

3. In the person of [God's] son,[10] Jesus, the firstborn[11] of every creature, the God becomes man. Emmanuel[12] suffers, bleeds, dies.[13] Wish you to see the ransom[?] Go to Gethsemane,[14] Gabbatha,[15] and Golgotha.[16]

   Surely, Jesus at the resurrection,[17] ascension,[18] and each day of his glory, doth utter these glorious words.

III. WHEN RANSOMED WHAT THEN?

1. We are slaves no longer.[19]

2. The pit is not our doom.

3. Everlasting glory is our portion.

Application.

1 Repenting, Downcast sinner – may this be as honey to thee. like wine to thy heavy heart – thou deservest hell. but – but He has found a ransom !!!

2. Doubting believer – backsliding has caused thee grief – unbelief belabours thee. Satan, & thy heart, in an infernal league are united – fear not, thou worm, the Lord saith I ! I !! am with thee – fear not for I have found a ransom

3. Believer trembling at death. Dismiss thy fears – why tremble – the pit could not hold thee, it is not big enough to hold a child of God – when thou passeth through the rivers remember He has found a ransom

Lord. I entreat thee let not the word be spoken in vain but help thou me. For Jesus Christ's sake

383. 385. 386.

APPLICATION.[20]

1. Repenting, Downcast sinner[,] may this be as honey to thee, like wine to thy heavy heart.[21] Thou deservest hell, but, but

<u>He has found a ransom!!!</u>

2. Doubting believer, backsliding has caused thee grief. Unbelief belabours thee. Satan and thy heart in an infernal league are united. Fear not, thou worm,[22] the Lord saith <u>I</u>! <u>I</u>!! am with thee.[23] Fear not, for

<u>I have found a ransom!</u>

3. Believer, trembling at death. Dismiss thy fears. Why tremble? The pit could not hold thee.[24] It is not big enough to hold a child of God. When thou passeth through the rivers, remember[25]

<u>He has found a ransom[.]</u>

Lord, I entreat thee, let not the word be

spoken in vain[26] but help thou me.

For Jesus Christ's sake.

383. 385. 386.

1. Other sermons for which Charles cited an entire chapter of Scripture as his text include "The Second Psalm" (Notebook 2, Sermon 101); "The Seven Cries on the Cross" (Notebook 3, Sermon 142); "Jacob's Dream" (Notebook 4, Sermon 194); and "Vision of the Man with the Inkhorn" (Notebook 5, Sermon 256).

2. Cf. 1 Cor 1:23.   3. Cf. Ps 46:1.

4. Gill spoke of redemption this way: "The delivery of a debtor from prison, by paying his debts for him, is an emblem of deliverance and redemption," and "The ransoming of persons out of slavery, by paying a ransom-price for them, to give an idea of the redemption of the Lord's people by Christ" (John Gill, *A Body of Doctrinal Divinity* [London: 1769, The Spurgeon Library], 2:720–25).

5. "1. Different; distinct from one another. . . . 3. Particular; single" (Johnson's *Dictionary*, s.v. "several").

6. Charles appears to use "dust" as a small unit of measure, similar to a "mite." This usage finds possible support from Charles's use of "mite" in his sermon, "Justification by Imputed Righteousness" (Notebook 2, Sermon 117), in which he noted that "Justice herein abates not a mite," with reference to the strictness of the law.

7. Cf. Matt 5:18.   8. Cf. Job 33:24.

9. "Surely, when God creates a man, it is but a matter of right that the man created should answer to the call of his Maker. When the Creator saith, 'Seek ye my face,' it is the natural duty of the creature to reply, 'Thy face, Lord, I will seek.' And the more this is so, because our Creator renews our obligations hourly, by exercising his sustaining power, and maintaining our existence" (*MTP* 13:469).

10. "The matter of satisfaction, or what that is which gives satisfaction to the justice of God; so that a sinner upon it, or in consideration of it, is acquitted and discharged; and this is no other than Christ's fulfilling the whole law, in the room and stead of sinners. . . . Does it require an holy nature? it has it in him, who is *holy, harmless*, and *undefiled*; does it require perfect and sinless obedience? it is found in him, who did no sin, never transgressed the law in one instance, but always did the things which pleased his Father" (Gill, *A Body of Doctrinal Divinity*, 2:765, italics in the original). Cf. Isa 52:13–53:12; Matt 20:28; Mark 10:45; John 1:29; 2 Cor 5:21; Eph 1:7; 1 Pet 1:18–19.

11. Cf. Col 1:15.   12. Cf. Isa 7:14; Matt 1:22–23.

13. Cf. Matt 26:30–27:66; Mark 14:26–15:47; Luke 22:39–23:56; John 18:1–19:42.

14. Cf. Matt 26:36–56; Mark 14:32–50.

15. Cf. John 19:13.

16. Cf. Matt 27:33; Mark 15:22; Luke 23:33; John 19:17.

17. Cf. Matt 28:1–10; Mark 16:1–8; Luke 24:1–12; John 20:1–10.

18. Cf. Luke 24:50–53; Acts 1:6–11.

19. Cf. Rom 6:15–23.

20. Other sermons in which Charles concluded with "application" include, "Take Heed How Ye Hear" (Notebook 2, Sermon 81); "Prove Me Now Herewith" (Notebook 2, Sermon 109); "By Faith Jericho Fell" (Notebook 2, Sermon 133); "The Unclean Spirit Returning" (Notebook 3, Sermon 168); "Leaning on Jesus['s] Bosom" (Notebook 3, Sermon 183); and "God's Care of the Stars" (Notebook 4, Sermon 189).

21. Cf. Ps 104:14–15.   22. Cf. Isa 41:14.

23. Cf. Isa 41:10; 43:2, 5; Matt 28:20.

24. Cf. Acts 2:24.

25. Cf. Isa 43:2.   26. Cf. Isa 55:11; 2 Cor 6:1.

225.   Matt IX. 2.   Son, be of good cheer.

Note the circumstances of this poor mans case.

SON, BE *of* GOOD CHEER [1]

Matthew 9:2

"And, behold, they brought to him a man sick of the palsy,[2] lying on a bed: and Jesus seeing their faith said unto the sick of the palsy; Son, be of good cheer; thy sins be forgiven thee."

Note the circumstances of this poor man's case.

387. 388. 396

387. 388. 396.

1. Charles did not finish this sermon, nor did he complete three other sermons in this volume: "He Filleth the Hungry with Good Things" (Sermon 226); "He Will Bring Every Work into Judgment" (Sermon 228); and "As One Whom His Mother Comforteth" (Sermon 229). Charles would preach on the text of Matt 9:2 three other times in his ministry: "The Physician Pardons His Palsied Patient" (*MTP* 39, Sermon 2337); "Good Cheer from Forgiven Sin" (*MTP* 52, Sermon 3016); and "The Secret of Happiness" (*MTP* 56, Sermon 3227).

2. "A privation of motion or feeling, or both, proceeding from some cause below the cerebellum, joined with a coldness, flaccidity, and at last wasting of the parts" (Johnson's *Dictionary*, s.v. "palsy").

226.   Luke I. 53   He filleth the Hungry with good thi...

362.

HE FILLETH *the* HUNGRY *with* GOOD THINGS [1]

Luke 1:53

"He hath filled the hungry with good things; and the rich he hath sent empty away."

362.

1. This sermon is the second of four Charles did not complete in this volume. The other three blank sermons are "Son, Be of Good Cheer" (Sermon 225); "He Will Bring Every Work into Judgment" (Sermon 228); and "As One Whom His Mother Comforteth" (Sermon 229). Charles would preach twice more on this text in "Alto and Bass" (*MTP* 44, Sermon 2582) and "The Hungry Filled, the Rich Emptied" (*MTP* 52, Sermon 3019).

John. XIX. 5   Behold the Man

Pilate led Jesus forth to some conspicuous place.
He pointed to his head & face — turned back the
cloth & shows. his bloody back.
I. What did Pilate intend by this.
1. To clear himself from the charge of aiding
   and abetting Jesus as an usurper.
2. To keep the mob quiet by gratifying them
3. To excite their pity & procure Jesus a release.
II. This is our message too
Behold.   not ourselves
            nor yourselves } but Jesus.

III. How men regard him.
May with a look of contempt
______________________ carelessness
______________________ curiosity
                        admiration
A few with the eye of hope.
Fewer still with real faith.
Then comes a look of Love &c.

IV Let me address certain characters.
Christian standing firm — keep thine eye there.
Backslider — return & look to the man.
Doubters trust the man, not man
Great Sinner   Behold the man

394. 395.

BEHOLD *the* MAN[1]
John 19:5

"Then came Jesus forth, wearing the crown of thorns, and the purple robe.
And Pilate saith unto them, Behold the man!"

Pilate led Jesus forth to some conspicuous place. He pointed to his head and face, turned back the cloth, and show[ed] his bloody back.[2]

I. WHAT DID PILATE INTEND BY THIS?

1. To clear himself from the charge of aiding and abetting Jesus as an [*sic*] usurper.[3]

2. To keep the mob quiet by gratifying them.

3. To excite their pity and procure Jesus a release.

II. THIS IS OUR MESSAGE TOO.

Behold not ourselves

    nor yourselves[4]   } but Jesus.

III. HOW MEN REGARD HIM.

Many with a look of contempt.

———————————— carelessness[5]
———————————— curiosity[6]
———————————— admiration[7]

A few with the eye of hope.[8]

Fewer still with real faith.[9]

Then comes a look of Love etc.[10]

IV. LET ME ADDRESS CERTAIN CHARACTERS.

Christian standing firm, keep thine eye there.

Backslider – return and look to the man.

Doubters trust <u>the</u> man, not <u>man</u>.

Great Sinner, <u>Behold the man</u>.[11]

394. 395.

1. Charles never again preached on this text.

2. "[H]is body appearing to be almost of the same colour with the purple or scarlet robe, thro' the stripes and lashes he had received, when that was thrown back" (John Gill, *An Exposition of the New Testament*, vol. 2 [London: printed for the author, 1747, The Spurgeon Library], 99).

3. "[Pilate knew] very well the jealousies and suspicions of *Tiberius*, and fearing lest it would turn to his own disrepute and disadvantage, immediately *he brought Jesus forth*; out of the judgment-hall, the place where [he] had been examined in; not to declare his innocence, not to move their pity, nor to release him, but to pass sentence on him" (Gill, 2:102, italics in the original).

4. 2 Corinthians 4:5: "For we preach not ourselves, but Christ Jesus the Lord; and ourselves your servants for Jesus' sake."

5. "But worse enemies than [infidelity] we have. We shall have to deal with the indifference of the masses round about us, and with their carelessness concerning Gospel truth – we shall have to deal with prevailing sin and corruption. . . . And how shall we deal with it? Will we bring in some Socialist system? Shall we preach up some new method of political economy? No! the cross, the old cross is enough. . . . We will but preach Christ as the sinner's Saviour, the Spirit of God as applying Christ's truth to the soul, and God the Father in his infinite sovereignty saving whom he wills" (*MTP* 7:167).

6. "Herod was in such a state of mind that he furnishes me with a typical character which I would use for the instruction and admonition of you all. He is a type of some who frequently come to this Tabernacle, and go to other places or worship occasionally,—people who were once under religious impressions, and cannot forget that they were so, now hardened into vain curiosity: they wish to know about everything that is going on in the church and kingdom of Christ, but they are far enough from caring to become part and parcel of it themselves" (*MTP* 28:99).

7. "'We preach Christ crucified': we preach him glorified, and delight to do so; but still the main point upon which the eye of a sinner must rest, if he would have peace with God, must be Christ crucified for sin. 'God forbid that I should glory

save in the cross of our Lord Jesus Christ.' Do, then, my dear hearer, let the very foundation of your faith in Christ be your view of him as ransoming you from the power of sin and Satan. Some say the[y] admire Christ as an example, and well they may; they can never find a better: but Jesus Christ will never be truly known and followed if he be viewed only as an example, for he is infinitely more than that" (*MTP* 27:67–68).

8. "I know, and you know who have believed in him, that you could not if you saw him trust him more really than you do now. His death is the unbuttressed pillar of your confidence and the sole foundation of your hope. In Christ you have believed, and you know that your sin is forgiven, that his righteousness is imputed to you, and that you stand accepted in the Beloved. This is not to you a matter of hope; it is a matter of firm conviction" (*MTP* 12:365–66).

9. "Oh, we have not seen him yet! Our views of him are too dim to be worth calling sights. The eyes of faith have looked through a telescope and seen him at a distance, and it has been a ravishing vision; but when the eyes of the soul shall really see him – him, and not another, him for ourselves, and not another for us, oh, the sight! Is not the thought of it a burning coal of joy? The sight of his very flesh will charm us, his wounds still fresh, the dear memorials of his passion still apparent. The perception of his soul will also delight us, for our soul will commune with his soul, and this is the soul of communion. The sight of his Godhead, so far as created spirit can see it, will also ravish us with joy. And then we shall have a brighter knowledge of him. Here we know in part – we know the names of his offices, we know what he has wrought, we know what he is working for us; but there those offices will shine in their splendour, and we shall see all that he did for us in its real weight and value; we shall comprehend then the height and depth, and know the love of Christ which passeth knowledge, as we do not know it at this hour" (*MTP* 19:572).

10. "Without love too, you are without the transforming force. Love to Christ is that which makes us like him. The eyes of love, like windows, let in the Saviour's image, and the heart of love receives it as upon a sensitive plate, until the whole nature bears its impress. You are like that which you love, or you are growing like it. If Christ be loved[,] you are growingly becoming like him; but without love you will never bear the image of the heavenly. O Spirit of God, with wings of love brood over us, till Christ is formed in us" (*MTP* 22:130).

11. Charles's emphasis on seeing Christ is reminiscent of his conversion experience at the Primitive Methodist Chapel, Colchester, in January 1850 (*Autobiography* 1:105, 107). That morning with the preacher absent, a regular man, "a shoemaker, or tailor" ascended the pulpit and endeavored to preach from Isaiah 45:22, "Look unto me and be ye saved, all the ends of the earth" (*Autobiography* 1:105). At one point in the sermon the man looked at Charles, and addressing him, said, "Young man, look to Jesus Christ. Look! Look! Look! You have nothin' to do but to look and live." Charles, in his own words, "saw at once the way of salvation. . . . The darkness had rolled away, and [at] that moment I saw the sun; and I could have risen that instant, and sung with the most enthusiastic of them, of the precious blood of Christ, and simple faith which looks alone to him" (*Autobiography* 1:106).

228

He will bring every work into judgment

HE WILL BRING EVERY WORK *into* JUDGMENT[1]

1. This title appears to be from Eccl 12:14, which is the text for "Every Work to Be Judged" (Sermon 231). Charles never again preached from Ecclesiastes 12.

Is. 66.13   As one whom his Mother comforteth. 229

AS ONE WHOM HIS MOTHER COMFORTETH [1]

Isaiah 66:13

"As one whom his mother comforteth, so will I comfort
you; and ye shall be comforted in Jerusalem."

1. Charles left three previous sermons unfinished in this volume: "Son, Be of Good Cheer" (Sermon 225); "He Filleth the Hungry with Good Things" (Sermon 226); and "He will Bring Every Work into Judgment" (Sermon 228). Charles preached again on this text in his sermon "The Tenderness of God's Comfort" (*MTP* 56:133–41).

230   1 Cor. XVI. 13.   Courage recommended.

The Christian character should mainly consist in the
quiet & patient graces, but there must also be some
of the manly, lionlike graces.

I.   The nature & necessity of Christian fortitude.
II. Certain times when much needed.
III. How it may be maintained.

I. The nature & necessity of Christian fortitude.
It is not reckless & careless daring.
It is not idle presumption, — where there is no ground.
It is not love of giving offence — nor mere boast.
It is a firm determination to do right, come
what may. —
It is much needed seeing we are in an enemies
country, have much fight to do, are very weak,
have many duties &c &c —

II. Certain times when much needed.
1. When praying aloud whether in the family
   or the prayer meeting.
2. When desirous of joining a Church
3.   At Baptism.
4. When enduring trials from God or for God.
5. In maintaining truth before gainsayers.
6. In wrestling with spiritual enemies —
7. In reproving evil men, bad living
   professors.
8. In the hour of death.

COURAGE RECOMMENDED[1]

1 Corinthians 16:13

"Watch ye, stand fast in the faith, quit you like men, be strong."

The Christian character should mainly consist in the quiet and patient graces,[2] but there must also be some of the manly, lionlike graces.[3]

I.   THE NATURE AND NECESSITY OF CHRISTIAN FORTITUDE.

II.   CERTAIN TIMES WHEN MUCH NEEDED.

III. HOW IT MAY BE MAINTAINED.

I.   THE NATURE AND NECESSITY OF CHRISTIAN FORTITUDE.[4]

It is not reckless and careless daring.[5]

It is not idle presumption[6] where there is no ground.

It is not love of giving offence,[7] nor mere boast.[8]

It is a firm determination to do right, come what may.[9]

It is much needed, seeing we are in an enemies [*sic*] country, have much fight to do,[10] are very weak, have many duties[11] etc. etc.

II.   CERTAIN TIMES WHEN MUCH NEEDED.

1.   When praying aloud, whether in the family or the prayer meeting.[12]

2.   When desirous of joining a Church.[13]

3.   At Baptism.[14]

4.   When enduring trials from God or for God.[15]

5.   In maintaining truth before gainsayers.[16]

6.   In wrestling with spiritual enemies.[17]

7.   In reproving evil men, bad living professors.[18]

8.   In the hour of death.[19]

III. How this must be maintained.
  1. By the grace of the Holy Spirit working in us — by this alone can it be done.
  2. Meditation on Saints who have gone before
  3. Searching the Scriptures, especially seeking the promises which are great. —
  4. Faith in Jesus, prayer to him & a diligent use of the means.
  5. Love of God shed abroad will be the death of cowardice —
    Quit yourselves like men — be strong

402.

III. HOW THIS MUST BE MAINTAINED.

1. By the grace of the Holy Spirit working in us. By this alone can it be done.[20]

2. Meditation on Saints who have gone before.[21]

3. Searching the Scriptures, especially seeking the promises which are great.[22]

4. Faith in Jesus, prayer to him, and a diligent use of the means.[23]

5. Love of God shed abroad[24] will be the death of cowardice.

     Quit[25] yourselves like men. [B]e strong.

402.

1. Charles never again preached on this text. Further, as noted below, it appears he copied most of his content and structure from John Gill's chapter on Christian fortitude in his work, *A Body of Practical Divinity* (John Gill, *A Body of Practical Divinity; or, a System of Practical Truths, Deduced from the Sacred Scriptures. Which (with the Two Former Volumes) Completes the Scheme of Doctrinal and Practical Divinity*, vol. 3 [London: printed for the author and sold by George Keith in Grace-church-street, 1770, The Spurgeon Library]).

2. "[S]aints are to be humble, self-denying, submissive to the will of God, and patient towards all men" (Gill, 3:190).

3. "[A] manly spirit . . . they should play the man, act the manly part, shew themselves to be men, as of wisdom, so of courage" (Gill, 3:190).

4. "The Nature and Necessity of Christian Fortitude" is borrowed from Gill's outline (Gill, 3:191).

5. "[W]hen a man . . . rushes into [dangers] unnecessarily, without any consultation and deliberation, and without having any good end in view to be answered. This is no other than audaciousness, or rather *temerity*, or rashness; and not true fortitude" (Gill, 3:191, italics in the original).

6. "But what can I do unless, with due care and caution, ye yourselves walk guardedly[?] Oh, my brethren; be much more in prayer than ever. Spend more time in pious adoration. Read the Scriptures more earnestly and constantly. Watch your lives more carefully. Live nearer to God. . . . On, Christian, with care and caution! On, with holy fear and trembling! On yet, with faith and confidence, for thou shalt not fall" (*NPSP* 1:172).

7. Cf. 2 Cor 6:3.

8. Cf. Prov 27:1–2; 1 Cor 1:31; 3:18–23; 4:7; Eph 2:8–9; Jas 4:13–17.

9. "Since the [C]hristian has so many difficulties and dangers to encounter with; so many discouragements in the way; so many trials, temptations, tribulations, and afflictions from various quarters, he must be a man of fortitude not to be moved with these things; bearing all with an invincible courage and constancy" (Gill, *A Body of Practical Divinity*, 3:191–92).

10. "To which may be added, the numerous enemies he has to grapple with; enemies mightier than he, who are lively and strong; some not flesh and blood, as he is, but above his match; even principalities and powers, and spiritual wickedness in high places" (Gill, 3:192). Cf. John 15:18–27; 17:16–26; Rom 8:36; Phil 2:14–16.

11. "Now of such fortitude there is a necessity in the [C]hristian life. When we consider the many duties of religion to be performed by us, and that with constancy and perseverance, both public and private, relative, social, and personal" (Gill, 3:191).

12. "In family worship; which undoubtedly is incumbent on the people of God: but now for a man to distinguish himself in a neighbourhood from all about him, and so to say in his practice . . . let others do what they will; this shews religious fortitude of mind: and in particular when a man first sets up family-prayer in his house" (Gill, 3:192).

13. "In a man's giving up himself to a church of Christ, to walk with it in all the commandments and ordinances of the Lord" (Gill, 3:192).

14. "Especially if such a man comes into a church in a regular manner, by previously submitting to the ordinance of baptism, and to that as it was first delivered and practised" (Gill, 3:193).

15. "Christian fortitude shews itself in bearing afflictions with constancy, and enduring sufferings with a firmness of mind, whether from the hands of God or men; and which may be called passive fortitude" (Gill, 3:194).

16. "From the hands of men; and especially for the sake of the gospel, the truths and ordinances of it; as when saints are called to suffer shame and reproach for the sake of Christ, they in imitation of him, despise the shame, and account it an honour to bear reproach for his sake" (Gill, 3:194).

17. "Christian fortitude appears in the spiritual warfare of the saints. There is a warfare for men on earth, and especially for good men, who are soldiers, and must endure hardness, as good soldiers of Christ" (Gill, 3:195).

18. "This also appears in fighting against spiritual enemies; as sin, and the lusts of it, which war against the soul; the law in the members warring against the law of

the mind; the flesh lusting against the spirit; which are, as it were, a company of two armies" (Gill, 3:195).

19. "Christian fortitude manifests itself in the hour of death. Death is very terrible to natural men; the philosopher calls it 'the most terrible of all terribles;' and no wonder he should call it so. . . . To Christless sinners death is the king of terrors, and even some gracious persons have been all their life-time through fear of death subject to bondage" (Gill, 3:196).

20. "The efficient cause of [C]hristian fortitude of mind is God, Father, Son and Spirit" (Gill, 3:197).

21. "The patterns of courage, the examples of fortitude in the saints who have gone before us, of the prophets, apostles, primitive [C]hristians and martyrs in all ages, may be a means of promoting a like disposition" (Gill, 3:198).

22. "The word of God is the means of producing and increasing [C]hristian fortitude; it is not only a part of the spiritual armour, called the sword of the Spirit, but having a place and abiding in the heart, fortifies it against spiritual enemies, and by it victory is gained over them" (Gill, 3:197).

23. "Such a temper and disposition of mind is attainable by faith, prayer, and waiting upon God" (Gill, 3:197–98).

24. "The love of God, and a sense of that, a persuasion of interest in it, and that nothing shall separate from it, casts out fear, and inspires with fortitude against every enemy" (Gill, 3:198). Romans 5:5: "And hope maketh not ashamed; because the love of God is shed abroad in our hearts by the Holy Ghost which is given unto us."

25. "1. To discharge an obligation; to make even." . . . or "3. To carry through; to discharge; to perform" (Johnson's *Dictionary*, s.v. "quit").

231   Eccles. XII. 14.   Every work to be judged.

after death comes the season of tribulation & anguish
to evil doers — may they be wise betimes to think
upon it —

I. When will the judge call us before him?
1. As soon as man dies he undergoes a judgment
2. But the decree of the great day will more confirm it.
When this shall be no man knoweth.

II. Who shall be judge?   The Son.
Here is cause for joy to Christians & for grief
to despisers. Not as once he came but with vengeance.

III. What shall we be judged for?
1. All our works.
Labours for food &c — constant acts of life.
Acts of pleasure, mirth, jollity &c.
Acts of religion shall be sifted too.

2. Every secret thing.
All our nightly actions & unseen deeds.
All our opinions, doctrines, wishes, thoughts.

IV. Why judged for these?
It is not fair that some should go free for ever therefore
this judgment will touch those who escape man.
Sin would revel too much unless checked.
Every man ought to reap a harvest from his seed.
This judgment will find out secret sinners, hypocrite
liars, cheats, thieves, formalists &c —   Bless, Bless

444.

EVERY WORK *to* BE JUDGED[1]
Ecclesiastes 12:14

"For God shall bring every work into judgment, with every secret thing,
whether it be good, or whether it be evil."

After death comes the season of tribulation and anguish to evil doers.[2] May they be wise betimes[3] to think upon it.

I. WHEN WILL THE JUDGE CALL US BEFORE HIM?

1. As soon as man dies, he undergoes a judgment.[4]

2. But the decree of the great day will more confirm it. When this shall be, no man knoweth.

II. WHO SHALL BE JUDGE? THE SON.[5]

Here is cause for joy to Christians and for grief to despisers. Not as once he came, but with vengeance.[6]

III. WHAT SHALL WE BE JUDGED FOR?

1. All our works.[7]

    Labours for food etc. Constant acts of life.

    Acts of pleasure, mirth, jollity etc.

    Acts of religion shall be sifted too.

2. Every secret thing.[8]

    All our nightly actions and unseen deeds.

    All our opinions, doctrines, wishes, thoughts.

IV. WHY JUDGED FOR THESE?

It is not fair that some should go free for ever. Therefore, this judgment will touch those who escape man. Sin would revel too much unless checked. Every man ought to reap a harvest from his seed.[9] This judgment will find out secret sinners, hypocrite liars, cheats, thieves, formalists, etc.

<u>Bless. Bless.</u>

400.

1. This sermon appears to be the completed version of Charles's unfinished one, "He Will Bring Every Work into Judgement" (Sermon 228).

2. Cf. Job 15:20–24; Rom 2:9–11.

3. "2. Soon; before long time has passed. 3. Early in the day" (Johnson's *Dictionary*, s.v. "betimes").

4. Cf. Heb 9:27.

5. Cf. John 5:22, 27; 9:39; Acts 10:42; 17:31; Rom 2:16; 2 Cor 5:10; 2 Tim 4:8; Jas 5:9; Rev 19:11.

6. Cf. 2 Thess 1:7–9.

7. Charles appears to be following Gill's similar division in his commentary on Eccl 12:14 (John Gill, *An Exposition of the Old Testament*, 4:587).

8. Cf. Eccl 12:14; Luke 8:17.

9. Cf. Gal 6:7–9.

Rev. XXII. 16. Jesus the Morning Star. 232

Nature fails to provide an object worthy to
set forth the matchless charms of Jesus. All her
most excellent works together fail to express
the lustre of his matchless character.

I Jesus is a Star.

1 Great men are sometimes called stars &
surely he is the greatest of all in every
particular in which men excel.

2. Stars give light, so does Jesus give us
comfort, knowledge &c.

3. Stars guide the traveller, the mariner
the freedom-seeking slave.

II. Jesus is the Morning Star.

1. Because that is the brightest star.

2. Because that heralds the day.
So did he dispel legal, ceremonial shadows.
So does he drive clouds & fears from sinners
So does he promise us eternal glory.

Have we seen the star, are we following
it, if so we are safe. ——
Look poor soul —

452. 453.

JESUS *the* MORNING STAR.[1]
Revelation 22:16

"'I Jesus have sent mine angel to testify unto you these things in the churches. I am the root and the offspring of David, and the bright and morning star.'"

Nature fails to provide an object worthy to set forth the matchless charms of Jesus.[2] All her most excellent works together fail to express the lustre of his matchless character.[3]

I. JESUS IS A STAR.

1. Great men are sometimes called stars, and surely he is the greatest of all in every particular in which men excel.

2. Stars give light. So does Jesus give us comfort, knowledge etc.[4]

3. Stars guide the traveller, the mariner, the freedom-seeking slave.

II. JESUS IS THE MORNING STAR.[5]

1. Because that is the brightest star.[6]

2. Because that heralds the day.

    So did he dispel legal, ceremonial shadows.[7]

    So does he drives [*sic*] clouds and fears from sinners.

    So does he promise us eternal glory.[8]

Have we seen the star? Are we following it? If so, we are safe.

Look poor soul—

452. 453.

1. Charles never again preached on this text.

2. "Not only is his teaching attractive, his doctrine persuasive, his life irreproachable, his character enchanting, and his work a self-denying labour for the common good of all his people, but he himself is altogether lovely" (*MTP* 24:661). "Oh that we might love our Lord for his own sake, love him because he is so supremely beautiful that glimpse of him has won our hearts, and made him dearer to our eyes than light. Oh that all true and faithful disciples of our beloved Lord would press forward towards that state of affection, and never rest till they reach it!" (*MTP* 24:662).

3. "[T]hink of the matchless character of Christ Jesus! Were there ever such perfections as meet in him? He hath not the excellency of one man, but of all men, without the faults of any. He is not merely the Rose of Sharon, but he is the Lily of the Valley. He may not only be compared at one time to the citron among the trees of the wood, but anon he is the goodly cedar. All types of beauty fail, and 'apples of gold in pictures of silver' lose their force when we come to treat of him. We must coin new words before we can describe the excellencies of Christ" (*NPSP* 6:312).

4. Cf. John 8:12; 1 Cor 1:30; Eph 1:3; Phil 2:1–3.

5. Cf. 2 Pet 1:19; Rev 2:28; 22:16.

6. "The planet Venus when she shines in the morning" (Johnson's *Dictionary*, s.v. "morning-star"). A handbook in Charles's library addresses Venus as the brightest "star" and references both 2 Pet 1:19 and Rev 22:16 when describing Venus (*The Heavens and the Earth. A Popular Handbook of Astronomy* (Thomas Milner, Edwin Dunkin, rev., *The Heavens and the Earth. A Popular Handbook of Astronomy*), new ed. [London: The Religious Tract Society, n.d., The Spurgeon Library], 85–86).

7. "[Christ] was then the day spring from on high, put an end to the night of *Jewish* darkness, and sprung the great Gospel day" (John Gill, *An Exposition of the New Testament*, vol. 3 [London: printed for the author, 1748, The Spurgeon Library], 811, italics in the original).

8. "[Christ's] glory being the glory of the only begotten of the Father, and he having a glory, as mediator, which his saints will ever behold, and be delighted with," and that Christ "shewed the way to eternal life by himself" (Gill, 3:811).

[blank]

ABOUT THE PROJECT AT MIDWESTERN SEMINARY

In 1857, Charles Spurgeon—the most popular preacher in the Victorian world—promised his readers that he would publish his earliest sermons. For almost 160 years, these sermons were lost to history. But with these volumes, these rediscovered sermons can finally be read, studied, and enjoyed by the millions around the world who admire Spurgeon's spiritual insights and literary grace.

This multi-volume set includes full-color facsimiles of Spurgeon's original handwriting, transcriptions of his outlines and sermons, biographical introductions, and editorial commentary that further illuminates Spurgeon's work. Taken together, *The Lost Sermons of C. H. Spurgeon* will add approximately 10 percent more material to Spurgeon's total body of literature, making it a must-have for pastors and scholars as well as the multitude of Spurgeon enthusiasts around the world.

The Lost Sermons project is overseen by a team of scholars and researchers at Midwestern Baptist Theological Seminary in Kansas City, Missouri, home of The Spurgeon Library, which houses nearly 6,000 volumes from Charles Spurgeon's personal library. Managers of spurgeon.org, Midwestern Seminary, under the leadership of President Jason K. Allen, are honored to steward these early works of Spurgeon as they seek to contribute to Spurgeon scholarship and research for the next generation.

ABOUT SPURGEON'S COLLEGE

Spurgeon's College was founded by the great Victorian preacher and philanthropist Charles Haddon Spurgeon in 1856. He recognised the injustice and frustration faced by those who desired to serve churches as ordained ministers but who had not benefited from the academic education required to gain entry for professional training. Charles Spurgeon wanted to embrace natural talents and abilities and looked for potential and passion, rather than academic privilege and family connections, when recruiting his students. The college remains thoroughly committed to these principles.

Today Spurgeon's College continues to prepare candidates for ordination to Baptist ministry within the Baptist Union of Great Britain. It also trains pastors from other denominations and those called to pioneer ministry and missional work. Since its foundation, more than 5,000 churches worldwide have been served by Spurgeon's ministers, and its trained ministers are active in more than thirty-five countries. The college has an exciting postgraduate programme and a thriving postgraduate research community composed of students from around the world.

Charles Spurgeon derived the college's motto from a book by nineteenth-century poet and essayist Dora Greenwell: "We labour to hold forth the Cross of Christ with a bold hand among the sons of men, because that Cross holds us fast by its attractive power. Our desire is that every man may both hold the Truth, and be held by it; especially the truth of Christ crucified." *Et Teneo Et Teneor*—"I hold and I am held"—is embedded in the crest of Spurgeon's College. To find out more please visit www.spurgeons.ac.uk.

SCRIPTURE INDEX

SUBJECT INDEX